PAT BROWN, MBA

Ultra Affluent

ABRAM 47 BROWN

First published by AbramBrown47 2025

First edition

ISBN: 978-1-967737-40-6

This book was professionally typeset on Reedsy.
Find out more at reedsy.com

Contents

Preface

Mastering Wealth Beyond Seven Figures

If you're holding this book, you already know something most people don't. You know that money alone doesn't solve everything. You know that wealth isn't just about how much you have — it's about how well you can manage it, protect it, grow it, and pass it on. You understand success is different at this level. At some point along your journey, you realized that building wealth was only the first mountain. There's a second mountain — the mountain of stewardship, mastery, and legacy. And that second mountain is steeper, harder, and even more important.

I wrote *Ultra Affluent* for those who have achieved much — and yet still feel the weight of uncertainty. Because no one talks about what happens after you "make it." No one tells you how isolating wealth can feel. No one tells you how complicated it becomes. No one hands you a blueprint for how to steward wealth without being consumed by it. The truth is, the ultra-affluent have their own challenges. And while the rest of the world might think, "it must be nice," you know the real story. You know the complexity. You know the responsibility. You know the invisible pressures. And most of all — you know that wealth can either be a blessing or a burden. This book is about making it a blessing.

For over two decades, I've sat across the table from people like you. People who built businesses, led companies, innovated, invested wisely, inherited legacies, or rode the rollercoaster of entrepreneurship to the top. People whose net worths would make headlines — but whose real lives are quieter, more complex, and more human than the headlines could ever show. And in those conversations, I saw the same questions again and again:

Am I protecting what I've built?

Am I overcomplicating it — or underthinking it?

Am I really in control — or just surrounded by people who say they're "taking care of it"?

Are my children prepared — or entitled?

Will my legacy be a blessing — or a burden?

What happens if I get tired, bored, or just want out?

Can I actually enjoy what I've built — or will I always worry?

The ultra-affluent have more options — and more at stake. This book is not just about financial literacy. It's about wealth mastery. It's about stepping into the role you've earned — owner of your future, architect of your legacy. Not a passive participant. Not a bystander. An active steward of everything you've worked so hard to build.

This is not a basic finance book. You already know how to balance a checkbook. You already know what a 401(k) is. You already understand compounding. This is not *Financial Literacy 101.* This is *Ultra Wealth Mastery.*

This is not a lecture.

It's not a guilt trip.

It's not a sales pitch.

It's a guide.

It's a conversation.

It's the manual you should have gotten with your first major liquidity event.

It's the manual you wish you had before you built a family office, before you bought your third property, before you set up that dynasty trust you're not even sure is working the way you intended.

This book will not tell you what to do. It will show you how to think. It will give you a framework for making the big decisions — with clarity, confidence, and calm. It will arm you with the questions that matter. It will strip away the noise. Because when you're ultra-affluent, you don't need more information. You need better filters. You don't need more options.

You need better decision-making tools. This book is your filter. This book is your tool. This book is your permission slip to take full ownership of the wealth you've created — and to make sure it serves you, not the other way around.

This book is for you if:

- You have a net worth of $10 million, $20 million, $50 million, or more — and realize the real challenges are just beginning.
- You've sold a business or had a major liquidity event — and wonder, what's next?
- You've inherited significant wealth — and want to be a wise steward, not a cautionary tale.
- You're first-generation wealth — and you're determined to get it right.
- You've seen friends make expensive mistakes — and you're committed to avoiding them.
- You're quietly successful — and want to quietly master the next phase.

It's for you if you care about freedom more than flash. If you value peace of mind more than public image. If you're less interested in the yacht race — and more interested in building something that lasts.

You don't have to read this book cover to cover. Each chapter is designed to stand on its own. Each chapter tackles one pillar of wealth mastery. Read the parts that call to you now. Come back to the rest as you need them. This is a reference. A guide. A conversation starter.

Each chapter will:

Break down complex topics in plain language.

Lay out the pros and cons of different strategies.

Give you action steps to move from insight to implementation.

We're not here for theory. We're here for traction. We're here to help you:

Protect what you've built.

Grow what you've built.

Enjoy what you've built.

Pass on what you've built — wisely.

And most importantly — we're here to help you master your wealth. Not just manage it.

Mastery doesn't mean complexity. Mastery means clarity.

Mastery means:

Knowing what you own and why.

Understanding your risk — not fearing it.

Delegating wisely — not blindly.

Building structures that serve you — not entrap you.

Creating a family culture of stewardship — not entitlement.

Being free — truly free — to live the life you want.

Mastery means being in control. Mastery means sleeping well. Mastery means legacy without the drama. This is the path to a life not just of wealth — but of dignity, peace, and power.

If you're reading this, you already have the raw materials. You've built.

You've achieved. You've created. Now it's time to master.

Consider this book your invitation.

An invitation to think differently. To act intentionally. To lead boldly. An invitation to build a legacy you're proud of. An invitation to step fully into your next chapter. No guilt. No shame. No fear. Just clarity. Just confidence. Just freedom.

Welcome to Ultra Affluent.

What It Really Means to Be Ultra Affluent

Let's Start by Getting Something Straight

If you're sitting here, book in hand, chances are you've already realized something most people never will: ultra affluence isn't just about how many zeroes trail your balance sheet. It's not a number on a screen. It's not a headline in a magazine. It's not a trophy you can place on the shelf. Ultra affluence is an entirely different world — a different mindset, a different set of challenges, and, most importantly, a different set of responsibilities and opportunities.

Sure, society loves to define wealth with numbers. Maybe $30 million qualifies. Maybe it's $50 million, $100 million, or more. But at this level, the number is almost irrelevant. It's not what you have; it's what your wealth allows you to do. It's not the size — it's the meaning. Wealth at this level means you have options that few others ever will. It means you have responsibility that most can't fathom. It means you have power — and with power comes the obligation to use it with wisdom and intent.

Let's start with the real asset here: control. At this level, money itself stops being the point. Control over your time, control over your decisions, control over your impact — these are the real currencies. Ultra wealth gives you the ability to say "no" without apology and "yes" without hesitation. It lets you design a life based on purpose rather than paycheck. But here's the catch — it only does so if you master it. Without control, wealth can quickly morph from blessing to burden. With control, it becomes a launchpad — a platform from which you can shape your world.

Beyond control, ultra wealth brings a profound sense of responsibility. It's not just about what you can buy — though buying power is real. It's about what you can build. The responsibility to protect your family, to grow your assets wisely, to guard your reputation, to steward your influence. This isn't about the next quarter or even the next decade. This is about the next generation, and the ones that follow. When you're ultra affluent, you're no longer playing for today — you're playing for centuries.

Now let's talk about options. At its core, wealth buys freedom. It buys you the chance to start businesses, fund causes, travel the world without restriction, take sabbaticals when others have to grind, and say no to anything — and anyone — that doesn't align with your values. Options are the real currency of the ultra wealthy. And if you manage your wealth well, you maximize those options. You buy back time. You buy back possibilities. You set the terms of your own life.

But eventually — inevitably — the question shifts. It's not "how much can I make?" but "what will I leave behind?" Legacy isn't about cash balances or property holdings. It's about values, wisdom, character. It's about the opportunities you create, the family culture you foster, the impact you make beyond your own lifespan. Being ultra affluent means you have the chance — the duty — to shape lives, not just lifestyles.

And here's the truth very few will tell you: you are not just an owner. You are a steward. Ownership says, "This is mine." Stewardship says, "This is my responsibility." Ownership hoards and clings. Stewardship cultivates and prepares. Ultra wealth demands a shift from possessiveness to purposefulness. The ultra affluent who find true peace and satisfaction are those who understand that wealth is not a trophy — it's a tool. It's not an identity — it's an opportunity. It's not just a right — it's a responsibility.

This distinction matters because if you think wealth is just about accumulation, you'll stay stuck. You'll stay reactive. You'll stay trapped in the very success you worked so hard to build. But if you recognize that ultra wealth is about stewardship — about using what you have to build something larger than yourself — then you unlock the true potential of what you've created. You stop thinking in terms of transactions and start thinking in terms of transformation.

This is the difference between being merely "rich" and being powerful. Not loud power. Not flashy power. Quiet, generational, transformative power. The kind that doesn't need to be broadcast to be felt. The kind that doesn't show up on social media feeds but shows up in the lives you shape, the communities you touch, and the family culture you foster. The kind of power that frees your children — not entraps them. The kind that lifts your family for generations.

The ultra affluent who master this understand something crucial: wealth is a platform, not a prison. Managed well, it offers freedom, purpose, and impact. Managed poorly, it becomes a cage — gilded, sure, but a cage nonetheless. And the difference lies not in how much you have, but in how well you steward it.

So here's the first real challenge I'll leave you with: Are you managing your wealth, or are you mastering it? Are you reactive, or are you deliberate? Are you trapped in complexity, or have you built clarity? Are you building a balance sheet, or are you building a legacy?

Because the world doesn't need more rich people. It needs more stewards. It needs more leaders who understand that wealth is not just a measurement — it's a mandate.

The Ultra Affluent Dilemma

The World Sees Wealth and Assumes Ease

The world sees wealth and assumes the journey stops there. As if arriving at the ultra-affluent level solves everything. You and I know better. Wealth doesn't erase problems — it magnifies them. It doesn't clear the path — it complicates the terrain. The moment you move from success to significance, from mere accumulation to stewardship, a new set of challenges emerges. These aren't the problems the world imagines — they are quieter, heavier, and much more complex. Let's step into the real dilemmas — the ones that live under the surface of every ultra affluent life.

Complexity vs. Simplicity

At the early stages of wealth building, the game is simple: make more, save more, invest wisely. But as your wealth scales, so does its complexity. You layer in trusts, holding companies, private equity stakes, hard assets like art collections and real estate, perhaps a family office. Each layer protects—but each layer also complicates. Each advisor brings expertise—but also, sometimes, conflicting advice. What was once a straightforward portfolio is now a labyrinth.

The greatest risk? That the structures built to protect your wealth trap you instead. You become a prisoner of your own design, tangled in operating agreements, compliance documents, and governance protocols. Sophistication without clarity becomes confusion. The art — and it is an art — is to build structures elegant enough to last, yet lean enough to live with. True mastery lies in clarity, in simplicity. Wealth that is engineered to serve, not suffocate.

Privacy vs. Isolation

One of wealth's greatest perks is privacy. You can insulate your life, build gates, employ security teams, create layers of protection that keep the world at bay. But walls that protect can also isolate. You begin to question motives. Old friendships shift. Family dynamics strain. New connections feel transactional.

You find yourself asking: who knows me — really knows me — without the filter of my net worth? The danger is real: privacy turning into loneliness, discretion mutating into isolation. The solution isn't further withdrawal; it's careful curation. It's about building circles of trust — genuine, intentional communities where you are seen not for what you have, but for who you are. Where conversations are candid, not calibrated. Where wealth is neither a barrier nor a badge.

Opportunity vs. Risk

One of the more exhilarating aspects of wealth is access. Deals, investments, ventures, experiences — doors swing open that most people never even see. But not all that glitters is gold. Ultra affluence attracts not just opportunities, but opportunists. Deals appear that seem too good to pass up. Partners promise returns that defy reality. Ventures look brilliant on the surface, but underneath, hidden risks fester.

Mastery at this level means learning to say "no" more often than "yes." It means prioritizing diligence over excitement, strategy over impulse. Wealth creates the illusion that every door must be walked through. But the real winners at this level are those who understand that the best opportunities are not always the loudest or flashiest — they are the ones most aligned with your mission, your values, your legacy.

Legacy vs. Entitlement

You want your wealth to outlast you — to be a blessing, not a burden. Yet you've seen the cautionary tales: inherited wealth draining ambition, safety nets turning into hammocks, legacy dissolving into entitlement. How do you ensure that what you leave behind strengthens, not weakens, the generations that follow?

The answer lies not in dictating from beyond the grave but in fostering stewardship while you're alive. It's about education, communication, and culture. Teaching not just financial literacy but emotional resilience. Building structures that deliver not just assets but also accountability. Legacy is not what you leave to them; it's what you leave in them — values, wisdom, principles that endure longer than any trust distribution schedule.

Why This Matters

Recognizing these dilemmas won't solve them outright. But recognition is the first step toward mastery. Wealth at this level is a different game, with different rules. Those who succeed in the long term — who build true dynasties — aren't the ones who simply accumulate. They are the ones who navigate these tensions wisely, intentionally, courageously.

The complexities, the isolation, the flood of opportunities, the fear of entitlement — these are not burdens to be avoided. They are invitations to a higher level of leadership. They are the real work of being ultra affluent.

This is why I wrote Ultra Affluent — not to celebrate wealth, but to help you master it. To help you see that success is not a destination but a responsibility. To help you build a legacy that extends far beyond balance sheets and asset valuations. A legacy built on clarity, courage, and conviction.

The Call to Action

If you're reading this, you've already begun the journey. But reading is not enough. Understanding without action is the beginning of regret. So I offer you a simple challenge: identify one area — complexity, isolation, opportunity, or legacy — where you know you are vulnerable. One area where you've accepted "good enough" instead of demanding "world-class."

Write it down.

And then commit — before the week is out — to one deliberate action to improve it.

Call the advisor.

Book the meeting.

Start the conversation with your family.

Audit the structures you've outgrown.

Say no to the next deal that doesn't align.

Because wealth, at this level, is not self-sustaining.
It demands vigilance.
It demands stewardship.
And above all, it demands leadership.

How to Use This Book

This Isn't a Novel

If you've made it this far, let's get one thing clear: this isn't a novel. It's not a quick-hit self-help manual promising overnight transformation. It's not a lecture designed to make you feel guilty for what you have or anxious about what's next. This book is a guide—an operating manual for wealth mastery at the ultra affluent level. It's built not for speed, but for precision. For people like you, who don't need more noise — but sharper tools, clearer frameworks, and better questions.

You don't have to read this book cover to cover. In fact, I don't recommend it. You're free to move through it the way you move through the world: intentionally, strategically, with purpose. Each chapter is a standalone playbook. Each section is a tool. Each idea is designed to be immediately practical, immediately powerful. No fluff. No filler. Just the insights you need, when you need them.

This is not entertainment. It's not here to impress you with complicated charts or dazzling technical jargon. It's a reference. A blueprint. A field guide to navigating wealth, freedom, and legacy at the highest levels. It's the resource you'll wish you had every time you stare down a major decision — a liquidity event, a generational transfer, a family governance challenge. It's built to grow with you, to meet you wherever you are in your wealth journey — whether you're fresh off an exit or managing a family office that spans continents and decades.

How to Navigate This Book

Start Where You Are: Open the table of contents. Scan the chapters. What resonates right now? What question is sitting in the back of your mind — or maybe gnawing at you every time you wake up at 3 AM? Start there. The order doesn't matter — relevance does.

Use It as a Toolkit: Are you preparing for a liquidity event? Jump to the sections on investment strategy, tax mitigation, or liquidity planning. Thinking about legacy? Dive into the family governance chapters. Grappling with asset protection or wealth transfer? Head to the advanced estate planning sections.

Come Back Often: Wealth mastery isn't a one-time event. As your wealth grows and life evolves, so will your questions. New challenges will surface — market volatility, family transitions, philanthropic opportunities. This book is designed to meet you again and again — to be as dynamic as your life.

Apply As You Go: Don't wait to finish every page before acting. Implement one idea. Make one decision. Adjust one habit. Momentum matters more than perfection. In wealth — as in life — action creates clarity.

What You'll Find Inside

Clarity Over Complexity: Complex wealth strategies don't have to come in dense, unreadable packages. We break down sophisticated concepts into plain language — not because we think you can't understand them, but because the goal is not just comprehension, but application.

Principles Over Prescriptions: You're too experienced to settle for one-size-fits-all advice. You deserve frameworks that flex with your situation. This book gives you a way to think, not a checklist to blindly follow.

Action Over Theory: Every chapter includes practical steps you can take immediately. No ivory tower theories here. It's all about real-world application — what actually works, not what sounds good.

Freedom Over Fear: Wealth shouldn't breed anxiety. It should enable freedom. Every section is designed to help you use wealth to create more life — not more worry.

A Note on Style

We've kept this book intentionally clean. No clutter. No jargon. No endless footnotes sending you down rabbit holes you don't have time for. Just clear, honest, empowering conversation. Imagine you're sitting with a trusted advisor — someone who respects your intelligence, your accomplishments, and your time — and who wants to equip you to move forward with more clarity and more confidence.

That's the voice of this book. Direct, respectful, and actionable.

Final Thought

This book isn't about accumulating more. You already have more. More assets. More options. More responsibility. This is about mastering what you already have — turning wealth into freedom, clarity, legacy. It's about using wealth as a tool to unlock dignity, autonomy, and purpose — not just for you, but for the generations that follow.

It's about becoming the architect of your next chapter. Not a passive participant in your own life. Not a bystander while others steer the ship. But the deliberate designer of your financial future, your family culture, your broader legacy.

Why Most Wealth Advice Fails the Ultra Affluent

The Wealth Management Industry Is Built on Assumptions

The wealth management industry is built on assumptions. Assumptions about what people need. Assumptions about what success looks like. Assumptions about what advice works. But if you're holding this book, you already know: most of that advice wasn't built for you.

It was built for the mass affluent. For the "high-net-worth." For those measuring their wealth in millions — not tens or hundreds of millions. For people still climbing the mountain, not for those who've already summited and are now tasked with building a fortress, a family legacy, and a future. At the ultra affluent level, most traditional advice doesn't just feel off — it breaks down completely. Here's why.

Cookie-Cutter Strategies Fall Apart

Most financial advice runs on models. Asset allocation models. Monte Carlo simulations. Rule-of-thumb calculators for retirement income. These models work well when the financial picture is simple: a 401(k), some mutual funds, a mortgage, a few insurance policies. They're designed for scale — to help the masses.

But what happens when your balance sheet no longer fits inside a traditional framework? When your assets include operating businesses, private equity stakes, real estate portfolios across multiple geographies, fine art collections, yachts, aircraft, and a matrix of trusts and holding companies? What happens when you're not just managing retirement income projections — you're managing generational influence and global assets?

Cookie-cutter models collapse under that complexity. They weren't designed for your world. Your life doesn't fit neatly into their spreadsheets. You need strategies that are bespoke, custom-built for your complexity, your values, your goals. Strategies designed not just for wealth building — but for wealth architecture.

Most Advisors Aren't Trained for This

Here's another reality: most financial advisors are trained to do one thing — help people accumulate wealth. They are good at guiding someone from zero to their first million, even their first ten million. But they aren't trained to navigate the complexities that come with true ultra affluence.

They're not trained to orchestrate family governance across generations. They're not trained to structure multi-generational wealth transfer that considers not just taxes but family harmony. They're not trained to craft philanthropic strategies that align with both tax optimization and mission impact. They're not trained in private placements, bespoke insurance solutions, or navigating the emotional landmines of preparing heirs without enabling entitlement.

At this level, you're not just managing money. You're managing capital. Reputation. Legacy. Risk. Family dynamics. Influence. The conversations aren't about beating the market by 50 basis points — they're about designing a structure that lasts longer than a lifetime. You need advisors who understand that — and who have the humility to collaborate across disciplines, not dictate from a singular viewpoint.

Sophistication Without Complexity

There's a dangerous myth that more wealth demands more complexity. That somehow success is measured by how many layers deep your structures go. That more LLCs, more SPVs, more offshore trusts automatically mean better planning. That's not sophistication. That's confusion with a price tag.

True sophistication is clarity. It's simplicity on the far side of complexity. It's structures that are robust, elegant, and understandable. It's not about how many pieces you have — it's about how well they fit together, how gracefully they move when the winds of change blow.

At the ultra affluent level, you don't need more moving parts. You need better coordination. Cleaner structures. Smarter risk management. Sharper strategies. Tighter family governance. A cohesive architecture that is as beautiful in its design as it is powerful in its execution.

An architect doesn't just add beams and bricks. An architect thinks about foundation, structure, flow, and legacy. An architect builds not just for today — but for generations. That's the mindset this book is built on.

Why This Matters

When traditional, mass-market advice fails you, it's not because you're difficult. It's because the advice was never designed for your life. You've outgrown the standard models. You've entered a world where the stakes are different, where the playbook has to change.

You need a new blueprint. A blueprint for mastery. Stewardship. Freedom. Legacy. A blueprint that's worthy of your complexity — and of your aspirations.

This book isn't about cramming you back into a standard mold. It's about giving you the frameworks and tools to design a wealth strategy that fits you — your life, your family, your vision.

Because ultra wealth deserves ultra wisdom. And you're ready for both.

Pros and Cons

Pros of Bespoke Wealth Management:

- Customized strategies tailored to your goals and complexity
- Integrated planning across investments, tax, estate, risk, and philanthropy
- Greater alignment between your wealth and your legacy vision
- Peace of mind knowing your structures are built to last

Cons of Bespoke Wealth Management:

- Requires finding the right experts — not all advisors are qualified
- Demands ongoing oversight and coordination
- May involve higher upfront complexity before reaching true simplicity
- Higher professional fees for specialized services — but worth the value

Action Steps

Start by conducting a full audit of your current wealth architecture. Is your financial life being managed by mass-market models — or is it being designed by true architects? Evaluate your advisory team. Are they orchestrating a holistic plan, or operating in silos?

Interview your advisors the way you would interview a CEO. Do they understand family governance? Philanthropy? Private markets? Risk beyond portfolio volatility? Are they willing to collaborate — or are they guarding their turf?

If not, it's time to upgrade.

Define your objectives beyond net worth targets. What legacy do you want to leave? What values do you want to instill? What risks do you want to eliminate?

Set a 90-day goal: realign your team, your strategy, or both. Complexity unmanaged becomes a burden. But complexity architected becomes a legacy.

Real-Life Scenarios

Consider the family who transitioned from traditional wealth management to a true family office structure. Initially, their life was a patchwork — different advisors managing slices of the pie. After restructuring, they gained holistic oversight: tax, investment, risk, philanthropy, family governance — all aligned. Their wealth wasn't just managed. It was mastered.

Contrast this with another family who stayed in mass-market models too long. They faced unnecessary estate taxes, fractured family relations, and governance gaps that took years to repair.

The difference wasn't intelligence. It was architecture.

Final Note

This chapter is your permission slip to demand better — not out of arrogance, but out of responsibility. You've outgrown the old models. It's time to architect something worthy of the life — and the legacy — you're building.

Mastery isn't about knowing everything. It's about knowing enough to ask better questions, to hire better teams, and to build better structures.

Ultra Affluent isn't just a label.

Your Wealth Mastery Blueprint: What's Inside

Ultra Affluence Demands More Than Just Good Investments

If you're holding this book, you already know something essential: success at the ultra affluent level isn't just about having more—it's about mastering more. You've outgrown simple portfolio theory and basic estate planning. Ultra affluence demands a deeper discipline. It demands mastery—not just of money, but of complexity. Mastery not just of strategy, but of legacy. Mastery not just of growth, but of resilience. This isn't about incremental improvement. It's about transformational clarity. It's about building the kind of wealth structure that can weather markets, time, and even generations.

This book is your blueprint for that mastery. Here's what you're going to build.

Building Your Wealth Command Center

At this level, winging it is not a strategy. The stakes are too high, and the complexity too great. You need a system—a centralized command center that provides real-time clarity on your wealth architecture. What you own. Where your risks are. How your cash flows. What's working—and what's eroding quietly beneath the surface. Think of it like the cockpit of a private jet. Without it, you're flying blind.

Your Wealth Command Center integrates your asset classes, legal entities, trusts, cash flow models, risk structures, and legacy plans into a single, coordinated dashboard. It's how you shift from reacting to proactively leading your wealth strategy. From confusion to clarity. From stress to sovereignty. This is the foundation on which true wealth mastery is built.

Action Step: Audit your current reporting system. Can you see your full financial landscape on one page? If not, start there. Demand better.

Creating Liquidity Without Losing Growth

One of the most underestimated risks at the ultra wealthy level is illiquidity. You can be worth $200 million on paper and still be cash poor. Real estate, private equity, fine art, operating businesses—they're impressive. But they're also illiquid. And in a liquidity crunch, prestige won't pay the bills.

Wealth mastery requires a liquidity strategy—one that balances growth with flexibility. This means setting up smart credit lines secured against appreciating assets. It means keeping strategic dry powder in tax-advantaged, easily accessible structures. It means understanding the liquidity profile of every asset and how quickly it can be converted, if necessary, without significant value destruction.

Real-Life Scenario: A tech founder with a net worth north of $500 million found himself unable to close on a once-in-a-lifetime real estate opportunity because his capital was locked up in illiquid venture funds. Contrast that with another family who maintained a strategic liquidity sleeve—allowing them to pounce when opportunity knocked.

Action Step: Assess your current liquidity profile. What percentage of your assets could you access within 30 days without penalties? Without sacrifice? Adjust accordingly.

Managing Risk Like a Billionaire

The ultra affluent think about risk differently. They understand that wealth magnifies exposure. More assets mean more targets. More visibility means more vulnerability.

The solution isn't just more insurance. It's more structure. More foresight. More discipline. It's about designing trust frameworks, asset protection entities, and contingency plans. It's about conducting comprehensive risk audits—legal, financial, reputational—and shoring up weaknesses long before they're tested. It's about ensuring your risk management strategy evolves with your life—not two steps behind it.

Action Step: Schedule a full-scope risk audit. Include cybersecurity, legal structures, estate planning gaps, and reputational vulnerabilities. Defense wins dynasties.

Mastering Advanced Investment Opportunities

Public markets are only one small corner of the ultra affluent investing universe. At your level, you have access to the private markets: private equity, venture capital, direct deals, real assets, hedge funds, private credit. But access is not a strategy. Selectivity is.

Mastery means understanding that not every direct deal deserves your capital. Not every venture fund is worth your time. It's about developing a personal investment filter that aligns opportunities with your core objectives and risk appetite. It's about saying "no" far more often than "yes." It's about due diligence, discipline, and a refusal to be seduced by shiny objects.

Real-Life Scenario: One entrepreneur diversified into a venture fund that failed spectacularly due to poor due diligence. Meanwhile, a peer developed a robust investment filter, allocating only to funds and projects where they had both informational advantage and alignment of values. The difference in outcomes? Astronomical.

Action Step: Refine your investment filters. What must an opportunity meet—strategically, financially, ethically—before you even consider it?

Structuring Generational Legacies and Philanthropic Plans

Wealth is fleeting. Legacy is engineered. Without structure, your estate could be a tax disaster and your heirs could be targets for entitlement, resentment, or worse. Dynasty trusts, family governance councils, and values-based philanthropy are no longer luxuries. They are imperatives.

Legacy planning is about more than documents and legal frameworks. It's about conversations—structured, intentional, and ongoing—with heirs. It's about embedding purpose, mission, and vision into the very structure of your wealth.

Action Step: If you haven't already, draft a family mission statement. It should guide not just wealth distribution, but the stewardship of values, influence, and opportunity.

Curating an Elite Advisory Team Without Losing Control

You are the CEO of your wealth. Your advisors are your executive team. Too many ultra affluent individuals allow their advisory circle to become bloated, misaligned, or—worse—more loyal to each other than to the client.

Curate your team carefully. Vet rigorously. Insist on collaboration, not silos. Demand transparency and fiduciary alignment. But most importantly, never abdicate leadership. You must remain at the helm—not your lawyer, your CPA, or your investment advisor.

Action Step: Conduct a team audit. Are your advisors proactive or reactive? Collaborative or territorial? Upgrade where necessary.

Why This Matters

This book is not about giving you more to think about. You already have enough complexity. It's about giving you clarity. It's about building a system—a blueprint—that elevates you from wealth owner to wealth master.

Ultra affluence doesn't just give you more options. It gives you more at stake. More impact to make. More lives to shape. More legacy to protect.

You've already built wealth. Now it's time to master it.

Final Call to Action: Choose one action step from this chapter. Implement it before the month ends. Momentum, not perfection, will elevate you to the next level.

Because at this level, the difference between a fortune and a dynasty is not the size of your portfolio.

It's the sophistication of your stewardship.

Part I: Foundation — Financial Literacy for the Ultra Affluent

Wealth without wisdom is a house without a foundation.
It might look impressive.
It might stand tall.
But when the storms come—and they always do—it crumbles.
Part I is about building that foundation.
Because ultra wealth demands more than basic financial literacy.
It demands:

- A deeper understanding of how money, markets, and mechanisms really work.
- A broader view of risk, liquidity, leverage, and legacy.
- A sharper lens for evaluating advisors, strategies, and opportunities.

This is financial literacy designed for:

- The entrepreneur who sold their company and is sitting on a life-changing liquidity event.
- The family business owner managing transition and succession.
- The private investor juggling real estate, venture, and legacy portfolios.
- The inheritor who has wealth but needs wisdom.

In this section, we will:

- Redefine what "financial literacy" means when you're managing tens or hundreds of millions.
- Break down the advanced concepts that protect and grow wealth at scale.
- Equip you with the filters you need to separate noise from signal.
- Help you think about money not just as a resource—but as a responsibility.

We'll cover:

- Cash flow mastery
- Advanced liquidity management
- The truth about leverage
- How to think about risk like an institution
- Tax strategies the ultra affluent need to know
- Estate structures for lasting legacy

Financial literacy at this level isn't about balancing a checkbook.

It's about balancing:

- Freedom and security.
- Growth and preservation.
- Opportunity and risk.

It's about thinking not just in dollars—but in decades.

Before you build anything else—you must pour the right foundation.

Welcome to Part I.

Let's lay the groundwork for everything to come.

Chapter 1: Pat Brown, MBA, From Athlete to Wealth Manager for the Ultra Affluent

Pat Brown's journey from the gridiron to the boardroom is a testament to discipline, adaptability, and an unwavering commitment to excellence. As a former Division I football player, Pat learned early on the value of structure, preparation, and teamwork—principles that would later form the cornerstone of his approach to wealth management for the ultra-affluent. But make no mistake: this transition was not a straight line. It was a journey defined by lessons that have become integral to the way he serves those managing significant wealth today.

Athletics at the highest collegiate levels demand a unique blend of physical prowess and mental rigor. Pat's experience on the football field taught him about strategy under pressure, the importance of adaptability, and the relentless pursuit of incremental improvement. These traits served him well as he transitioned from sports to the world of finance—a field where stakes are high, markets are volatile, and the need for strategic clarity is paramount.

After his playing days, Pat pursued an MBA, recognizing that true mastery would require a deeper understanding of financial theory, investment strategy, and business dynamics. This academic foundation, combined with his competitive instincts, positioned him to navigate the complexities of wealth management with the same discipline and rigor he brought to athletics. But unlike the finite timelines of sports seasons, wealth stewardship is a multi-generational game. The objective is not merely short-term wins, but enduring, strategic success.

Pat's professional trajectory has always been guided by one principle: service to others. He understood early that managing significant wealth isn't just about numbers; it's about people—their ambitions, their family legacies, their deeply held values. Ultra-affluent clients are not seeking transactional relationships; they require trust, discretion, and a level of strategic insight that cuts through complexity. Pat's background instilled in him the ability to listen intently, communicate clearly, and execute decisively—traits that have made him a trusted advisor to some of the nation's most successful individuals and families.

His client engagements are not boilerplate. Each relationship begins with a conversation—an in-depth dialogue to understand not just assets and liabilities, but goals, fears, family dynamics, and long-term aspirations. From there, Pat orchestrates a highly personalized strategy, integrating estate planning, tax efficiency, investment management, insurance optimization, liquidity event preparation, and philanthropic planning. His aim is not to overwhelm clients with complexity, but to replace confusion with clarity, and to transform risk into resilience.

Real-life scenarios demonstrate the depth of Pat's impact. One founder approached him post-liquidity event with a sprawling portfolio—stock options, real estate, venture capital holdings—and no coherent strategy for consolidation or risk management. Pat's disciplined approach involved coordinating with estate attorneys, CPAs, and investment managers to build a comprehensive, tax-optimized, legacy-focused plan. The result was not just financial security but a sense of control and direction that had previously been lacking.

Another family office sought Pat's guidance to transition leadership and wealth to the next generation. Sensitive to the nuances of family governance and the challenges of multi-generational wealth transfer, Pat facilitated a series of family meetings, helped articulate a shared family mission, and put governance structures in place to ensure unity and strategic alignment. It wasn't just about preserving wealth; it was about preserving the family's identity and purpose.

The pros of working with a wealth manager like Pat are evident: strategic clarity, coordinated execution, risk mitigation, and legacy enhancement. The cons? There are few, but clients must be ready to engage deeply, to have frank conversations about their goals and fears, and to trust the process. Strategic wealth management at this level demands active participation and a willingness to think beyond immediate horizons.

Action Step: If you find yourself navigating the complexities of significant wealth—liquidity events, multi-generational planning, concentrated asset positions, philanthropic initiatives—engage a professional who brings both technical expertise and personal commitment. Seek out someone who doesn't just manage money but manages complexity, emotion, and legacy with equal skill.

The call to action is clear: Do not leave your financial life—and by extension, your family's future—to chance or partial planning. Insist on working with an advisor who brings discipline, rigor, and a strategic framework tailored to your specific situation.

Pat's journey from athlete to wealth manager underscores a larger truth: success, whether on the field or in finance, is rarely about luck. It's about preparation, execution, and resilience. It's about having a game plan—and the right coach to help you navigate it.

While this book is designed to inform and inspire, if you are ready to elevate your wealth strategy and want personalized guidance, Pat Brown is available for consultation. With years of experience serving ultra-affluent individuals and families, he stands ready to help you move beyond complexity toward clarity, from uncertainty toward a future of enduring wealth and impact.

The goals—wealth preservation, strategic growth, risk mitigation, legacy planning—are within reach. But they require more than good intentions; they demand action. Whether you can accomplish this on your own or need the guidance of a seasoned professional, the next move is yours to make.

Chapter 2: The Ultra Affluent Mindset, Preservation Over Growth

At the ultra-affluent level, the conversation about wealth shifts fundamentally. For those who have crossed a certain threshold, it becomes less about growth at all costs and more about preservation—about sustaining, protecting, and extending wealth across generations. Growth is still important, but it is not the north star; the focus shifts to endurance, resilience, and intentional legacy. This is the ultra-affluent mindset: preservation over growth.

When you first built your wealth, chances are the mindset was aggressively growth-oriented. Whether through entrepreneurship, investments, innovation, or inheritance, success was fueled by risk-taking, strategy, and expansion. That mentality, however, does not simply scale linearly once wealth reaches a level where risk carries vastly different consequences. Losing 20% of $500,000 is painful; losing 20% of $50 million can be catastrophic not just for your lifestyle, but for future generations and philanthropic ambitions.

Preservation does not mean becoming risk-averse or passive. It means being strategic, recognizing that the primary goal now is sustainability and stability. It means shifting from the "growth at all costs" mentality to one that carefully calibrates risk and return with the long-term picture in mind. Real-Life Scenario: A first-generation entrepreneur who had built a $200 million fortune remained overly concentrated in his company's stock. A major downturn in his sector erased a significant portion of his wealth—wealth he had planned to pass on to his children and earmark for philanthropic endeavors. Had he adopted a preservation-first mindset earlier, he could have gradually diversified without sacrificing overall growth.

The pros of prioritizing preservation are clear: reduced risk of catastrophic loss, enhanced financial resilience, smoother wealth transfer, and greater peace of mind. The cons? The returns may not be as spectacular in bull markets. You might not "outperform" speculative investors in high-growth environments. But for the ultra-affluent, the true goal is not beating the market year-to-year—it's ensuring that wealth endures, serves a purpose, and maintains its impact across decades.

A preservation mindset demands several critical shifts. First, diversification becomes non-negotiable. Concentrated bets that might have worked during the wealth accumulation phase are now dangerous. Strategic asset allocation, exposure to alternative investments, and a global approach are essential. Second, liquidity planning rises in importance. Having ready access to capital allows you to navigate market downturns without selling distressed assets. Third, tax efficiency becomes a core part of the strategy—it's not just what you earn, it's what you keep.

Another pillar of the preservation mindset is governance—both personal and family governance. Wealth without governance can quickly become a source of conflict or decline. Families that successfully preserve wealth across generations often have clear governance structures, articulate shared values, and instill financial literacy early. Real-Life Scenario: A multigenerational family with a $500 million fortune implemented a family council, annual retreats, and formal succession planning. As a result, they not only preserved their financial capital but also their human and intellectual capital, maintaining unity and purpose.

Insurance also plays a more prominent role. At the ultra-affluent level, comprehensive insurance—covering life, property, liability, and specialized risks like cyber threats—becomes a critical tool for wealth preservation. Many overlook the role insurance plays not just in protecting assets but in optimizing estate transfer strategies through tools like irrevocable life insurance trusts (ILITs).

Philanthropy is another key component. Beyond personal fulfillment, structured giving through donor-advised funds (DAFs) or private foundations can enhance tax efficiency, perpetuate family values, and leave a lasting legacy. Philanthropy, when integrated into the broader wealth strategy, is not just charity—it's a vehicle for meaning and impact.

Action Step: Begin by reassessing your current strategy. Are you still operating with a "growth-first" mindset that served you well early in your journey but may now be misaligned with your current objectives? Conduct a thorough audit: review asset allocations, liquidity reserves, estate plans, governance structures, and risk protections. Where are the vulnerabilities? Where might the old playbook be putting your wealth at risk?

The call to action is both simple and profound: Shift your mindset. Understand that wealth preservation is not about playing it safe—it's about playing it smart. It's about designing a financial ecosystem resilient enough to withstand market cycles, adaptable enough to evolve with new opportunities, and strategic enough to serve multiple generations.

The goals—sustainability, resilience, impact, legacy—are entirely achievable. But they require a recalibration of mindset and strategy. Whether you choose to navigate this transition on your own or engage seasoned professionals to assist, the first step is recognizing that preservation is the true measure of enduring wealth.

While this chapter provides the framework, if you find yourself seeking a deeper, customized approach to shifting from a growth-first to a preservation-first strategy, Pat Brown is available to provide guidance. With years of experience helping ultra-affluent individuals and families manage wealth with precision and purpose, he brings the clarity, structure, and vision necessary to turn complexity into confidence.

Chapter 3: From Wealth Creator to Wealth Steward: A Different Financial Playbook

There is a profound transition that every ultra-affluent individual must face at some point: the evolution from wealth creator to wealth steward. The financial strategies that build wealth are not the same ones that sustain it. The skillset that drove growth and success is often ill-suited to the complexities of preservation, stewardship, and legacy. Understanding this shift is not a matter of capability—it is a matter of recognizing that a different financial playbook is required.

In the wealth creation phase, the emphasis is on risk, innovation, and opportunity. Entrepreneurs, executives, and investors thrive in environments where bold moves and calculated risks generate outsized rewards. But the stewardship phase demands a reversal in priorities. The focus turns to risk management, wealth preservation, tax efficiency, intergenerational planning, and legacy creation. Wealth stewards must think not just about growing assets, but about sustaining and transferring them—while maintaining family unity, purpose, and privacy.

A fundamental mindset shift is required. Growth is no longer the primary driver—stability, resilience, and intentionality are. Real-Life Scenario: A tech entrepreneur who amassed considerable wealth through high-risk startups struggled post-exit to adjust his approach. Without recalibration, his aggressive growth strategies exposed his portfolio to unnecessary risks, leading to significant losses during a market downturn. Once he embraced the stewardship mindset, focusing on diversified allocations, estate planning, and structured philanthropy, his financial life regained stability and purpose.

The pros of embracing wealth stewardship are clear: enhanced financial security, smoother wealth transition to future generations, preservation of family harmony, and a more significant, lasting impact through philanthropy or values-based initiatives. The cons? It demands giving up some of the adrenaline and excitement that comes with aggressive growth strategies. It requires patience, planning, and a willingness to engage with complex structures and professional teams.

The steward's playbook starts with governance—not just personal discipline, but family governance as well. A clear mission statement, a set of shared values, and structured family meetings can prevent the most common causes of wealth destruction: miscommunication, entitlement, and conflict. Action Step: Draft a family constitution or mission statement that articulates shared goals and values. Implement family councils and annual retreats to foster unity and communication.

Next is asset allocation and risk management. Diversification is no longer optional—it is mandatory. Private investments, real estate, global equities, fixed income, and alternative assets must be balanced with liquidity needs and tax considerations. Stewardship requires a disciplined investment policy statement that prioritizes capital preservation while allowing for reasonable growth. Action Step: Review your current asset allocation and rebalance it to align with long-term goals and risk tolerance appropriate for a multi-generational strategy.

Tax efficiency becomes an art form in the stewardship phase. Wealth creators often focus on topline returns; stewards focus on after-tax returns and wealth transfer efficiency. Advanced strategies like grantor retained annuity trusts (GRATs), spousal lifetime access trusts (SLATs), dynasty trusts, and family limited partnerships (FLPs) are powerful tools when used correctly. Real-Life Scenario: A family that implemented a series of GRATs successfully moved significant wealth out of the estate tax system while maintaining access to income streams, preserving their legacy with far greater tax efficiency.

Philanthropy takes on new meaning. It evolves from occasional giving to structured, mission-aligned initiatives. Private foundations, donor-advised funds (DAFs), and impact investing allow stewards to align capital with values while optimizing tax outcomes. Philanthropy, when integrated into the financial strategy, enhances legacy and fosters a sense of purpose among younger generations. Action Step: Develop a formal philanthropic strategy that aligns with your family's mission and long-term objectives.

Stewardship also demands rigorous privacy and risk management. Ultra-affluent families are increasingly targets for cyber threats, litigation, and reputational attacks. Comprehensive risk audits—encompassing personal security, digital security, insurance, and legal structures—are no longer luxuries; they are necessities. Action Step: Conduct a full personal and family risk audit, updating insurance, digital security protocols, and legal protections.

The transition from creator to steward is not about slowing down—it is about elevating the game. It requires engaging with a new set of advisors: estate attorneys, tax strategists, investment specialists, family governance consultants, and philanthropic advisors. It requires discipline, but also opens the door to deeper fulfillment—not just in growing wealth, but in securing a legacy that endures.

The call to action is clear: Recognize that the strategies that built your wealth are not the ones that will sustain it. Embrace a new playbook—one centered on stewardship, governance, diversification, tax efficiency, risk management, and impact.

The goals—financial resilience, family unity, enduring legacy, and impactful philanthropy—are achievable. But they require a deliberate shift in mindset and strategy. Whether you undertake this transition on your own or with the guidance of seasoned professionals, understand this: True wealth is not measured solely by accumulation, but by endurance, purpose, and the ability to empower generations to come.

While this chapter provides the strategic framework, if you find yourself ready to transition from wealth creator to wealth steward and would like tailored guidance, Pat Brown is available to help. With extensive experience advising ultra-affluent individuals and families, he brings the clarity, structure, and vision necessary to help you write the next chapter of your wealth story—one defined by enduring impact and legacy.

Chapter 4: Wealth is a Family Business: Teaching the Next Generation

Wealth, at its highest levels, is not just a private resource—it is a family enterprise. The ultra-affluent quickly realize that managing significant wealth is more than asset allocation and tax efficiency; it is about teaching, preparing, and empowering the next generation to sustain and elevate the family legacy. Wealth is a family business, and like any enterprise, it requires leadership development, strategic planning, governance structures, and cultural stewardship.

The first generation of wealth creators often focuses on building the empire—businesses, investments, real estate portfolios. The next challenge is even greater: ensuring that wealth is not only preserved but also productively utilized by generations who did not directly participate in its creation. Without intentional preparation, wealth can easily become a source of conflict, entitlement, or loss.

Studies consistently show that 70% of wealth transfers fail by the third generation. This failure is rarely due to poor financial advice or investment losses—it is due to breakdowns in communication, lack of preparation, and the absence of a shared family mission. Real-Life Scenario: A family with a nine-figure fortune lost nearly half its wealth within two generations because heirs lacked financial literacy, accountability structures, and a sense of purpose around the family's capital.

The pros of treating wealth as a family business are profound: greater cohesion, sustained wealth, a clear sense of shared purpose, and empowered heirs. The cons? It requires time, patience, and a willingness to engage in sometimes difficult conversations. Families must address differences in philosophy, aspirations, and capabilities openly and constructively.

The process begins with education. Financial literacy for the next generation must go beyond basic budgeting. It should encompass investment principles, risk management, philanthropy, business operations, governance, and the responsibilities of wealth. Action Step: Implement a formal family education curriculum—a "Family MBA"—that evolves as children mature, ensuring they develop both technical knowledge and emotional intelligence.

Next is governance. Families need a decision-making framework: councils, boards, and family constitutions that outline how decisions are made, how conflicts are resolved, and what principles guide the deployment of wealth. Governance creates clarity and prevents the chaos that can arise from unstructured, informal management. Action Step: Draft a family constitution and establish a family council to formalize governance structures.

Transparency is also key—not full transparency on all financial details, but age-appropriate visibility into the family's values, goals, and expectations. Children should understand not just that the family has wealth, but why, and what it is intended to achieve. Real-Life Scenario: A multi-generational family built annual retreats where financial education, philanthropic planning, and business updates were shared, fostering a deep sense of involvement and responsibility among younger members.

Philanthropy provides a powerful platform for engagement. Involving the next generation in charitable initiatives teaches not only financial stewardship but also the value of impact and responsibility. Structured giving programs, matching grants, and family foundations can serve as entry points for younger family members to learn about money management and social responsibility. Action Step: Launch a next-generation philanthropy committee within your family structure, giving heirs a voice in strategic giving.

Another pillar is leadership development. Just as a business develops a pipeline of future executives, families must cultivate leadership skills among younger generations. This includes not only financial acumen but also communication, negotiation, critical thinking, and decision-making. Action Step: Encourage heirs to gain external leadership experience—running businesses, engaging in professional careers, or managing philanthropic initiatives—before stepping into roles of greater family responsibility.

Lastly, ongoing review and adaptation are essential. Family dynamics change, laws evolve, markets shift. Governance frameworks, educational programs, and philanthropic strategies must be revisited and refined regularly to stay effective and relevant. Action Step: Conduct annual family summits to review governance policies, family goals, and the evolving roles of individual members.

The call to action is direct: Treat your family's wealth as the sophisticated enterprise it is. Recognize that without preparation, even vast fortunes can disappear. With deliberate education, governance, and leadership development, your wealth can become not just a financial asset but a platform for multi-generational growth, impact, and unity.

The goals—sustained wealth, empowered heirs, family cohesion, enduring legacy—are achievable. But they require a shift from passive inheritance to active stewardship. Whether you choose to guide this transition yourself or engage experienced advisors to assist, the first step is a mindset change: understand that wealth, wisely managed, is a family business.

While this chapter outlines the framework, if you are seeking tailored strategies to prepare your family for the responsibilities of wealth stewardship, Pat Brown is available for consultation. With years of experience working with ultra-affluent families, he brings the structure, insight, and discretion necessary to help turn financial success into a lasting family legacy.

Chapter 5: The Real Risks for the Ultra Wealthy: What Keeps Billionaires Up at Night

At the ultra-affluent level, risk has a different texture. For most, risk means the volatility of the markets or the possibility of not hitting a retirement savings target. But for billionaires and those managing generational wealth, the risks are deeper, more nuanced, and often invisible to the casual observer. It's not portfolio dips that keep billionaires up at night; it's the risks that threaten legacy, reputation, family unity, and the very foundations of their empire.

First and foremost, concentration risk is paramount. Many ultra-wealthy individuals created their fortune through a single business, investment, or asset class. Even after liquidity events, there can be an over-reliance on a few key holdings. While concentration built the wealth, it also represents a structural fragility. Real-Life Scenario: A tech founder with a significant post-IPO concentration in company stock saw billions evaporate when market sentiment turned. Action Step: Proactively diversify. Build a disciplined reallocation plan that acknowledges the emotional difficulty of selling legacy assets but prioritizes risk reduction.

Next is governance risk—not just corporate governance, but family governance. Without structured family governance, wealth often becomes a divisive force. Siblings squabble. Heirs grow resentful. Values dissipate. Real-Life Scenario: A billionaire industrialist died without clear succession planning; within a decade, his heirs were locked in litigation, and a once-proud family business was disassembled. Action Step: Build a family governance framework—councils, constitutions, decision-making bodies—to create clarity, unity, and sustainable leadership transitions.

Cybersecurity risk is increasingly a top concern. Ultra-wealthy families and their businesses are targets for sophisticated cyberattacks—phishing, ransomware, data breaches, identity theft. Beyond financial loss, breaches can cause reputational harm that is difficult to recover from. Action Step: Conduct a comprehensive cybersecurity audit, including personal devices, home networks, business systems, and family offices. Invest in robust cybersecurity protocols and education.

Another major risk is regulatory and political risk. Changes in tax law, wealth redistribution policies, or geopolitical instability can have significant impacts on ultra-affluent families. Smart wealth owners monitor legislative trends and diversify not only investments but also citizenship and residency options. Real-Life Scenario: An ultra-wealthy family with global real estate and business holdings leveraged second citizenships and jurisdictional diversification to mitigate country-specific risks. Action Step: Evaluate global mobility and second citizenship options to hedge against political and regulatory shifts.

Reputation risk looms large as well. In the age of social media and instant news cycles, reputational damage can erode not only personal standing but also business value. Crisis management strategies, media training, and proactive reputation management are no longer optional—they are essential. Action Step: Develop a crisis communication plan and regularly audit your digital and media presence.

Another underappreciated risk is the erosion of purpose. Wealth without mission can lead to complacency, entitlement, and generational decline. Many families struggle to instill the work ethic, values, and ambition that created the wealth in the first place. Real-Life Scenario: A billionaire established a family foundation with an open mandate, inviting the next generation to define philanthropic goals and strategies, instilling purpose and leadership skills. Action Step: Engage your heirs in defining a shared family mission that transcends wealth.

Liquidity risk cannot be ignored. Many ultra-wealthy individuals have significant assets tied up in illiquid holdings—real estate, private equity, venture capital. In times of market stress or personal need, liquidity shortages can force distressed sales. Action Step: Maintain a liquidity reserve—not just in cash but in quickly accessible investments—that can cover both opportunities and emergencies.

Finally, personal risk must be acknowledged—kidnapping, extortion, personal security threats. While unpleasant to discuss, personal safety for ultra-wealthy individuals and families is a real concern. Comprehensive security planning, including secure residences, travel protocols, and trained security personnel, is vital. Action Step: Engage a professional security consultant to evaluate vulnerabilities and implement a personalized security strategy.

The call to action is straightforward but profound: Think beyond the obvious. The real risks to ultra-wealthy individuals are rarely market-related alone. They involve people, purpose, reputation, regulation, security, and governance.

The goals—safeguarding wealth, preserving family unity, maintaining reputation, ensuring personal security—are attainable. But they demand a different level of vigilance and strategic planning. Whether you choose to address these risks on your own or partner with trusted experts, one thing is clear: success at the ultra-affluent level is not just about growing wealth—it's about protecting it against the risks that matter most.

While this chapter lays out the primary risks and strategies, if you seek deeper, customized risk assessments and solutions tailored to your unique profile, Pat Brown is available to help. With years of experience advising ultra-affluent individuals and families, he brings the insight, discretion, and comprehensive planning required to safeguard not just assets, but legacies.

Chapter 6: Building a Strong Financial Team, The Who's Who of Wealth

Wealth at the ultra-affluent level is not simply a number on a statement. It is an ecosystem, a responsibility, and a lifestyle that demands sophisticated, deliberate management. For those managing tens, hundreds of millions, or even more, the skills that built the wealth are not always the same ones that preserve and elevate it. Enduring wealth is a team sport, not a solo endeavor. Just as no championship team wins with a star player alone, no ultra-affluent individual sustains wealth without a team of specialized, coordinated experts.

The myth of the self-made individual persists, but it misses a crucial truth: true, multi-generational wealth is the product of teamwork—high-level professionals, all aligned to protect, grow, and steward a fortune. Imagine sitting here post-liquidity event, flush with success but aware that managing this new complexity is an entirely different game. This is where many falter—assuming that business acumen alone is enough. At this level, wealth management requires a different playbook, one less about speed and more about chess-like precision.

The first cornerstone of your wealth team is the wealth manager. Not just a financial advisor pitching funds, but a true strategist—someone who integrates investment management, tax strategy, estate planning, risk mitigation, and philanthropic endeavors into a coherent, personalized plan. They act as the quarterback, coordinating other professionals and ensuring that every decision serves your overall goals and preserves optionality.

Then comes the estate planning attorney—essential as wealth scales. While a will suffices for modest estates, the complexity of substantial wealth requires a more intricate architecture. Trusts, family limited partnerships, dynasty trusts, charitable vehicles—all require careful design and continuous updates to align with your family dynamics and evolving tax laws. Estate planning isn't just about minimizing taxes—it's about maintaining control, promoting family unity, and perpetuating values.

No team is complete without a seasoned CPA or tax strategist. At this level, taxes are not a once-a-year chore; they are a full-time strategic battleground. Structuring income, minimizing capital gains, optimizing charitable contributions, managing estate and gift taxes—these all demand proactive, sophisticated tax planning. The tax advisor should work hand-in-glove with your wealth manager and estate attorney to ensure full alignment.

A risk management specialist—often in the form of a high-net-worth insurance consultant—is non-negotiable. Ultra-affluent individuals face risks that others do not: targeted lawsuits, cyber threats, liability issues, property and asset risks on a global scale. Insurance must be comprehensive—covering property, liability, life, disability, and cyber risks—and must be reviewed regularly to evolve alongside your wealth footprint.

If you have operating businesses, a corporate attorney becomes vital—someone skilled not only in entity formation but in succession planning, regulatory compliance, and exit strategy design. Business and personal wealth are often deeply intertwined, and protecting one means protecting the other.

Strategic philanthropy is another cornerstone. Whether via a private foundation, donor-advised fund, or charitable trust, philanthropy should be integrated not only for its tax advantages but as a strategic component of your legacy. A skilled philanthropic advisor ensures that your giving aligns with your mission and maximizes impact.

Depending on scale, a family office—single or multi-family—can provide centralized management of investments, administration, and lifestyle services. A family office ensures continuity, professionalism, and the insulation needed to maintain privacy and efficiency across all aspects of your financial and personal life.

Real-world examples illustrate the difference this team makes. One entrepreneur, flush from a $400 million exit, initially operated with a solo financial advisor. Without a team, he missed critical tax strategies, failed to implement asset protection trusts, and made several uncoordinated philanthropic gifts that lacked tax optimization—costing tens of millions. In contrast, a peer who invested early in building a multidisciplinary team preserved far more wealth and created a structured, resilient legacy.

Or consider the family who neglected integrated risk management—they owned a substantial real estate empire but failed to place properties in protective entities. One lawsuit led to catastrophic liability. Contrast this with a neighboring family who'd restructured into a latticework of LLCs and trusts, emerging unscathed from similar threats.

The pros of assembling a coordinated, expert team are obvious: strategic clarity, risk mitigation, tax efficiency, peace of mind. You move from reactive to proactive management. You are no longer exposed to the whims of luck or market forces but insulated by structure and foresight.

The cons? Building and maintaining such a team requires trust, humility, and investment. You must be willing to delegate, to cede certain decisions to specialists. Good advice is expensive—but poor or fragmented advice is far costlier.

Action Steps: Begin by auditing your current advisory structure. List your existing advisors—wealth manager, CPA, estate attorney, risk consultant, philanthropic advisor, corporate counsel. Are there gaps? Are these professionals communicating, or operating in silos? Build a visual organizational chart of your team and identify weak spots.

Then, clarify your goals. Is your priority wealth preservation, strategic growth, multi-generational legacy, philanthropic impact, personal privacy? Different goals demand different team configurations. Set clear expectations for your advisors—coordination, communication, fiduciary duty.

Finally, commit to a full team review within 30 days. Interview new candidates if necessary. Challenge your existing advisors to step up collaboration. Wealth at this level demands nothing less.

The call to action is simple: Build your team before you need them. Don't wait for a crisis to highlight the gaps. At the ultra-affluent level, you're not just managing investments—you're orchestrating complexity.

Ultra Affluent isn't just a status—it's a responsibility.

This chapter has given you the blueprint. If you find yourself needing deeper guidance on assembling or upgrading your wealth management team, Pat Brown is available to assist. With years of experience guiding ultra-affluent individuals and families, he brings the clarity, structure, and leadership necessary to ensure your wealth does more than endure—it thrives.

Chapter 7: The Wealth Manager's Role: Architect, Quarterback, and Strategist

When you reach the echelon of ultra-high-net-worth status, the complexity of your financial life no longer resembles what most consider "wealth management." Your needs transcend basic investment advice and simple tax planning. Your wealth touches nearly every facet of your existence—family, business, philanthropy, legacy, security, reputation. At this level, the role of your wealth manager must expand beyond traditional boundaries. They are no longer merely an advisor; they must become your architect, your quarterback, and your strategist.

Imagine sitting across from me—an accomplished entrepreneur or executive who has recently navigated a liquidity event or crossed into nine-figure territory. You have advisors—perhaps several—but you sense something is missing. Each individual is excellent in their field, but together they are a collection of disconnected expertise. What you need now is not more specialists but a central figure who sees the entire chessboard and connects every move.

As an architect, the wealth manager designs the blueprint of your financial life. They start by listening—to your vision, values, and long-term objectives—and then translate those aspirations into an integrated structure of investments, trusts, insurance frameworks, liquidity solutions, and philanthropic vehicles. Every pillar must align with your overarching goals. No detail is too minor, no legacy assumption too sacred. The architect ensures that each element supports and strengthens the next.

As a quarterback, the wealth manager coordinates your team—estate attorneys, CPAs, risk advisors, philanthropic strategists, business managers. Each is critical, but without a leader to orchestrate, they risk working at cross purposes. The wealth manager ensures everyone is executing against a cohesive, dynamic plan. They call the plays, ensuring that tax strategies complement estate plans, that investment portfolios reflect liquidity needs, and that philanthropic endeavors align with tax optimization. When circumstances shift—a tax law changes, a business opportunity arises, a family dynamic evolves—the quarterback adjusts the playbook in real-time.

As a strategist, the wealth manager navigates the terrain ahead. Markets evolve. Regulations shift. Family needs transform. The strategist looks forward, not backward—anticipating risks, identifying opportunities, and recalibrating plans proactively. They help you prepare for the unseen and unexpected, providing the foresight needed to preserve and grow wealth sustainably.

Consider the real-life scenario of a tech founder who exits with $200 million. His initial focus is investment, allocating funds into public markets, venture capital, and private equity. Without an architect, his estate plan lags behind, leaving him exposed to massive estate taxes. Risk coverage is insufficient, and his advisory team offers fragmented, sometimes conflicting, advice. When a recession strikes, liquidity issues emerge. Contrast this with another founder who engages a wealth manager in the architect-quarterback-strategist role. This manager orchestrates an updated estate plan, structures asset protections, integrates liquidity and tax strategies, and ensures proactive adjustments. When market turmoil hits, this founder not only weathers the storm but is poised to capitalize on dislocations.

The pros of having a wealth manager in this expanded role are clear: clarity amidst complexity, proactive risk management, family harmony through governance, and philanthropic impact through strategic giving. Your wealth becomes a tool to achieve a broader mission, not just an accumulation of assets.

The cons? Finding a wealth manager who can truly operate at this level is challenging. Not all advisors have the breadth of knowledge, collaborative mindset, or strategic sophistication required. Entrusting someone with this level of oversight demands profound trust—sharing not just financial statements but intimate family dynamics, aspirations, and vulnerabilities.

Action steps? Begin with an audit of your current advisory structure. Identify whether you have a central figure connecting the moving parts or whether your advisors operate in silos. Interview potential candidates—not just for credentials, but for their ability to integrate, communicate, and lead. Review your financial blueprint—does it feel like a cohesive plan or a patchwork of disjointed strategies? Evaluate how well your advisors collaborate—is coordination occurring, or is everyone operating independently?

Set clear goals. Are you building a multi-generational legacy? Are you maximizing tax efficiency? Are you optimizing philanthropic impact? Are you ensuring family governance and continuity? Your goals will shape the team you build and the leader you require.

Ask yourself: Can I realistically achieve these goals with my current setup? Do I have the right architect-quarterback-strategist? Can I manage this complexity alone, or is it time to hire out?

Here's your bold call to action: Within the next thirty days, commit to identifying and engaging a wealth manager capable of fulfilling this expanded role. Or, if you already have one, schedule a comprehensive review to ensure they are operating at the level your wealth demands.

Because managing significant wealth is not just about safeguarding a portfolio.

It's about orchestrating a legacy.

Ultra Affluent is your permission slip to demand more—more clarity, more strategy, more integration—from those entrusted with your financial future.

If you are ready to elevate your approach to wealth management, Pat Brown is available to guide you through this transition. With years of experience advising ultra-affluent individuals and families, Pat offers the clarity, structure, and strategic leadership required to turn complexity into enduring, meaningful success.

Chapter 8: The Wealth Management Process: Discovery to Execution

Reaching a point of ultra-affluence—the moment when wealth shifts from being a tool for living to a structure that must be carefully managed—requires a fundamental change in how you think about money. At this level, wealth is not simply invested; it is architected, protected, directed, and stewarded. Success here is not measured solely by return on investment, but by the successful alignment of wealth with the life you envision for yourself, your family, and future generations. And to accomplish that, a deliberate process must guide you—from discovery to execution.

Imagine you are seated across from me. You're highly successful, perhaps freshly minted from a liquidity event or after years of diligent building and investing. The bank accounts and portfolios are sizable. And yet, as substantial as the numbers are, the complexity is even greater. You're facing questions you've never confronted before: How do I protect what I've built? How do I transition from growth to preservation? How do I align my financial strategy with my life's purpose?

That's where the wealth management process begins—with discovery.

Discovery is about far more than assets and liabilities. A true wealth manager begins by understanding you. Your goals. Your fears. Your ambitions. Your values. It's a deep dive—an exploration into what wealth means to you and what you want it to accomplish. In these conversations, the surface numbers quickly give way to deeper truths. Wealth management at this level is about life management. It's about aligning financial strategies with personal philosophies.

During discovery, we ask questions—not just about what you have, but about what you want. What is your vision for your family's future? What philanthropic causes do you care about? What risks keep you awake at night? What legacy do you want to leave? Discovery is a conversation, not a questionnaire. It is the foundation upon which every future strategy is built.

Once discovery is complete, the next phase is design. Here, the wealth manager synthesizes the information gathered and begins to construct a customized wealth blueprint. This is not a one-size-fits-all portfolio allocation or a boilerplate estate plan. It is a bespoke strategy—integrating investment management, tax planning, estate structuring, risk mitigation, philanthropic endeavors, and family governance.

The design phase also includes modeling. Various scenarios are constructed to stress-test the plan against market downturns, changes in tax policy, life events, and other uncertainties. Monte Carlo simulations, cash flow projections, tax impact assessments—these are not academic exercises; they are tools to ensure the plan is resilient.

Once the design is vetted and finalized, we move to implementation. Here, strategy becomes action. Investment portfolios are restructured. Trusts are created. Insurance policies are adjusted or initiated. Philanthropic vehicles—such as donor-advised funds or private foundations—are established. Family meetings are scheduled to discuss governance frameworks and succession plans.

Implementation is not a one-time event; it is a series of coordinated actions—often over months—ensuring that every part of the plan is executed with precision. Communication among your team of advisors is critical during this phase. The wealth manager acts as quarterback, coordinating among attorneys, CPAs, investment managers, and insurance specialists.

Finally, we reach the ongoing management phase. Wealth management at this level is dynamic. Life changes. Markets evolve. Tax laws shift. Family dynamics transform. Regular reviews—quarterly, annually—ensure that the plan adapts. Adjustments are made proactively, not reactively.

Consider the real-life example of a family that accumulated $500 million through a combination of entrepreneurship and savvy investing. Initially, they managed their wealth with ad hoc strategies, engaging experts piecemeal. Over time, the lack of coordination led to inefficiencies—duplicate estate planning structures, missed tax planning opportunities, an investment portfolio that lacked cohesion.

When they engaged in a true discovery-to-execution wealth management process, the transformation was remarkable. Their wealth manager conducted an in-depth discovery process, understanding not just their assets, but their values and vision. A unified strategy was developed: investments were reallocated for greater diversification and tax efficiency, estate plans were streamlined, a family office was established, and a philanthropic foundation was launched to formalize their giving.

Contrast that with another family—net worth north of $300 million—who never undertook a coordinated discovery process. Instead, they treated wealth management as a series of transactions—buy this property, invest in that fund, set up that trust. When the patriarch passed away unexpectedly, the disjointed nature of their planning became painfully apparent. Disputes among heirs, inefficient tax structures, and liquidity crises ensued.

The pros of a comprehensive wealth management process are clear. You gain clarity, coordination, and confidence. Risks are mitigated before they materialize. Opportunities are seized. Family harmony is preserved through thoughtful governance and communication.

The cons? It requires time—meaningful, introspective time. It requires vulnerability—sharing not just financial information, but hopes, fears, and dreams. And it requires trust—entrusting your vision to a wealth manager who can translate it into actionable strategy.

Action steps? If you haven't engaged in a thorough discovery process, initiate one. Insist that your wealth manager's first priority is to understand you—not just your assets. Review your current strategy: Is it comprehensive or piecemeal? Are your advisors coordinated or siloed? Schedule a review meeting focused specifically on integration and alignment.

Set clear goals. Do you want a cohesive wealth strategy that aligns with your life's purpose? Do you want to ensure tax efficiency, investment resilience, and a legacy that endures? Do you want to prepare the next generation for the responsibilities of wealth?

Ask yourself: Can you realistically design, implement, and manage such a comprehensive strategy on your own, or do you need to hire experts who can guide you through the discovery-to-execution process?

Here's your bold call to action: Within the next 30 days, conduct a full audit of your current wealth management approach. Identify gaps. Engage in a true discovery conversation—with yourself, your family, and your advisors.

Because wealth at this level is not just about having more.

It's about being more—more thoughtful, more strategic, more intentional.

Ultra Affluent is your permission slip to move from managing money to mastering legacy.

Chapter 9: Doing It Yourself vs. Hiring a Wealth Manager: Pros and Cons

Reaching the ultra-affluent level presents a distinct and formidable question—do you manage your wealth yourself, or do you entrust it to a professional wealth manager? It's not a decision to be taken lightly. The stakes are higher, the complexity deeper, and the risks more nuanced. At this level, wealth is no longer just a series of accounts and investments; it's an ecosystem, interconnected and dynamic. Managing it demands time, expertise, and a disciplined process.

Imagine you are sitting across from me. You are sharp, sophisticated, and capable. You've built a business, navigated intricate markets, and made tough decisions. Why shouldn't you manage your own wealth? After all, no one knows your goals and risk tolerance better than you do. This sentiment is common among the ultra-affluent. But wealth management at this level is not about competence; it's about bandwidth, specialization, and architecture.

Let's first explore doing it yourself. The clear advantage is control. You maintain direct oversight of every decision. You avoid the fees associated with professional management. You remain intimately involved in the allocation, risk management, and strategic direction of your capital. For someone who has built a fortune through decisive action and personal involvement, this is deeply appealing.

Another advantage is alignment. You answer only to yourself. You do not have to worry about conflicts of interest or question whether your advisor's incentives align with yours. The goals are your goals, uncompromised and unfiltered.

There's also a learning aspect. Managing your own wealth deepens your understanding of financial markets, tax law changes, estate planning nuances, and investment opportunities. For the intellectually curious, this can be deeply satisfying.

But now, let's consider the cons. Time is the first and most glaring cost. Wealth management is not a set-it-and-forget-it endeavor. It demands constant attention—to markets, to changing laws, to shifting family dynamics, to evolving economic conditions. Every hour spent managing wealth is an hour not spent elsewhere—on business ventures, family, philanthropy, or personal growth.

Complexity is the next hurdle. At the ultra-affluent level, your financial world encompasses not just stocks and bonds, but real estate holdings, private equity, hedge funds, venture investments, art collections, aircraft, yachts, trusts, foundations, and operating businesses. Each asset class brings unique risks, tax considerations, legal structures, and liquidity challenges.

Tax optimization alone can be a full-time job. International holdings add another layer of complexity—currency risk, jurisdictional tax laws, geopolitical exposure. Estate planning requires constant updates to reflect changes in the law and family situations. Risk management—ensuring adequate and appropriate insurance coverage, asset protection structures, and cybersecurity measures—is more critical than ever.

Emotion is another hidden risk. Self-managed wealth is vulnerable to behavioral biases—overconfidence, loss aversion, herd behavior, and short-termism. Even seasoned entrepreneurs can fall prey to these cognitive traps, especially when managing personal wealth where emotions run high.

Now let's shift to hiring a professional wealth manager. The primary benefit is expertise. A top-tier wealth manager brings deep knowledge across investment management, tax strategy, estate planning, philanthropy, and risk management. They integrate these domains into a cohesive strategy tailored to your unique goals.

Time efficiency is another key benefit. Delegating wealth management frees you to focus on what you do best—whether it's growing businesses, leading philanthropic initiatives, or simply enjoying life. It's a recognition that your time is your most valuable asset.

A wealth manager provides emotional distance. They offer a disciplined, objective perspective, helping to mitigate the behavioral biases that can erode returns and compromise decision-making. They bring process, structure, and accountability.

Coordination is also critical. A wealth manager acts as the quarterback, coordinating the efforts of estate attorneys, tax advisors, risk specialists, and philanthropic consultants. This integrated approach ensures that all elements of your financial life work together harmoniously.

Real-life scenarios illustrate the difference. Consider a tech founder who managed her own $250 million fortune. Initially, she thrived, but as complexity grew, cracks appeared. Estate taxes loomed large because her estate plan was outdated. Private investments lacked diversification. Philanthropic efforts were scattered and tax-inefficient. Ultimately, she hired a wealth manager who restructured her plan, optimized her philanthropic vehicles, and coordinated her advisory team.

Contrast that with another individual who insisted on managing his $300 million fortune alone. He resisted professional advice, made aggressive private equity bets, and lacked proper asset protection structures. When an unexpected lawsuit struck, his personal assets were exposed. Years of careful building were jeopardized by an oversight a seasoned professional would have prevented.

Of course, there are cons to hiring a wealth manager. Cost is an obvious one. Professional management fees can range from 50 to 100 basis points annually, sometimes more depending on the complexity and scope of services. Trust is another. You must be sure that the advisor acts as a fiduciary, placing your interests first.

Not all advisors are created equal. Some lack true multi-disciplinary expertise. Others may be more focused on asset gathering than on holistic wealth management. Due diligence in selecting a wealth manager is critical.

Action steps if you're considering doing it yourself? Conduct an honest time audit. Do you have the bandwidth to monitor markets, coordinate advisors, stay abreast of tax law changes, and manage family governance? Evaluate your own expertise. Do you have the depth and breadth of knowledge to manage all aspects of your financial ecosystem?

If you're considering hiring a wealth manager, conduct rigorous due diligence. Interview multiple candidates. Assess their credentials, experience, and philosophy. Ensure they operate as fiduciaries. Understand their fee structures. Seek references.

Set clear goals. Do you want to maximize investment returns, minimize taxes, preserve family harmony, and leave a legacy? Do you want to free yourself from day-to-day financial management to focus on what matters most?

Ask yourself: Can you realistically achieve these goals on your own, or does the complexity demand a professional team?

Here's your bold call to action: Within the next 30 days, decide—commit to either developing a rigorous self-management plan with dedicated time and discipline or engage a wealth manager who meets your standards.

Because managing ultra-affluent wealth is not just about growing numbers.

It's about growing freedom, impact, and legacy.

Ultra Affluent is your permission slip to choose wisely—with clarity, strategy, and confidence.

Chapter 10: How a Wealth Manager Coordinates the Complex Web: Estate, Tax, Insurance, Investments

When you arrive at the upper echelons of wealth, life becomes a delicate orchestration. Managing wealth at this level is no longer a straightforward exercise of selecting a few investments or filing a tax return once a year. It is an intricate web, a network of decisions and consequences that must be coordinated carefully, deliberately, and intelligently. Estate planning, tax strategy, insurance, investments—each strand is critical. Each requires specialized expertise. But without a conductor to oversee the orchestra, the result is discordant noise, not harmonious music.

Imagine you are sitting across from me. You're highly capable—you've built businesses, made smart investments, and navigated complex markets. You have a CPA, an estate attorney, an insurance agent, an investment advisor. Each does good work. Yet, despite the competency of each, your overall financial life feels disjointed. Decisions are made in isolation. Opportunities are missed. Risks are overlooked. What you need now is not more specialists working separately; it's a wealth manager who sees the whole.

A skilled wealth manager does exactly that. They coordinate the complex web of estate, tax, insurance, and investments—bringing coherence, synergy, and strategic alignment. Their role is not to replace your other advisors but to harmonize them.

Estate planning is often the starting point. Many ultra-high-net-worth individuals have outdated or fragmented estate plans. Perhaps you have a revocable trust drafted years ago, a few powers of attorney, maybe even a charitable foundation. But is your estate plan integrated with your current life situation, your tax strategy, your business interests, and your philanthropic goals? A wealth manager works closely with your estate attorney to ensure that your estate plan is not just a static document, but a living, breathing structure that adapts to changes in law, family, and personal objectives.

Tax strategy is next. Tax planning at the ultra-wealthy level is a year-round endeavor, not a once-a-year scramble. It's about income tax optimization, estate and gift tax minimization, capital gains management, charitable giving, and international tax issues. A wealth manager coordinates with your CPA to ensure that investment decisions are tax-aware, that estate structures minimize transfer taxes, and that philanthropic efforts are structured for maximum impact and efficiency.

Insurance is another vital, often overlooked, component. It's easy to think of insurance as a commodity—just another premium to pay. But at this level, insurance is a strategic tool. It protects against liabilities that could threaten your fortune. It ensures liquidity for estate tax obligations. It secures income streams. A wealth manager coordinates with insurance advisors to audit coverage, identify gaps, and integrate insurance into the overall wealth plan.

Investments, of course, are at the core. But investment management for the ultra-affluent goes beyond asset allocation. It's about aligning investments with cash flow needs, tax strategies, philanthropic goals, and legacy planning. Private equity, real estate, hedge funds, municipal bonds, venture capital—each asset class must be carefully selected, sized, and integrated into a broader portfolio strategy. A wealth manager ensures that investment decisions are not made in a vacuum but are coordinated with all other aspects of your financial life.

Consider the real-life example of a family with $500 million in assets. Initially, they worked with excellent individual advisors—a top-tier investment manager, a reputable CPA, a respected estate attorney. Yet, without coordination, redundancies and inefficiencies crept in. Their estate plan failed to leverage GST exemptions fully. Investment portfolios lacked tax-efficiency. Insurance coverage was outdated, exposing them to unnecessary risk. When they engaged a wealth manager to coordinate the web, the transformation was profound. Estate plans were updated, investment strategies were restructured for tax efficiency, and insurance coverage was aligned with overall risk management.

Contrast this with another family who insisted on managing their advisors separately. Over time, small misalignments snowballed. A lack of communication between their CPA and investment manager led to significant, unnecessary tax liabilities. Estate planning documents conflicted with business succession plans. When the family patriarch passed away, the lack of coordination resulted in legal disputes and avoidable tax burdens.

The pros of having a wealth manager coordinate your financial web are undeniable. You gain clarity, integration, and proactive management. Risks are mitigated before they become problems. Opportunities are identified and seized. Your wealth strategy becomes cohesive, not fragmented.

The cons? It requires selecting the right wealth manager—someone with the expertise, humility, and leadership skills to coordinate complex teams of advisors. It requires transparency and trust—sharing your complete financial picture and your broader life goals.

Action steps? Begin with a financial life audit. Are your estate plan, tax strategy, insurance coverage, and investment management coordinated? Are your advisors communicating effectively? Identify gaps and inefficiencies. Interview wealth managers who specialize in holistic coordination. Ensure they operate as fiduciaries and have experience managing complex, multi-disciplinary wealth strategies.

Set clear goals. Do you want to optimize tax efficiency, protect family harmony, ensure strategic philanthropy, and preserve legacy wealth? Do you want to sleep better at night knowing that your financial life is not a patchwork but a cohesive strategy?

Ask yourself: Can you realistically coordinate this complex web yourself, or do you need to hire a professional who can?

Here's your bold call to action: Within the next 30 days, initiate a review of your entire financial ecosystem. Assess coordination, identify gaps, and commit to hiring a wealth manager if needed.

Because managing wealth at this level is not just about protecting assets.

It's about orchestrating a legacy.

Ultra Affluent is your permission slip to elevate your wealth management—from fragmented to flawless.

Part II: Wealth Preservation & Protection

After wealth is created, the true challenge begins: preserving it across time, markets, and generations. This section unpacks the sophisticated strategies ultra-high-net-worth individuals must master to defend their capital against erosion, taxes, lawsuits, and poor planning. It explores the importance of transitioning from growth-focused mindsets to risk management frameworks, emphasizing resilience over returns. Topics include liquidity management, asset protection structures, advanced estate planning techniques, concentrated position strategies, and the disciplined diversification required to safeguard wealth. Real-world examples and plain-language breakdowns illuminate how the ultra-affluent can avoid common pitfalls and ensure their wealth becomes a durable foundation for freedom, not a source of future risk or regret. Part II is about securing what has already been won—protecting wealth not just for today, but for decades and generations to come.

Chapter 11: Advanced Estate Planning: GRATs, SLATs, IDGTs, and FLPs Explained

When you reach the level of wealth where your net worth moves into eight, nine, even ten figures, the conversation around estate planning transforms. Basic wills and revocable trusts, while important, no longer offer the strategic edge or protection that you need. At this level, preserving your wealth, minimizing taxes, and securing your legacy requires more advanced tools. Names like GRAT, SLAT, IDGT, and FLP start to surface—acronyms that can feel opaque at first but are essential instruments in the architecture of ultra-affluent estate planning.

Imagine you're sitting across from me. You're a seasoned entrepreneur or investor who has spent decades building a substantial fortune. You understand hard work, risk management, and growth. Yet when it comes to ensuring that your wealth transfers smoothly to the next generation—without a 40% estate tax haircut or family disputes—things feel less certain. This is where advanced estate planning enters the picture, providing strategies to protect your life's work, preserve family harmony, and maintain control across generations.

Let's start with a Grantor Retained Annuity Trust, or GRAT. In its simplest form, a GRAT allows you to transfer appreciating assets to your heirs while minimizing gift tax liability. You place assets into a trust and receive annuity payments for a term of years. If the assets appreciate faster than the IRS's assumed rate of return (the Section 7520 rate), the excess growth passes to your beneficiaries free of additional tax. The GRAT is particularly effective when asset values are depressed or volatility is high—precisely the kinds of conditions that ultra-wealthy individuals can strategically leverage. The pros of a GRAT are clear: significant potential tax savings and the ability to transfer appreciation outside your estate. The cons? If you pass away during the term, the assets revert to your estate. This risk can be managed by setting short GRAT terms—sometimes as short as two years—but it remains a factor to consider.

Next, consider the Spousal Lifetime Access Trust, or SLAT. A SLAT allows you to make a gift to an irrevocable trust for the benefit of your spouse (and potentially other family members) while removing the gifted assets from your taxable estate. The beauty of the SLAT is twofold: you reduce your estate tax exposure while retaining indirect access to the assets through your spouse. It's a sophisticated balance of control and generosity. However, there are risks. If your spouse dies or you divorce, your access vanishes. Therefore, SLATs must be constructed carefully, often in conjunction with prenuptial or postnuptial agreements and thoughtful planning around liquidity and future needs.

The Intentionally Defective Grantor Trust, or IDGT, is another powerful tool. Despite the confusing name, an IDGT is essentially a trust that is "defective" for income tax purposes—meaning you, the grantor, continue to pay income taxes on trust assets even though they are no longer part of your estate. Why is this advantageous? Because by paying the taxes personally, you are effectively making additional, tax-free gifts to the trust beneficiaries—accelerating the growth of the trust's assets without triggering gift tax consequences. Moreover, IDGTs often involve a sale of appreciating assets to the trust in exchange for a promissory note, locking in current valuations and shifting future appreciation outside your estate. The pros are substantial tax savings and enhanced legacy transfer. The cons are complexity and the need for careful valuation and structuring to withstand IRS scrutiny.

Family Limited Partnerships, or FLPs, offer another strategic layer. By transferring assets into an FLP, you can maintain control over the investments while gifting minority interests to your heirs. Because minority interests lack control and marketability, they are often valued at a discount for gift and estate tax purposes, allowing you to leverage your lifetime exemptions more effectively. FLPs also provide creditor protection and centralized management of family assets. However, FLPs must be operated as bona fide businesses with proper formalities; otherwise, the IRS may challenge the valuation discounts. Careful administration is key.

Real-world examples bring these strategies to life. Imagine a family who used a series of short-term rolling GRATs to transfer millions in private equity interests to the next generation, saving tens of millions in estate taxes. Or the entrepreneur who set up a SLAT and an IDGT in tandem, balancing immediate family access with long-term estate planning goals. Or the multi-generational family office that used an FLP structure to manage real estate holdings, preserving operational control while efficiently transferring wealth across generations.

Advanced estate planning isn't just a technical exercise—it's a profound expression of leadership. The pros are undeniable: minimized estate taxes, enhanced asset protection, greater control over wealth transfer, and alignment with family legacy goals. The cons, equally real, are the complexity, cost, and necessity for ongoing management and review. These strategies are not set-and-forget; they require annual audits, potential adjustments as laws change, and clear communication with family members to prevent misunderstandings. At this level, neglect is not an option. Lack of proper structure invites risk, confusion, and unnecessary tax burdens.

The action steps? Conduct a comprehensive review of your current estate plan. Engage an estate planning attorney experienced in advanced strategies. Model the impact of GRATs, SLATs, IDGTs, and FLPs under different assumptions about asset growth, tax rates, and family needs. Stress-test your plan for scenarios like early death, divorce, or liquidity crunches. Coordinate with your wealth manager, CPA, and insurance advisors to ensure full integration. These structures do not exist in silos—they must interact seamlessly with your overall wealth architecture.

Set clear goals. Do you want to maximize the wealth transferred to heirs? Maintain control of family assets? Minimize tax exposure? Protect assets from creditors and ex-spouses? Support philanthropic causes in perpetuity? These goals will dictate which structures are appropriate. Importantly, think about how your wealth will serve not just your children, but generations you will never meet. Legacy is not an accident; it is engineered through careful planning, conscious leadership, and continuous stewardship.

Now ask yourself: Can you navigate this advanced planning landscape on your own, or do you need to hire experts to guide you? Even the most financially savvy ultra-wealthy individuals benefit from assembling a team—estate attorneys, tax strategists, wealth managers—to design, implement, and manage these sophisticated structures. Wealth of this magnitude deserves—demands—professional-level protection and strategy. The stakes are simply too high to leave to chance or half-measures.

Here's your call to action: Within the next 60 days, commit to an estate plan review. If you don't already have advanced strategies in place, explore which tools—GRATs, SLATs, IDGTs, FLPs—align best with your goals and initiate the implementation process. Challenge yourself to think beyond preservation toward the intentional design of a legacy. Think about the impact you can have—not just tomorrow, but a hundred years from now. At the ultra-affluent level, estate planning isn't just about avoiding taxes. It's about ensuring that your wealth endures—with purpose, clarity, and impact.

Ultra Affluent is your permission slip to elevate your estate planning from basic to brilliant.

Chapter 12: Asset Protection Trusts: Domestic and Offshore Strategies

When you reach a level of wealth where you can't measure your financial security by salary or even investment returns alone, a different kind of conversation needs to happen. You begin to realize that wealth, while a source of freedom, is also a target. As an ultra-high-net-worth individual, you are more visible, more vulnerable, and often more exposed than you might expect. Threats come not just from market volatility or tax policy changes, but from litigation, creditors, business disputes, divorce, and even reputation risks. This is why serious wealth requires serious defense, and few tools are more effective in that defense than asset protection trusts, both domestic and offshore.

Imagine you are seated across from me, reflecting on the empire you've built—a thriving business portfolio, a carefully constructed investment strategy, multiple homes, perhaps a yacht or two, and a growing philanthropic footprint. You know you've worked hard, sacrificed, and planned well. Yet you also know that in today's litigious society, a single lawsuit—whether meritless or legitimate—could jeopardize it all. You need to build a fortress around your wealth, and that fortress starts with understanding how asset protection trusts operate.

A domestic asset protection trust (DAPT) is a structure created under the laws of certain U.S. states that allows you to place assets into a trust and protect them from future creditors. States like Delaware, Nevada, South Dakota, and Alaska are often cited as leaders in this field. The beauty of a

DAPT is that it allows you, the grantor, to be a discretionary beneficiary—meaning you can still receive distributions at the trustee's discretion—while the trust shields the assets from claimants. There is no federal law governing DAPTs, so their effectiveness is largely determined by state statutes and how well they can stand up under scrutiny in court. Done correctly, a DAPT can provide robust protection against personal liability, professional malpractice claims, and even business disputes.

The pros of a DAPT are clear. It offers domestic familiarity—U.S. legal systems, U.S. trustees, U.S. asset locations. It can often be simpler and less costly to administer than an offshore trust. And it's a powerful deterrent to would-be litigants who realize that the assets they hope to seize are behind a significant legal firewall. The cons? Not every state recognizes DAPTs, and creditors may engage in jurisdictional challenges. Moreover, courts may apply their own state's laws under certain circumstances, which can erode the trust's protective features. Proper planning and choice of jurisdiction are critical.

Offshore asset protection trusts take the strategy one step further. These trusts are established under the laws of foreign jurisdictions—such as the Cook Islands, Nevis, or the Cayman Islands—that are well-known for their creditor-unfriendly statutes. Offshore trusts can provide an even higher level of protection because the jurisdictional hurdles for creditors are steeper: shorter statutes of limitation, higher standards of proof, and legal systems less inclined to recognize U.S. judgments. In the right situation, they offer unparalleled insulation against liability.

The pros of offshore trusts are their formidable asset protection statutes and the difficulty for creditors to reach those assets. They can be designed to include duress clauses, preventing trustees from complying with foreign court orders. However, they are not without their drawbacks. Offshore trusts are subject to heightened scrutiny from the IRS and must comply with reporting requirements such as Form 3520 and FBAR filings. Failure to comply can result in significant penalties. They also carry reputational risks if not properly structured and disclosed—no ultra-affluent individual wants to be on the front page of the news for the wrong reasons.

Consider the real-life scenario of a successful tech entrepreneur who sold his company for $500 million. Early in his career, he had an unfortunate brush with litigation that left him wary of future risks. After his liquidity event, he worked with his advisors to establish a DAPT in Nevada, moving a portion of his wealth into the trust. A few years later, a former business partner attempted to sue over a long-ago business dealing. Thanks to the DAPT, the assets were well beyond reach, and the case was settled favorably. Contrast this with another high-net-worth individual who, despite warnings, opted not to set up any asset protection structures. A messy business dispute led to a judgment that forced him to liquidate real estate holdings at a loss, dramatically eroding his net worth.

There are hybrid structures as well. Some individuals set up both domestic and offshore trusts to diversify their protection strategies. A domestic trust can hold assets that are more straightforward to manage within the U.S., while offshore trusts can safeguard international investments or excess capital not needed for immediate use. The key is coordination—ensuring that the structures are integrated into the broader wealth plan, consistent with estate and tax strategies.

Beyond asset protection, the conversation shifts to something more profound—mastery. Mastery at this level isn't just about preserving what you have. It's about advancing your wealth, your legacy, and your influence in a way that is durable and deliberate. The ultra-wealthy who master their financial position do so by thinking not in terms of assets, but in terms of architecture. They build structures that weather market storms, political shifts, legal risks, and generational changes. Asset protection trusts are just one piece of this architecture, but they are a foundational one.

The action steps to consider are clear. Conduct a full risk audit: where are you exposed? Review your business interests, real estate holdings, personal liabilities, and even reputation risks. Engage a specialist attorney experienced in asset protection planning. Evaluate whether a DAPT, an offshore trust, or a hybrid structure aligns with your goals and risk profile. Understand the reporting requirements and be prepared to maintain compliance meticulously. Build a structure that does not merely exist, but is integrated tightly with your estate plan, your investment strategy, your family governance structures, and your philanthropic objectives.

Set clear goals: Do you want to shield assets from creditors? Protect against future business risks? Provide a secure legacy for heirs? Are you willing to accept the higher complexity and cost of offshore strategies in exchange for greater protection? Are you aiming for autonomy and control, or are you ready to entrust professionals to manage parts of this complex machinery? Can you truly handle this level of structuring and ongoing compliance on your own, or do you need to hire out a seasoned attorney, a trusted wealth manager, and a meticulous CPA to architect and manage your protection strategy?

Here's your bold call to action: Within the next 60 days, conduct a comprehensive vulnerability assessment of your current financial structure. If you find exposure—and you likely will—commit to establishing a robust asset protection trust strategy. Whether domestic, offshore, or hybrid, make sure your fortress is as strong as the wealth it protects. Take action deliberately, not reactively.

Because at the ultra-affluent level, wealth isn't just about numbers. It's about security, dignity, and freedom. It's about creating a legacy that is not only formidable but also protected against the tides of life and law. Mastering wealth beyond seven figures means understanding that freedom is not given—it is constructed, defended, and perpetuated with precision.

Ultra Affluent is your permission slip to protect what you've built—deliberately, strategically, and confidently.

Chapter 13: Dynasty Trusts: Building Multigenerational Wealth

When you reach a level of wealth where you can't measure your financial security by salary or even investment returns alone, a different kind of conversation needs to happen. You begin to realize that wealth, while a source of freedom, is also a target. As an ultra-high-net-worth individual, you are more visible, more vulnerable, and often more exposed than you might expect. Threats come not just from market volatility or tax policy changes, but from litigation, creditors, business disputes, divorce, and even reputation risks. This is why serious wealth requires serious defense, and few tools are more effective in that defense than dynasty trusts.

Imagine sitting across from me. You have built companies, scaled investments, donated to causes close to your heart. You know financial statements like the back of your hand, yet when it comes to estate planning — true multigenerational estate planning — there's a recognition that this terrain requires a different playbook. Dynasty trusts are not basic instruments; they are financial architecture designed to weather the storm of time, taxation, family dynamics, and legislative change.

A dynasty trust is essentially a perpetual or long-term irrevocable trust designed to pass wealth from generation to generation without incurring transfer taxes like estate, gift, or generation-skipping transfer (GST) taxes. Historically, the rule against perpetuities limited trust duration, but many states — such as South Dakota, Nevada, Delaware, and Alaska — have abolished or extended these limits, making it possible to structure trusts that last hundreds of years, if not indefinitely. For families intent on creating not just financial security but a legacy, dynasty trusts offer the ultimate vehicle for enduring wealth.

The primary benefit of a dynasty trust is the ability to eliminate estate taxes at each generational transfer. In the absence of planning, each time wealth moves — from parent to child, and child to grandchild — it could be reduced by estate taxes of up to 40%. A dynasty trust bypasses this erosion by keeping assets outside of individual estates. Moreover, assets within the trust can appreciate and compound tax-free, allowing for greater wealth accumulation over time. The trust can also provide significant protection from creditors, lawsuits, and divorcing spouses, shielding family wealth from external threats that grow as wealth becomes more visible.

However, with great power comes great complexity. Dynasty trusts are not plug-and-play instruments. They require meticulous drafting, skilled trustees, and ongoing maintenance. Poorly designed trusts can lead to rigidity, family disputes, or, ironically, wealth destruction. Flexibility must be carefully balanced with control. For example, the trust should include provisions allowing trustees to adapt to changing tax laws and family circumstances without jeopardizing the integrity of the plan. Equally important is avoiding the "trust fund baby" syndrome — when beneficiaries lose motivation because they are provided wealth without expectation or responsibility.

One of the most significant advantages of a dynasty trust is the ability to embed family governance structures within the trust itself. Families can craft a mission statement outlining the purpose of the wealth, set educational and entrepreneurial goals for beneficiaries, and create family councils or advisory boards. This ensures that wealth is not just preserved but is actively managed and used in a manner consistent with the family's values and aspirations. The best dynasty trusts are not cold legal constructs; they are living expressions of family philosophy and purpose.

Consider the real-world example of the Johnson family, who sold a closely-held business for $500 million. Early planning allowed them to seed a dynasty trust with shares well before the liquidity event, freezing a low valuation for gift tax purposes. Over the decades, the trust has grown, funding multiple generations' education, entrepreneurial ventures, and charitable endeavors. The family gathers annually to review the trust's mission, revise guidelines, and onboard the next generation into leadership roles. Contrast this with another family who delayed planning, resulting in massive estate tax obligations and a subsequent sale of family assets to cover the liability — a poignant reminder that timing and proactive planning are essential.

Another less heralded benefit is asset protection. Assets within a properly structured dynasty trust are generally not considered part of the beneficiary's marital estate, insulating them from divorce proceedings. They are also typically shielded from creditors and lawsuits, provided the trust is administered in accordance with sound fiduciary principles and local law. In an era where litigation risk is omnipresent, this layer of protection is no small matter for the ultra-affluent family.

The cons, however, must be acknowledged. Dynasty trusts can be costly to set up, often requiring hundreds of hours of legal, tax, and financial planning expertise. Ongoing trustee fees and administrative costs must be factored in as well. Furthermore, the permanence of these trusts demands thoughtful design; inflexibility can become a burden if the trust doesn't allow for adaptations to unforeseen changes. Lastly, there is the philosophical risk: creating beneficiaries who see the trust not as an opportunity but as an entitlement. Proper structuring can help mitigate this risk by embedding incentives, education requirements, and phased distributions based on age or achievement.

Action steps? Start by defining the purpose behind your wealth. Is it to empower future generations to pursue education and entrepreneurship? To support philanthropy? To preserve family businesses or properties? Engage a seasoned estate planning attorney with expertise in multigenerational planning. Analyze state jurisdictions carefully — South Dakota, Nevada, and Delaware are often considered top choices due to favorable trust laws, privacy statutes, and creditor protection. Determine the governance structure early — will you appoint professional trustees, family members, or a hybrid? Will there be a family council or advisory board to guide the mission?

Then, work to create a family mission statement. Bring your heirs into the conversation early and often. Educate them not just about the trust, but about the responsibility that comes with it. Wealth without wisdom is a curse disguised as a blessing. Your dynasty trust should serve as a bridge — connecting the hard work and vision of your generation with the ambitions and dreams of the next.

Set clear goals: Do you wish to minimize estate taxes and maximize wealth transfer efficiency? Protect family assets from external threats? Embed your family's values into a formal governance structure? Support educational and entrepreneurial initiatives for generations to come? The clarity of your goals will dictate the blueprint of your dynasty trust.

Ask yourself honestly: Can you design, implement, and steward this structure on your own? Or do you need the guidance of expert estate planners, trust attorneys, tax strategists, and family governance consultants? At this level, expertise is not optional — it is the price of preserving what you've built.

Here's your bold call to action: Within the next 90 days, initiate a comprehensive review of your estate plan with the specific objective of evaluating whether a dynasty trust is appropriate for your goals. Draft your family mission statement and begin conversations with trusted advisors about the architecture and administration of your legacy.

Because real wealth is not just counted in dollars — it's measured in decades, even centuries.

Ultra Affluent is your permission slip to plan, to protect, and to purposefully build what others will only dream of leaving behind.

Chapter 14: Family Limited Partnerships (FLPs) and LLCs for Asset Control

When you cross into the ultra-affluent territory, wealth management begins to resemble architecture more than arithmetic. You're no longer merely investing and accumulating; you're constructing a financial structure built to last generations. In this architecture, control and protection are as vital as growth. Two of the most potent tools for those seeking to protect, consolidate, and transition wealth are Family Limited Partnerships (FLPs) and Limited Liability Companies (LLCs). When understood and deployed correctly, they offer not just tax efficiency and asset protection, but also something even more valuable: control.

Imagine you are seated across from me. You're a highly accomplished entrepreneur or investor. You've built a substantial portfolio — real estate, private equity, marketable securities — and perhaps you've sold a business or two. You're thinking not only about growth but about how to pass on your wealth without losing the values, discipline, and prudence that built it in the first place. You want to protect the wealth from external threats — creditors, divorces, lawsuits — and from internal ones — poor decision-making, entitlement, and family discord. This is where FLPs and LLCs step into the picture.

A Family Limited Partnership is, at its core, a partnership composed of family members. It has two classes of partners: general partners, who manage the partnership and control the assets, and limited partners, who have ownership interests but no control. Typically, parents or patriarchs and matriarchs hold the general partnership interest, and children or other descendants hold the limited partnership interests. The strategic advantage of this setup is profound: you can transfer ownership (and therefore, future appreciation) to your heirs while retaining full control over the assets during your lifetime.

The benefits of FLPs extend beyond control. One of the key features is valuation discounting. Because limited partners lack control and cannot readily sell their interests, the value of their partnership interests can be discounted for gift and estate tax purposes — often by 20% to 40%. This means you can transfer more wealth using less of your lifetime gift and estate tax exemption. Moreover, FLPs provide asset protection. Creditors of a limited partner cannot seize partnership assets directly; at most, they can obtain a charging order — a right to receive distributions, if any are made — but cannot force distributions or interfere with management.

However, FLPs are not without risks and responsibilities. The IRS scrutinizes FLPs closely, particularly when they are created primarily for tax purposes rather than for bona fide business or investment activities. To withstand such scrutiny, the FLP must be properly structured and operated as a real business entity, not merely as a tax shelter. This means keeping accurate records, holding annual meetings, adhering to partnership formalities, and maintaining separation between personal and partnership assets. Improperly managed FLPs risk being "pierced," losing their protective benefits and triggering adverse tax consequences.

LLCs, or Limited Liability Companies, are another flexible and powerful vehicle for asset control. Like FLPs, they offer liability protection, pass-through taxation, and centralized management. However, LLCs add a layer of simplicity and flexibility. An LLC can be managed by its members (owners) or by designated managers, and the operating agreement can be customized to set out the management structure, distribution policies, transfer restrictions, and dispute resolution mechanisms. LLCs are especially useful for real estate holdings, family businesses, and investment accounts.

The choice between an FLP and an LLC often depends on the specific goals and circumstances. FLPs have advantages in multigenerational planning because of the distinct general and limited partner structure, which can reinforce family governance and control over time. LLCs, meanwhile, may offer more flexibility and ease of administration, especially in states with favorable LLC laws like Delaware, Nevada, and Wyoming. In practice, many ultra-affluent families use both: FLPs for certain assets and governance goals, LLCs for others.

Real-life scenarios illustrate how these structures play out. Take the example of a family with significant real estate holdings who formed an FLP to consolidate the properties under one umbrella. They gradually gifted limited partnership interests to their children, achieving substantial estate tax savings while maintaining operational control. Later, when one child faced a divorce, the former spouse could not claim partnership assets — a testament to the asset protection benefits. Another example: a family who created a Delaware LLC to hold a large investment portfolio, designing the operating agreement to restrict transfers, prevent forced distributions, and outline clear succession planning, ensuring that the portfolio would remain intact and governed according to the family's values.

The pros of FLPs and LLCs are compelling: control without ownership, estate tax efficiency through valuation discounts, asset protection, and centralized management of complex wealth. But the cons must be respected: complexity in formation and operation, cost of legal and administrative maintenance, and the potential for legal challenges if the structures are not properly respected. These are not DIY tools; they require skilled legal, tax, and financial advisors to set up and maintain.

The action steps are straightforward but critical. Begin by conducting a thorough inventory of your assets and your estate planning goals. Engage experienced counsel to discuss whether an FLP, an LLC, or a combination makes sense for your situation. Carefully design the partnership agreement or LLC operating agreement to reflect your governance objectives, distribution preferences, and transfer restrictions. Think beyond today: anticipate family dynamics, potential disputes, and the need for flexibility as laws and circumstances change. Most importantly, operate the entity properly. Hold meetings, maintain records, file required documents, and avoid commingling personal and entity assets.

Set clear goals. Do you want to protect assets from creditors and ex-spouses? Transfer wealth efficiently to the next generation? Retain control over family investments and businesses? Foster a culture of stewardship and responsibility among heirs? Your answers to these questions will guide the structure and governance of your FLPs and LLCs. And then ask the hard question: can you realistically achieve all this on your own, or do you need the guidance of estate planners, tax experts, and family governance consultants to navigate this sophisticated terrain?

Here's your bold call to action: Within the next 90 days, conduct an asset protection and estate planning review. Identify which assets could benefit from consolidation and control under an FLP or LLC structure. Engage qualified advisors to begin designing and implementing the appropriate vehicles. Don't leave your wealth exposed or fragmented — build the architecture that will protect, preserve, and guide it for generations.

Because at the ultra-affluent level, true wealth is not merely amassed; it is deliberately structured.

Ultra Affluent is your permission slip to transform your financial life from successful to sustainable — built not just for today, but for tomorrow, and for the generations who will carry your name and your legacy.

Chapter 15: Risk Management for the Affluent: Why Umbrella Coverage Isn't Enough

When you reach a certain level of wealth — the kind where your net worth is measured not just in assets, but in influence, opportunity, and visibility — risk management takes on a whole new meaning. For the ultra-affluent, personal and financial risks don't just multiply — they compound, often in ways that traditional insurance and asset protection strategies can't fully capture. While umbrella coverage is a necessary foundation, it's merely that — a foundation. True risk management for the ultra-affluent requires a layered, strategic, and dynamic approach that goes far beyond a simple umbrella policy.

Imagine you are seated across from me, reflecting on the world you've built. You've acquired businesses, amassed properties, and cultivated a life rich in resources and relationships. You have the customary insurance in place: homeowners, auto, health, a basic umbrella policy to cover liabilities beyond the standard limits. But then imagine a lawsuit — not the routine kind, but a high-stakes, high-visibility suit tied to an incident at one of your homes or an accusation against one of your ventures. Suddenly, the limits on your umbrella policy feel laughably inadequate. You realize too late that what protected you when you had $2 million in net worth does not begin to suffice when you have $50 million or $250 million.

Umbrella insurance is often touted as the answer to liability protection, and for most people, it is. It extends liability coverage beyond the limits of your homeowners, auto, and watercraft policies, offering an extra layer of security against personal injury claims, property damage, and lawsuits. For the mass affluent, a $5 million or $10 million umbrella policy may seem generous. For you, however, it is a fraction of the exposure you face. High-profile individuals are magnets for litigation — real or frivolous — because your wealth signals the potential for a large payout. The more successful you are, the larger the target on your back.

The pros of umbrella coverage are clear. It is relatively inexpensive for the amount of additional coverage it provides. It is easy to purchase and, for middle-market individuals, can be sufficient to protect against routine risks. But the cons for the ultra-affluent are equally obvious. The coverage limits are often too low. The policies may have exclusions that you are unaware of — intentional acts, business-related liabilities, or claims related to employment practices at your household staff. And umbrella coverage is reactive. It responds after a claim has been made. It does not proactively shield assets or prevent litigation from being initiated in the first place.

True risk management for the ultra-affluent starts with understanding the full spectrum of risks you face — operational, reputational, financial, personal — and constructing a layered defense. Asset protection structures like LLCs, FLPs, and trusts can segregate assets and shield them from creditors. Employment practices liability insurance (EPLI) can protect against claims from domestic staff. Directors and officers (D&O) insurance is critical if you sit on corporate boards. Cyber liability insurance is increasingly non-negotiable as high-net-worth individuals become prime targets for cybercrime and data breaches. Kidnap and ransom insurance, though it sounds dramatic, can be vital for families who travel internationally or maintain a high profile.

Consider the real-world case of a tech entrepreneur who, after a liquidity event, maintained his existing $5 million umbrella policy but neglected to reassess his total exposure. A lawsuit filed by a former household employee quickly exhausted the umbrella limits, and the settlement was drawn directly from personal assets. Contrast this with a different family who, anticipating their expanded risk profile, created multiple asset-holding

LLCs for real estate, updated their insurance to include $50 million of umbrella coverage supplemented with D&O, EPLI, and cyber policies, and restructured their estate plan to place vulnerable assets into protective trusts. When litigation came, they were insulated — not immune, but fortified.

Another layer to consider is personal security and privacy. Wealth often invites attention — not all of it welcome. Physical security assessments, home security enhancements, and cybersecurity audits should be standard operating procedures. Families with ultra-affluence should think about reputation risk management — employing public relations firms on retainer, monitoring social media exposure, and having crisis communication plans in place. A reputation built over decades can be tarnished overnight in the age of viral news and cancel culture.

Pros of a sophisticated risk management strategy are substantial: comprehensive protection, reduced exposure, peace of mind, and the ability to defend wealth not just reactively, but proactively. The cons? Complexity, cost, and the need for ongoing management. High-level risk management is not a one-time event. It requires continual reassessment as wealth grows, laws evolve, and family dynamics change. It also demands assembling a team — insurance advisors, asset protection attorneys, cybersecurity experts, and security consultants who specialize in high-net-worth individuals.

Action steps are vital and non-negotiable. Begin with a comprehensive risk audit. Where are you exposed? What is insured, and what is uninsured? Evaluate your current umbrella policy not just for the limit but for the exclusions and underlying requirements. Expand your coverage thoughtfully — don't just buy more umbrella; layer in specialty coverages like EPLI, D&O, cyber, and kidnap/ransom insurance. Simultaneously, evaluate your asset structures. Are your real estate holdings, investment accounts, and business interests properly segregated and insulated? Conduct a personal security assessment and implement both physical and digital protections. Develop a media and reputation management plan, including monitoring systems and crisis protocols.

Set clear goals. Do you want to ensure that no single lawsuit could bankrupt you? Protect your family from targeted threats? Shield your public image from reputational harm? Create a defensive architecture that is seamless, adaptive, and unobtrusive? Your goals will dictate the tools and strategies you deploy. Then ask the essential question: can you realistically orchestrate this level of complexity on your own, or do you need to assemble a team of experts to guide you?

Here's your bold call to action: Within the next 60 days, initiate a comprehensive risk audit. Assemble the right team of advisors. Expand and deepen your insurance coverage thoughtfully, not reflexively. Upgrade your asset protection structures. Assess your personal security protocols. In a world where risks are expanding in volume, velocity, and visibility, deliberate risk management is not optional. It is the only responsible path forward.

Because at the ultra-affluent level, wealth is not just to be grown — it is to be guarded with vigilance, sophistication, and unwavering discipline.

Ultra Affluent is your permission slip to master risk — not just avoid it.

Chapter 16: Captive Insurance Companies: Entrepreneurial Risk Management

At a certain level of wealth, the strategies available to you begin to evolve. They become more sophisticated, less about "off the shelf" solutions and more about custom architecture — the same kind of architecture you applied to building your business or portfolio. One of the least understood, but most powerful tools in the ultra-affluent arsenal for both wealth preservation and risk management is the Captive Insurance Company (CIC). While traditional insurance may serve the mass market, captives are built for those who don't just want to purchase insurance — they want to own it.

Imagine you're seated across from me. You're an entrepreneur who has scaled businesses, taken risks, and controlled outcomes for decades. You're used to customizing everything — your investment strategy, your estate planning, even your philanthropic footprint. So why are you still outsourcing your risk management to third-party insurers who don't understand your business, don't price your risks correctly, and siphon away capital year after year in premiums that often don't get paid back? This is where the conversation shifts to captives — a strategy that lets you take control of your risk management and convert what used to be an expense into a profit center.

A Captive Insurance Company is, simply put, an insurance company that you own, designed to insure the risks of your operating businesses or personal wealth ecosystem. Instead of paying premiums to a traditional third-party insurer, you pay premiums to your own captive. If your loss experience is good — and if you're like most ultra-affluent entrepreneurs, you've built a career on managing risk intelligently — those premiums become profits inside your captive. This creates a powerful financial lever: you're converting what was once an expense into a form of retained earnings, growing tax-advantaged reserves that you control.

The pros of captives are compelling. First, they allow you to insure risks that traditional carriers may either overprice or refuse to cover altogether — things like supply chain disruption, cyber liability, reputational damage, or unique business interruptions. Second, they create a potential profit center: if claims are low, your captive retains the premiums. Third, captives can create tax advantages. Premiums paid to a properly structured captive are generally tax-deductible to the business and are not immediately taxed to the captive up to certain limits. Fourth, captives can be a significant tool in estate planning — using the captive to accumulate assets that are later transferred to heirs outside the estate, potentially avoiding estate tax.

But, of course, there are cons. Captives are complex to form and operate. They must be legitimate insurance companies under the law, not just a "cookie jar" to hold assets. They require careful actuarial analysis, underwriting discipline, regulatory compliance, and risk management protocols. The IRS closely scrutinizes captives, particularly small captives under Section 831(b) of the Internal Revenue Code, to ensure they are not merely tax shelters. Setting up a captive requires substantial upfront capital, ongoing management costs, and a willingness to engage with regulatory frameworks at the state, national, and even international levels.

Let's bring it to life with real-world scenarios. Consider a business owner in the construction industry, traditionally burdened with high premiums for liability and business interruption insurance. By creating a captive, he was able to underwrite these risks more accurately based on his firm's actual loss history. Over a decade, his captive accumulated millions in surplus — a reservoir of wealth that otherwise would have been lost to traditional insurance premiums. Another example: a family office that manages a complex array of real estate investments and operating businesses. They created a captive to insure against niche risks like environmental liability, tenant disputes, and loss of key contracts. When COVID-19 hit, and standard insurers denied many business interruption claims, their captive paid out, protecting family wealth when it mattered most.

Action steps for those considering a captive start with a feasibility study. Not every risk or every business is a candidate. Engage a professional team — captive management firms, tax advisors, and legal counsel — to assess your risk profile, loss history, and financial structure. Consider the jurisdiction carefully; states like Vermont, Delaware, and Montana are popular U.S. domiciles, but offshore options like Bermuda and the Cayman Islands may offer different advantages. Design the captive's risk pool intelligently: diversify the risks, price the premiums properly, and ensure that the captive is truly operating as an insurance company, with real underwriting, claims management, and regulatory filings.

Set clear goals. Are you looking to reduce insurance costs? Retain underwriting profits? Insure unique or hard-to-cover risks? Enhance your estate planning and legacy strategies? Your goals will inform the design of the captive. Then ask the critical question: can you realistically build and operate a captive on your own, or do you need to hire experienced managers, actuaries, and compliance experts? Captives are powerful, but they are not DIY projects. They require the same rigor, discipline, and oversight as any other regulated financial entity.

Here's your bold call to action: Within the next 90 days, if you haven't already, initiate a feasibility study to explore whether a captive insurance company could be a valuable tool in your wealth management and risk architecture. Don't dismiss it as an exotic strategy — captives have been used for decades by the largest corporations in the world. If you've reached the level of ultra-affluence, you deserve the same sophistication and control in your risk management. Convert insurance from a cost center to a profit center. Protect your wealth — not passively, but proactively.

Because at the ultra-affluent level, wealth isn't just accumulated — it's engineered.

Ultra Affluent is your permission slip to master your risk profile the same way you mastered your enterprise — with strategy, precision, and authority.

Chapter 17: Private Placement Life Insurance (PPLI): A Tax-Advantaged Growth Tool

At the level of ultra-affluence, the conversation about money stops being about accumulation and starts being about optimization. You've already earned, invested, and grown your wealth. Now the task is more complex — how do you protect it, enhance it, and transition it efficiently to the next generation? Taxes, regulatory changes, and portfolio drag become significant obstacles. And so the strategies must evolve, too. Enter Private Placement Life Insurance (PPLI), a tool that — while invisible to many — has become a centerpiece of wealth planning for families with substantial assets. For the ultra-affluent, PPLI is not about insurance in the traditional sense; it's about creating a highly efficient, tax-advantaged investment vehicle within a protective wrapper.

Imagine you're sitting across from me, a seasoned entrepreneur or investor who has built a $50 million or $250 million net worth. You have exposure to taxable investments: hedge funds, private equity, marketable securities, real estate. You've worked hard, but every year a silent partner takes a huge cut of your growth — the IRS. Capital gains taxes, interest income, dividend taxes — all leech away at your returns, slowing your compounding power. You've mastered business; you've mastered investing. Now the question is, have you mastered tax optimization at scale? For most, the answer is no — and this is where PPLI becomes a game-changer.

Private Placement Life Insurance is a life insurance contract, but not like the retail policies you're used to seeing. Unlike mass-market life insurance, which typically focuses on providing death benefits to middle-class families, PPLI is engineered for ultra-affluent individuals seeking to invest significant assets on a tax-deferred or even tax-free basis. In a PPLI structure, investments grow tax-free inside the policy. There are no annual taxes on interest, dividends, or capital gains. When structured properly, the death benefit can pass income-tax-free to beneficiaries. And if needed, policyholders can access cash value through tax-free loans and withdrawals. In short, PPLI marries high-end investment access with the formidable tax advantages traditionally associated with life insurance.

The pros of PPLI are striking. First, there's the tax deferral. Imagine compounding $20 million over decades without annual tax drag. Second, there's investment flexibility. Unlike traditional life insurance policies with cookie-cutter investment choices, PPLI allows policyholders to invest in customized separate accounts, including hedge funds, private equity, and other alternative investments, subject to IRS diversification rules. Third, PPLI offers asset protection. In many jurisdictions, the cash value inside a life insurance policy is shielded from creditors. Finally, when structured correctly, the death benefit can be used for wealth transfer, estate planning, and even liquidity creation for estate tax obligations — all without triggering income tax.

But PPLI is not without cons. It is complex. The policies must be carefully designed and maintained to comply with IRS guidelines on diversification and investor control. PPLI is also expensive to set up; typically, it requires minimum premiums of $2 million to $5 million, and the underlying investment and insurance costs must be evaluated carefully to ensure efficiency. Moreover, because PPLI is a life insurance product, underwriting is required — though many policies can be structured with minimal health requirements or via "guaranteed issue" for higher-net-worth individuals who face underwriting challenges. Finally, poor design can collapse the structure, creating taxable events and eroding the very benefits you sought to achieve.

Consider a real-world example: a family office with a $100 million portfolio heavily allocated to alternative investments. Every year, tax drag was reducing their net returns by more than 2%. By moving a portion of their investments into a PPLI structure, they eliminated the annual taxation, increased the after-tax return on their portfolio, and created a tax-free death benefit that could be used to cover estate taxes without forcing asset liquidation. Another case: an entrepreneur with a large concentration of illiquid real estate assets, facing significant estate tax exposure. By deploying PPLI, he was able to create liquidity outside the taxable estate, avoiding a fire sale of prized properties when the estate came due.

The action steps for those considering PPLI begin with a feasibility study. Not all assets are suitable for PPLI; highly liquid, tax-inefficient assets are prime candidates, while already tax-advantaged holdings (like municipal bonds or IRAs) are not. Engage a professional team — a PPLI specialist, estate planning attorney, and tax advisor — to conduct a full audit of your portfolio and wealth transfer goals. Evaluate the domicile carefully; policies issued in jurisdictions like Delaware or South Dakota can offer strong creditor protections and favorable tax treatment. Pay close attention to the insurance carrier's financial strength and the investment platform's flexibility and reputation.

Set clear goals. Are you primarily seeking tax-free growth? Asset protection? Estate liquidity? Multigenerational wealth transfer? The clarity of your objectives will dictate how the PPLI structure is designed — including the policy type (variable universal life is typical), investment allocations, and ownership structure (often a trust to keep the death benefit outside the taxable estate). Equally important: determine who will manage and administer the policy over time, ensuring compliance with IRS diversification rules and monitoring investment performance within the policy's separate account framework.

Now the essential question: can you construct and manage a PPLI strategy on your own? The answer is unequivocally no. PPLI requires specialized expertise — from selecting the right carrier, to building the right investment platform, to maintaining compliance with complex tax and legal standards. The costs of getting it wrong are catastrophic: collapsed policies, adverse tax consequences, and reputational damage. Hire out. Build a team that includes wealth managers experienced in PPLI, attorneys who understand private placement structures, and tax advisors who can integrate PPLI seamlessly into your overall wealth plan.

Here's your bold call to action: Within the next 90 days, conduct a tax-efficiency audit of your existing investment portfolio. Identify the assets suffering from the heaviest tax drag. Then, initiate a feasibility study to determine whether PPLI could increase your after-tax returns and provide additional estate planning benefits. The objective is simple: stop leaking unnecessary tax dollars and start building a structure where your wealth can grow unhindered, protected, and positioned for maximum impact.

Because at the ultra-affluent level, winning isn't about the highest gross returns — it's about the smartest net returns.

Ultra Affluent is your permission slip to elevate your wealth planning from good to exceptional — to move from reactive to proactive, from fragmented to integrated.

Part III: Tax Efficiency and Wealth Optimization

At the ultra-affluent level, the true measure of financial mastery is not simply how much wealth is created, but how efficiently it is preserved, grown, and transferred. Part III dives deep into the strategies that separate mere wealth accumulation from sophisticated wealth optimization. In this section, we move beyond surface-level tax planning and into the deliberate design of tax-efficient structures that protect and propel complex wealth. Readers will explore the power of advanced income tax minimization strategies, from entity structuring to deferred compensation and charitable planning. They will learn how Private Placement Life Insurance (PPLI) transforms tax drag into tax-free compounding and why captives and other alternative vehicles offer unparalleled advantages in risk and tax management.

This part also emphasizes the critical integration of tax strategy with overall wealth design — blending legal, financial, and investment disciplines into one cohesive system. Real-world scenarios and practical frameworks will illustrate how the ultra-wealthy legally reduce their tax burdens, accelerate after-tax returns, and position their assets for multigenerational success. By the end of Part III, readers will not only understand the available tools but also gain the strategic clarity to apply them with precision.

Tax efficiency at this level is not an option — it's a requirement for anyone serious about sustaining influence, freedom, and legacy. This section is the guidebook for those ready to convert tax from an inevitable cost into a powerful lever for lasting wealth.

Chapter 18: Income Tax Minimization Strategies for Complex Wealth

When you reach the ultra-affluent level, income taxes are no longer an annual nuisance. They are a persistent, strategic challenge that can erode your wealth over time if left unchecked. At this echelon, simple deductions and basic deferrals no longer move the needle. The complexity of your wealth — with its mix of business ownership, private investments, real estate holdings, and perhaps international interests — demands a different caliber of planning. The conversation must shift from tax compliance to tax optimization. It's not about avoiding taxes; it's about engineering your affairs so tax becomes a tool you control rather than a force that controls you.

Imagine you are seated across from me — a seasoned entrepreneur or investor who has built and navigated substantial financial success. You have C-corporations, LLCs, maybe a family office managing everything from venture capital stakes to commercial real estate. Your portfolio generates ordinary income, qualified dividends, short- and long-term capital gains. Each category is taxed differently and requires precision to minimize. You understand that left unmanaged, taxes could easily claim 40% or more of your earnings each year — a silent but steady drain on your compounding power. The question you now face is not whether you are successful, but whether you are efficient.

Income tax minimization for complex wealth begins with entity structuring. How you own your assets is just as important as what you own. Leveraging partnerships, S-corporations, and carefully designed LLCs allows for the allocation of income in ways that minimize taxation. For example, partnerships allow for flexible profit and loss allocations, letting you direct income to entities or individuals in lower tax brackets. S-corporations can help business owners avoid self-employment tax on a portion of their earnings through reasonable compensation planning. Advanced planning even includes tiered entity structures — using management companies and holding companies to separate activities and optimize income flows.

Another essential strategy is the use of deferred compensation and retirement structures. While 401(k)s and IRAs are pedestrian for the mass affluent, ultra-wealthy individuals leverage defined benefit plans, 412(e)(3) plans, and even captive insurance companies structured to include retirement benefits. For those with significant W-2 income, nonqualified deferred compensation plans can allow a substantial portion of income to be deferred until retirement, ideally at a lower tax rate. But these strategies are complex and require a strong understanding of ERISA rules, contribution limits, and investment design.

Private placement life insurance (PPLI), already discussed in another chapter, plays a powerful role here as well. By housing investment assets inside an insurance wrapper, you can achieve tax-free growth and avoid the annual drag of interest, dividends, and capital gains taxation. Structured correctly, PPLI can effectively convert taxable investments into a tax-sheltered compounding machine.

Charitable planning offers another dimension to minimize taxes while supporting causes you care about. Charitable remainder trusts (CRTs) allow you to defer capital gains taxes on the sale of highly appreciated assets while providing an income stream for life and leaving the remainder to charity. Donor-advised funds (DAFs) let you make large contributions — and take large deductions — in high-income years, smoothing your taxable income over time. For those with substantial philanthropic goals, private foundations can offer both tax deductions and ongoing control over charitable activities, though they come with stricter administrative and regulatory obligations.

Real estate, too, offers significant opportunities for tax minimization. Through cost segregation studies, you can accelerate depreciation deductions on commercial and residential real estate, front-loading tax benefits and improving cash flow. Like-kind exchanges under Section 1031 allow you to defer capital gains taxes when swapping investment properties. For families managing significant real estate portfolios, structuring ownership through LLCs and employing strategies like opportunity zone investments can further reduce tax liability and enhance after-tax returns.

International strategies should not be overlooked for those with global exposure. Offshore trusts, properly structured and disclosed, can offer asset protection and tax deferral opportunities. Foreign earned income exclusions and housing allowances can benefit expatriates. For those with operating businesses abroad, careful planning around controlled foreign corporations (CFCs) and global intangible low-taxed income (GILTI) rules is essential to avoid unexpected U.S. tax liabilities.

Real-world examples illuminate the power of these strategies. One entrepreneur, after selling a business for $200 million, used a combination of installment sales, charitable remainder trusts, and PPLI to dramatically reduce his effective tax rate. Another family office, managing diverse assets from commercial real estate to venture capital, deployed a tiered LLC structure with a family management company, creating legitimate business expenses and reducing overall taxable income. Yet another investor, anticipating a large capital gain, established a donor-advised fund in advance, offsetting the gain with a substantial charitable deduction while funding philanthropic initiatives for decades to come.

The pros of comprehensive tax minimization strategies are compelling: higher after-tax returns, enhanced cash flow, better compounding, and the ability to direct more wealth toward family and philanthropic goals rather than to the IRS. The cons? Complexity, upfront planning costs, and the ongoing need for compliance and adjustment as tax laws change. Missteps can be costly — improper structuring can result in penalties, interest, or audits. These strategies require not just technical knowledge but also the wisdom to integrate them seamlessly into a broader wealth plan.

The action steps are clear but rigorous. Start with a comprehensive tax audit. Map out your income sources, entity structures, and investment profiles. Engage an elite team — tax attorneys, CPAs, wealth managers — with deep experience in complex wealth structures. Identify opportunities to restructure ownership, defer income, shift assets into tax-advantaged vehicles, and align charitable giving with tax minimization. Stress-test your plan against different income scenarios, liquidity events, and legislative changes. Commit to an annual review — what works this year may not work next.

Set goals that are both quantitative and qualitative. Do you want to reduce your effective tax rate below a certain threshold? Maximize after-tax investment returns? Create liquidity for estate taxes without forced asset sales? Fund a philanthropic legacy? The clarity of your goals will inform the sophistication of your strategy. Then ask yourself: can you realistically navigate this terrain alone? Or do you need to hire specialists who live and breathe this level of complexity every day?

Here's your bold call to action: Within the next 90 days, complete a forensic tax audit of your current structures and strategies. Identify the biggest sources of tax drag and the most immediate opportunities for optimization. Then, assemble the right team to architect a tax minimization plan that matches the scale and sophistication of your wealth. Taxes are a certainty — but overpaying them is not.

Because at the ultra-affluent level, it's not what you make — it's what you keep.

Ultra Affluent is your permission slip to transform tax from a threat into a tool — a tool for growth, preservation, and enduring impact.

Chapter 19: Navigating Private Equity, Hedge Funds, and Venture Capital Taxation

When wealth reaches the level where traditional investments are no longer sufficient, the world of private equity, hedge funds, and venture capital beckons. These alternative investments promise higher returns, access to exclusive opportunities, and portfolio diversification that can weather volatile markets. But with those opportunities comes a new frontier of complexity — especially in taxation. For the ultra-affluent, the financial gains of these asset classes are only meaningful if they are managed with tax sophistication. High returns can quickly erode when tax drag, obscure structures, and mismanaged distributions are ignored.

Imagine you are sitting across from me — a highly accomplished entrepreneur, investor, or executive who has successfully allocated millions into alternative assets. You've backed promising startups, funded buyouts, and committed capital to hedge fund strategies designed to capture alpha. Yet every K-1 you receive each spring brings a familiar sense of dread — long lists of taxable gains, phantom income, foreign disclosures, and multistate tax filings. The allure of outsized returns is undeniable, but the complexity of managing the tax consequences can feel overwhelming. The question is not whether these investments belong in your portfolio — they do — but whether you are managing their taxation with the same intentionality you brought to your wealth creation.

Private equity investments typically generate returns through capital appreciation and carried interest, but they also create taxable events along the way. When a portfolio company is sold, capital gains are realized — but because funds are structured as partnerships, you, as an investor, receive a portion of that gain even if you weren't involved in the sale timing. Moreover, many private equity funds invest across state lines, exposing limited partners to state income taxes in jurisdictions they otherwise have no connection to. The allocation of income, gains, and losses on the K-1 can be complex, and the deductibility of expenses — management fees, for example — can vary depending on structure and planning.

The tax pros of private equity are clear: long-term capital gains rates, typically lower than ordinary income tax rates, apply to most investment profits if assets are held longer than a year. Qualified small business stock (QSBS) exemptions under Section 1202 can allow for exclusion of up to $10 million in gains per investment in qualifying startups. Funds structured properly can also provide opportunities for tax deferral or installment sales. However, the cons are equally present: phantom income — where tax is owed before cash is distributed — state and local tax exposure, and the complexity of tracking basis, especially when funds engage in recapitalizations or restructurings.

Hedge funds bring their own unique tax considerations. Many hedge funds engage in high-turnover strategies, triggering short-term capital gains, taxed at the higher ordinary income rates. Others invest in derivatives, options, and foreign securities, creating further layers of complexity. The famed "carried interest loophole" benefits fund managers but does little for limited partners who must contend with the annual tax hit on gains that may or may not be distributed in cash. Some hedge funds attempt to "structure" around high tax burdens by organizing as offshore funds or using blockers, but these tactics require careful planning to avoid running afoul of the IRS or creating adverse personal tax consequences.

Pros of hedge funds include the potential for high returns uncorrelated to public markets and access to sophisticated strategies like global macro, long-short equity, and event-driven investing. Some funds use "in-kind" redemptions to minimize taxable events upon withdrawal. But the cons — high fees, limited liquidity, and complex tax reporting — must be weighed carefully. It's not uncommon for investors to face state tax filings in multiple jurisdictions or to receive late K-1s that disrupt their tax filing timelines.

Venture capital investments — the most speculative of the trio — also offer unique tax planning opportunities. Early-stage investments, if held for five years and qualifying under Section 1202, may be eligible for QSBS exclusions. Additionally, Section 1045 allows investors to roll over gains from the sale of QSBS into another qualifying investment, deferring taxes further. But venture investments often come with high failure rates, complicated valuation issues, and the need for precise record-keeping to substantiate tax positions in the event of an audit.

Real-life scenarios highlight these challenges. Consider the entrepreneur who invests in several venture funds, only to find that, despite strong paper returns, few exits materialize on schedule. Meanwhile, taxable income — phantom income — must be reported based on fund activity, not actual cash flow. Another case: a family office with substantial private equity exposure finds itself filing in 18 different states because of the funds' multistate investment footprints. Without careful planning, they pay state taxes on income that, when aggregated, exceeds federal taxable income due to differing apportionment rules.

The action steps for investors at this level are clear but nontrivial. Start with a thorough review of current alternative investment holdings. Analyze the structures of each fund — domestic versus offshore, LP versus blocker — and the expected tax consequences. Engage a tax advisor experienced in partnership taxation and multistate filings. Evaluate the potential benefits of placing alternative investments inside tax-advantaged vehicles like PPLI or deferred compensation plans where permissible. Consider the use of charitable vehicles, like charitable lead trusts (CLTs) or donor-advised funds (DAFs), to offset large gains with charitable deductions. And always insist on transparency from fund managers about tax reporting timelines and expectations.

Set clear goals: Is your priority maximum after-tax return? Diversification? Liquidity management? Legacy building? These priorities will shape which funds you invest in and how you structure those investments. Perhaps you're willing to accept complex K-1s and multistate filings in exchange for high alpha, or perhaps you prefer more tax-efficient strategies even at the cost of lower gross returns. In either case, align your tax strategy with your broader wealth strategy, not as an afterthought but as a core pillar.

Then ask yourself the inevitable question: Can you realistically manage this complexity on your own? Even the most capable entrepreneurs and investors benefit from an elite team — tax attorneys, CPAs, wealth managers — who specialize in alternative asset taxation. Without this expertise, it's not a question of if you'll leave money on the table through unnecessary taxes; it's a question of how much.

Here's your bold call to action: Within the next 90 days, conduct a tax impact analysis of your private equity, hedge fund, and venture capital holdings. Identify the biggest sources of tax drag and the biggest opportunities for tax deferral or exclusion. If necessary, restructure ownership through more efficient vehicles. Alternative investments should be an engine of wealth creation — not an engine of tax inefficiency.

Because at the ultra-affluent level, returns are measured not just by how much you make, but by how much you keep after taxes are done with you.

Ultra Affluent is your permission slip to elevate your alternative investment strategy from opportunistic to optimized — from merely sophisticated to truly efficient.

Chapter 20: Domicile Optimization: Moving to Save Millions

When you have crossed into the realm of ultra-affluence, every decision must be viewed through a wider lens. You no longer think in terms of incremental changes; you think in terms of strategic moves that can shift millions — even tens of millions — over a lifetime. Nowhere is this more evident than in the concept of domicile optimization. In simple terms: where you live can be one of the single largest financial decisions you make. At this level, state taxes, inheritance laws, asset protection statutes, and residency requirements are not minor details — they are major levers of wealth optimization.

Imagine you are seated across from me. You're a successful entrepreneur, a private equity partner, or perhaps a real estate magnate with a significant net worth. You've spent your life building businesses, investing wisely, and creating a legacy. But now you realize that your home state — the place you started, grew up, or built your company — is also one of the highest-taxed, most litigious states in the country. You're facing the reality that staying where you are could cost you 10% to 15% of your income annually in state taxes alone, not to mention estate taxes and exposure to lawsuits. What's the solution? You need to rethink not just how you invest, but where you live.

Domicile optimization is the strategic act of relocating your legal residence — and often your actual lifestyle — to a jurisdiction that aligns better with your wealth preservation goals. The pros of this move can be enormous: zero state income tax, no state-level estate tax, stronger asset protection laws, and more favorable trust and privacy statutes. States like Florida, Texas, Nevada, Wyoming, South Dakota, and Tennessee have become magnets for the ultra-affluent precisely because they offer these advantages. A move to one of these states can save millions in taxes over a lifetime and even more in estate taxes when transferring wealth to heirs.

But the cons are real and must be carefully weighed. Relocating isn't just about forwarding your mail or changing your driver's license. States with high income taxes — think California, New York, New Jersey, and Massachusetts — are aggressive in challenging domicile changes. They look at a mosaic of factors: where you spend your time, where your business interests are located, where your family is based, where you receive mail, where your doctors and financial advisors are located, and even where your pets live. If you don't make a bona fide, well-documented, and thorough relocation, you could find yourself still on the hook for taxes — even after you've moved.

A real-world example brings this to life. A tech entrepreneur based in California with a $100 million pending IPO realized that a move to Texas could save him nearly $13 million in state income taxes on his liquidity event alone. But California's Franchise Tax Board scrutinizes moves aggressively. Simply buying a house in Texas was not enough. He had to sell his California home, register to vote in Texas, move his primary banking relationships, update his estate planning documents to reflect Texas law, and document his presence through travel logs, credit card statements, and cellphone records. It was not just a move — it was a complete reinvention of his legal and financial life. Done properly, it resulted in full recognition of his Texas domicile and a massive tax savings.

Another case involved a family with significant real estate holdings and business interests in New York. They decided to relocate to Florida, drawn by the absence of a state income tax and favorable trust laws. They not only moved their residence but also restructured their trusts under Florida law, transferred their voter registration and driver's licenses, and even moved some of their board meetings for the family business to Miami. New York challenged their move but ultimately had to concede because the family had meticulously documented every aspect of their transition.

The action steps for domicile optimization are not to be taken lightly. First, conduct a full analysis of your current and projected income streams, estate tax exposure, and asset protection needs. Identify which jurisdictions align best with your goals. Engage a team — tax attorneys, estate planners, and relocation consultants — who specialize in high-net-worth domicile transitions. Prepare a checklist: sell or rent out your current primary residence, acquire a home in the new state, update all your professional and personal documents, and track your physical presence rigorously. Some families even go as far as hiring audit consultants who simulate an aggressive audit to ensure they would withstand scrutiny.

Set clear goals: Is the objective to reduce ongoing income taxes? Minimize estate taxes? Strengthen asset protection? Improve privacy? Or perhaps a combination of all these? Your priorities will dictate not just where you move, but how you structure the transition. For some, a move to Florida for income tax purposes makes sense, while others may choose South Dakota or Nevada for their superior trust and asset protection laws, even if it requires maintaining property or business entities there.

Now, the inevitable question: Can you do this on your own? Absolutely not. The cost of a failed domicile change can be catastrophic — years of back taxes, penalties, interest, and potentially litigation. Even if you succeed in moving your physical residence, without proper documentation and strategy, you could still be considered a resident by your former state for tax purposes. The stakes are simply too high. Assemble a team of experts — people who have done this hundreds of times for families like yours — and let them guide you through the maze.

Here's your bold call to action: Within the next 90 days, initiate a domicile optimization study. Review your current state's tax burdens and legal environment. Identify jurisdictions that offer the advantages you need to protect and grow your wealth. Engage qualified advisors to design and implement a comprehensive plan to relocate your domicile in a way that withstands scrutiny, achieves your goals, and positions your family for multigenerational success.

Because at the ultra-affluent level, where you live — legally and financially — matters just as much as how much you have.

Ultra Affluent is your permission slip to move strategically, deliberately, and with precision — not just to a new house, but to a new financial reality.

Chapter 21: Charitable Tax Strategies: CRUTs, CLTs, Donor-Advised Funds

When you reach a certain level of wealth, the relationship between philanthropy and taxes evolves. Giving is no longer just about writing a check or donating appreciated stock; it becomes a strategic exercise in legacy building, tax optimization, and personal values alignment. For the ultra-affluent, charitable giving can — and should — be an extension of the overall wealth management plan, designed with the same precision and sophistication as the rest of your financial architecture. It's here where tools like Charitable Remainder Unitrusts (CRUTs), Charitable Lead Trusts (CLTs), and Donor-Advised Funds (DAFs) come into play, turning generosity into a dynamic force for wealth preservation, tax efficiency, and impact.

Imagine you are sitting across from me. You're a seasoned entrepreneur, investor, or executive who has amassed significant wealth. You have causes you care about — education, healthcare, social justice, the arts — and you also have real, tangible concerns about taxes: income taxes, capital gains taxes, and looming estate taxes. You want to make an impact, but you also want to be strategic. You understand that unchecked taxes can erode your wealth over time and compromise your ability to leave a lasting legacy. The good news? You don't have to choose between generosity and tax efficiency. With the right structures, you can have both.

Let's start with Charitable Remainder Unitrusts (CRUTs). A CRUT allows you to transfer assets into a trust that provides you, or other designated beneficiaries, with a stream of income for life or for a term of years. At the end of the term, the remainder goes to charity. When you contribute appreciated assets — like stock or real estate — to a CRUT, you get a charitable deduction based on the present value of the remainder interest, avoid immediate capital gains tax, and remove the assets from your estate. The trust can sell the appreciated assets without incurring capital gains tax and reinvest the proceeds. The result? A lifetime income stream, an immediate tax deduction, and an eventual charitable gift — all from one strategy.

The pros of a CRUT are significant: deferral of capital gains taxes, current income tax deductions, and reduction of estate tax exposure. Additionally, CRUTs can be customized — you can set the payout rate, name multiple beneficiaries, and even allow for future contributions. The cons? CRUTs are irrevocable — once you place assets into the trust, you can't get them back. The income stream is taxable to the beneficiaries, and the administrative burden — annual valuations, filings, trust management — requires ongoing attention. Nevertheless, for those looking to generate income and leave a charitable legacy, CRUTs can be a powerful tool.

Charitable Lead Trusts (CLTs) work in the opposite direction. With a CLT, you contribute assets to a trust that provides an income stream to charity for a term of years, after which the remainder passes to your heirs. In a low-interest-rate environment, CLTs are particularly powerful because they allow you to "freeze" the value of the assets for estate tax purposes. If the trust's investments outperform the IRS's assumed rate of return (the Section 7520 rate), the excess growth passes to your heirs free of additional gift or estate tax. CLTs can be structured to provide significant estate tax savings while simultaneously supporting your charitable interests.

The pros of a CLT include immediate impact for charities, potential estate tax reduction, and the ability to transfer wealth to heirs at a discount. However, CLTs also have drawbacks. They are complex to set up and administer, require a strong investment strategy to outperform the IRS hurdle rate, and like CRUTs, they are irrevocable. Additionally, depending on the structure, you may not receive an immediate income tax deduction

— only a gift tax benefit. But for families concerned with estate taxes and interested in substantial charitable giving, CLTs represent a strategic solution.

Donor-Advised Funds (DAFs) offer a simpler, more flexible alternative. A DAF is like a charitable investment account: you make a contribution, receive an immediate tax deduction, and then recommend grants to charities over time. DAFs allow you to "pre-fund" your philanthropy, taking deductions in high-income years and pacing your giving over future years. They are particularly valuable for individuals facing a large liquidity event, such as the sale of a business, who want to maximize deductions in a single year but disburse charitable gifts gradually. DAFs are easy to set up, require no ongoing administration on your part, and offer investment options to grow your charitable dollars tax-free.

The pros of DAFs are clear: immediate deductions, flexibility in grantmaking, professional management, and no minimum distribution requirements. The cons? Once you contribute to a DAF, you relinquish control over the funds — although you can recommend grants, the sponsoring organization legally owns the assets. Additionally, DAFs do not provide the same level of legacy control or family engagement that a private foundation might offer. Nevertheless, for most ultra-affluent families, DAFs provide a streamlined, effective way to engage in strategic philanthropy without the administrative burden of a foundation.

Real-world examples illustrate the power of these strategies. Consider a family who sold their business for $250 million. Facing a massive capital gains tax bill, they contributed $20 million of appreciated stock to a CRUT, securing a substantial income tax deduction, deferring capital gains, and creating an income stream for their retirement years. Another case involved a multi-generational family office that used a CLT to transfer $50 million in real estate holdings to heirs, dramatically reducing estate taxes while directing millions to charitable causes over the life of the trust. A third example: a tech executive with a liquidity event who established a DAF with $5 million, using it to fund a decade's worth of planned giving while optimizing the deduction in the high-income year of the IPO.

The action steps for integrating charitable tax strategies into your wealth plan are both simple and critical. Begin with a philanthropic vision: what causes matter most to you? What legacy do you want to leave? Then, conduct a tax and estate planning review to identify opportunities to integrate CRUTs, CLTs, or DAFs into your broader strategy. Engage with experienced advisors — estate attorneys, tax planners, and charitable planning specialists — to design the right structures. Evaluate whether a single strategy or a combination of tools is most appropriate given your goals, liquidity events, and family dynamics.

Set clear goals: Do you want to maximize income tax deductions in a particular year? Reduce estate tax exposure? Generate a lifetime income stream while benefiting charity? Create a family legacy around giving? These goals will guide the choice and design of your charitable vehicles. And then, ask yourself honestly: can you structure, implement, and manage these complex strategies alone? The answer, if you value compliance, efficiency, and impact, is no. A sophisticated team is essential to navigate the legal, tax, and administrative nuances that come with high-level charitable planning.

Here's your bold call to action: Within the next 90 days, formalize your philanthropic strategy. Define your charitable priorities, review your potential tax exposure, and initiate conversations with advisors about implementing CRUTs, CLTs, DAFs, or a combination thereof. Strategic philanthropy isn't just about giving — it's about giving smart, giving efficiently, and giving in a way that amplifies your impact while preserving your wealth.

Because at the ultra-affluent level, generosity should not be random or reactive — it should be intentional, structured, and deeply aligned with your legacy.

Ultra Affluent is your permission slip to elevate your giving — to transform charity from an act of kindness into an instrument of enduring impact and tax efficiency.

Chapter 22: Generation-Skipping Transfer Tax (GST) Planning Demystified

For the ultra-affluent, the journey toward wealth mastery is not just about preserving wealth during their lifetime, but also about ensuring its efficient transfer across generations. As families grow and expand, so too does the challenge of transferring wealth without it being eroded by taxation at each generational handoff. Enter the Generation-Skipping Transfer Tax, or GST tax — a federal tax designed specifically to prevent the wealthy from circumventing estate and gift taxes by passing assets directly to grandchildren or great-grandchildren. While it sounds complicated — and often is — strategic GST planning can unlock profound advantages for families aiming to sustain wealth across multiple generations.

Imagine you are seated across from me — a highly accomplished individual who has built an estate worth tens or hundreds of millions of dollars. You are contemplating not just your children's inheritance, but how your grandchildren and their descendants will be provided for. You recognize that without careful planning, your estate could be subjected to estate taxes in each successive generation — a devastating one-two punch of federal and potentially state taxes, which could strip away more than half of your family's wealth with every transfer. This is where GST planning becomes essential. It's not a loophole — it's an intentional strategy, sanctioned by the IRS, to preserve family wealth beyond just your immediate heirs.

In essence, the GST tax is an extra layer of tax imposed on transfers to "skip persons" — generally grandchildren or individuals more than 37.5 years younger than the donor — that would otherwise avoid estate or gift tax at an intervening generation. The GST tax rate is steep — it matches the top federal estate tax rate, currently 40%. However, every individual is afforded a GST exemption amount — approximately $13.61 million per person in 2024 — that can be allocated strategically to shield certain transfers from GST tax altogether. Proper use of this exemption is critical, and poor planning can result in catastrophic, unnecessary taxation.

The pros of GST planning are significant. When done correctly, it allows you to "pre-fund" future generations with substantial assets while avoiding estate tax at each generational level. Dynasty trusts, which leverage the GST exemption, can hold assets in perpetuity for your descendants, protected from creditors, divorce, and additional estate taxes. Such trusts not only shelter the principal from taxation but also provide controlled distributions according to the parameters you set — ensuring responsible stewardship of wealth. Furthermore, GST-exempt trusts can grow outside the taxable estates of future beneficiaries, magnifying the impact of compound returns across generations.

Of course, there are cons to be mindful of. GST planning is complex and requires meticulous record-keeping and tax filings. Allocating GST exemptions incorrectly — for example, through poor documentation or timing mistakes — can trigger unintended tax liabilities. The legal structure must be crafted with care: trusts must meet specific requirements, including proper beneficiary designations and trustee provisions. Additionally, many states impose their own separate generation-skipping transfer taxes or have rules limiting the duration of trusts (known as the Rule Against Perpetuities), although some states like South Dakota and Nevada have abolished these rules, making them favorable jurisdictions for dynasty trust planning.

Real-world scenarios make the power of GST planning vivid. Consider a family that established a GST-exempt dynasty trust in the 1990s with an initial funding of $10 million. Over the decades, with prudent investment management and the power of tax-free compounding inside the trust, the assets have grown to over $100 million. Not only has the original wealth been preserved, but it has grown substantially, all while being insulated from estate taxes, creditor claims, and marital disputes for the family's heirs. Contrast this with a family who failed to engage in GST planning and whose wealth was cut nearly in half at each generational transfer due to compounding estate taxes, significantly reducing the overall family legacy.

The action steps for GST planning start with understanding your family's long-term goals. Are you seeking to provide for multiple generations? Are there concerns about heirs' financial maturity or external risks like divorce? Begin by working with estate attorneys and wealth advisors experienced in GST planning. Create dynasty trusts designed to be GST-exempt, ensuring proper allocation of your lifetime GST exemption. Choose favorable jurisdictions with no Rule Against Perpetuities to maximize the trust's lifespan. Design the trust with flexibility — including powers of appointment, trustee succession plans, and distribution guidelines — to accommodate changing family dynamics over the decades.

Set clear goals: Is your priority maximizing wealth transfer across multiple generations? Protecting assets from estate taxation, creditors, and marital disputes? Empowering future generations with financial resources while maintaining oversight? Once these goals are articulated, they can guide the design and implementation of your GST plan. It's not merely about saving taxes — it's about preserving family wealth, values, and opportunities over the long arc of time.

And here's the inevitable question: Can you do this alone? The honest answer is no. GST planning requires a coordinated team of estate planners, tax attorneys, and wealth advisors who specialize in multi-generational strategies. Mistakes — even seemingly small ones — can have multi-million-dollar consequences and reverberate across generations. Proper planning, rigorous documentation, and ongoing review are essential to ensure the plan remains effective in the face of changing laws, financial markets, and family circumstances.

Here's your bold call to action: Within the next 90 days, initiate a multi-generational wealth review. Assess your current estate plan for

GST exposure. Identify whether your existing trusts are GST-exempt and whether additional planning could leverage your GST exemption more effectively. Engage a specialized team to design or refine your dynasty trust structures to maximize wealth preservation for future generations.

Because at the ultra-affluent level, true wealth mastery is not just about growing assets — it's about ensuring that the fruits of your labor endure long after you're gone.

Ultra Affluent is your permission slip to think bigger, plan further, and protect deeper — to build a legacy that transcends generations.

Chapter 23: Carried Interest Planning for Private Equity and Venture Executives

When you've reached the ultra-affluent level, your wealth is no longer tied solely to salary or even traditional investment returns. It's often tethered to more complex, nuanced sources — and few are more influential, or more complicated, than carried interest. For private equity and venture capital executives, carried interest isn't just a bonus — it's the centerpiece of wealth creation. Properly structured and protected, it can catapult a career's worth of sweat equity into generational wealth. Poorly managed, however, it can trigger unnecessary tax consequences, liquidity crises, and erode the very advantages it was designed to provide.

Imagine you are sitting across from me — a successful private equity or venture capital partner, holding significant carried interest rights in one or more funds. You've spent years nurturing investments, guiding portfolio companies through growth, exits, and acquisitions. Now, your carried interest is on the cusp of crystallizing into real, tangible wealth. But lurking behind the celebration is a complex web of tax considerations. You've heard conflicting advice: some suggest holding your carry through a pass-through entity, others recommend trusts or offshore structures. You know that the decisions you make now will determine how much of this wealth stays with you — and how much vanishes into taxes.

At its core, carried interest is a profits interest — the right to a share of the profits generated by a fund's investments, typically without contributing significant capital upfront. The beauty of carried interest is that it transforms labor into capital — meaning, if structured correctly, gains are taxed at long-term capital gains rates rather than as ordinary income. This differential — currently 20% versus 37% federally — can mean millions in tax savings. But the IRS has taken note, and legislation like the carried interest "three-year rule" under the Tax Cuts and Jobs Act (TCJA) has added layers of complexity, requiring that investments be held for three years to qualify for favorable tax treatment.

The pros of carried interest are undeniable. It allows executives to participate in the upside of their fund's investments without the need for large capital commitments. When taxed at long-term capital gains rates, the wealth generated is highly tax-efficient. Carried interest can also be leveraged to build estate planning structures — such as gifting carry early to trusts when valuations are low — multiplying the potential wealth transfer benefits. Furthermore, carry offers a powerful alignment of incentives between executives and investors, reinforcing long-term thinking and performance.

Yet the cons are equally important to recognize. The taxation of carried interest remains a political target and could change, subjecting it to ordinary income tax rates in the future. The three-year holding period requirement means that some gains, particularly in venture capital where early exits are common, may not qualify for long-term rates. Liquidity timing can be unpredictable — carry often pays out in "lumpy" distributions that are difficult to plan around. Additionally, without proactive planning, the receipt of carry can complicate estate planning, exposing significant assets to estate taxes without sufficient liquidity to pay them.

Real-life scenarios drive these points home. Consider a private equity partner who gifted carried interest rights into a generation-skipping dynasty trust early in the fund's life. Because the carry was worth little at the time of the transfer — essentially a "hope" value — the gift used a minimal portion of his lifetime exemption. Years later, as portfolio companies were sold, the trust — outside his taxable estate — realized tens of millions in gains, free of estate taxes. Contrast that with another executive who failed to plan. His carried interest was fully included in his taxable estate, triggering a liquidity crisis for his heirs who had to sell illiquid assets at a discount to cover the estate tax bill.

Action steps for optimizing carried interest begin with structure. Many executives hold carry through limited liability companies (LLCs) or family limited partnerships (FLPs), enabling more flexibility for gifting, estate planning, and managing liability exposure. Early gifting of carried interest — while the interest has minimal ascertainable value — can "freeze" future appreciation outside the estate. Trust structures — particularly grantor trusts — allow executives to transfer carry without triggering immediate tax consequences while maintaining income tax responsibility, ensuring the trust grows undiminished.

Another strategy is the use of installment sales to intentionally defective grantor trusts (IDGTs). An executive can sell a portion of their carried interest to the trust in exchange for a promissory note, locking in today's value and transferring future appreciation outside the estate. Proper valuation — typically using discounts for lack of marketability and lack of control — is critical to withstand IRS scrutiny. Additionally, establishing a Delaware or Nevada dynasty trust can extend these benefits across generations, bypassing estate taxation at each level.

Set clear goals: Do you want to maximize after-tax proceeds from carry? Reduce estate tax exposure? Create a multi-generational wealth vehicle? Provide liquidity for heirs? Protect assets from future creditors or lawsuits? These goals will guide the planning — whether you prioritize early gifting, leverage trust structures, or opt for charitable strategies like setting up a charitable lead trust (CLT) funded by carry proceeds. Importantly, coordinate your carried interest strategy with your overall financial, tax, and estate plan to ensure seamless integration.

Now, the inevitable question: Can you handle this complexity alone? The reality is, no. Carried interest planning at the ultra-affluent level demands a team — tax attorneys, estate planners, valuation experts, and wealth advisors — all coordinated to manage the nuances and stay ahead of regulatory changes. Even small mistakes — undervaluing a transfer, misapplying discounts, failing to comply with gift tax reporting — can cost millions and unravel an otherwise solid plan.

Here's your bold call to action: Within the next 90 days, conduct a full review of your carried interest holdings. Identify funds nearing exit events, assess current valuations, and initiate discussions with estate and tax advisors about optimal structures. Determine whether gifting, sales to trusts, or other strategies align with your goals. Take proactive steps before liquidity events — not after — to ensure your hard-earned carried interest delivers maximum benefit to you and your family.

Because at the ultra-affluent level, the difference between good and exceptional wealth planning is measured in millions — and in the legacy you leave behind.

Ultra Affluent is your permission slip to stop reacting and start architecting — to transform your carried interest from a one-time windfall into a multigenerational wealth engine.

Part IV: Investment Access and Sophistication

At the ultra-affluent level, investing is no longer about basic asset allocation or chasing public market returns — it's about gaining access to opportunities and structures unavailable to the average investor. Part IV of Ultra Affluent is dedicated to unpacking the world of sophisticated investment strategies tailored for high-net-worth individuals who demand more than conventional portfolios. Here, we go beyond stocks and bonds, introducing readers to private equity, hedge funds, venture capital, direct investments, and bespoke portfolio construction.

This section will explore the intricate details of tax-aware investing, the real trade-offs between liquidity and higher returns, and the importance of manager selection and due diligence. Readers will learn how to think like an institution — balancing risk, return, and access — while building portfolios that align with long-term goals and multi-generational wealth preservation.

Throughout this part, we break down complex vehicles into plain language, analyze real-world case studies, and provide actionable frameworks for evaluating and integrating sophisticated investments into an overarching wealth strategy. By the end of Part IV, readers will understand how the ultra-wealthy move capital differently, why access often trumps alpha, and how thoughtful design can turn a portfolio into a powerful tool for freedom, growth, and legacy.

Chapter 24: Private Equity and Venture Capital for the Ultra Affluent

When you ascend to the level of the ultra-affluent, the investment opportunities available to you evolve dramatically. The familiar world of stocks, bonds, and mutual funds remains, but it is no longer sufficient to meet your goals for wealth growth, preservation, or diversification. You begin to enter a realm reserved for those who have both the capital and the patience to navigate more sophisticated, less liquid, but often far more rewarding investments. Chief among these are private equity and venture capital — asset classes that have historically fueled not only outsized returns but also significant influence in shaping industries, markets, and innovation itself.

Imagine you're sitting across from me. You've built substantial wealth — perhaps through entrepreneurship, executive leadership, or smart early investments. Now you're looking for more. You want your capital not just to work but to expand — quietly, deliberately, and with access to the kinds of deals the public markets cannot offer. You've heard about friends or colleagues investing in private companies before they went public, or backing buyouts that created household-name brands. You wonder how to enter this world, how it works, what the risks are, and most importantly, whether the rewards are worth it. The answer: for the ultra-affluent, private equity and venture capital aren't merely alternatives — they are essential components of a sophisticated portfolio.

Private equity, at its core, involves investing directly into private companies, often through buyouts, growth equity, or distressed asset strategies. These investments are typically made via pooled funds managed by seasoned general partners (GPs) who raise capital from limited partners (LPs) like you. The fund uses that capital to acquire, improve, and eventually exit companies, distributing profits back to the investors. Venture capital operates similarly but focuses on early-stage, high-growth startups. The appeal is simple: by accessing private markets, you gain exposure to companies before they go public or get acquired, capturing much of the value creation that traditional public markets no longer offer.

The pros of private equity and venture capital are compelling. Historically, these asset classes have outperformed public equities over long time horizons. They offer access to unique growth opportunities, diversification beyond traditional asset classes, and, for those willing to engage more directly, a chance to influence the companies they invest in. The illiquidity — often seen as a drawback — can actually be a strength, forcing long-term thinking and reducing the temptation to make impulsive moves based on market noise.

But the cons must be respected. These investments are illiquid, often locking up your capital for 7 to 10 years or more. They are complex, requiring a deep understanding of fund structures, fee arrangements (like the ubiquitous "2 and 20" model — 2% management fee, 20% carried interest), and the nuances of portfolio company operations. Access can also be a barrier; the top-performing funds are often closed to all but existing or institutional investors. There's also the inherent risk — especially in venture capital — that many, if not most, investments will fail, with only a few delivering the outsized returns that drive fund performance.

Real-world scenarios illustrate these dynamics. Take the example of a family office that committed $10 million to a top-quartile private equity fund specializing in healthcare buyouts. Over the fund's life, the investment doubled, despite a few portfolio companies underperforming. The family's patient capital allowed the GP to weather downturns, restructure companies, and eventually exit at favorable valuations. In contrast, consider a tech executive who gained early access to a venture fund investing in fintech startups. While several portfolio companies failed, two became unicorns and were acquired for billions, generating returns of 20x on invested capital — outcomes impossible to replicate in public markets.

The action steps for entering private equity and venture capital are clear. First, assess your liquidity needs. Private investments demand that you lock away capital for long periods; ensure you have sufficient liquidity elsewhere before committing. Next, seek access — either directly through your network, via a trusted wealth advisor with connections to top-tier funds, or through feeder funds that aggregate capital from qualified investors. Conduct rigorous due diligence on the GPs: evaluate their track records, investment theses, operational capabilities, and alignment of interests with LPs. Understand the fund's terms — management fees, carried interest, hurdles, and distribution waterfalls — as these materially affect net returns.

Set clear goals: Are you seeking absolute return maximization, diversification, exposure to innovation, or impact investing opportunities? Your goals will guide fund selection — for instance, a focus on late-stage venture capital if you want a balance between growth and risk, or distressed private equity if you seek contrarian opportunities in market downturns. Decide whether you want a hands-off approach — simply being an LP in blind pool funds — or a more active role through direct investments, co-investments, or even launching a personal fund or family office investment arm.

And now, the inevitable question: Can you navigate this world alone? Without a doubt, the answer is no. Private markets are opaque, relationships matter, and access is as much about who you know as what you know. Top-performing funds often limit their investor base to trusted partners. Conducting proper due diligence requires expertise not only in finance but also in legal structuring, operational analysis, and industry-specific knowledge. Engaging with an advisor, family office, or investment consultant with deep private market experience is essential to avoid costly missteps and optimize opportunities.

Here's your bold call to action: Within the next 90 days, evaluate how much of your portfolio is allocated to private investments. If it's under 10% — and your liquidity allows — start exploring top-tier private equity and venture capital opportunities. Build relationships with trusted advisors who can provide access and insight. Commit to a strategy that aligns with your long-term goals, and approach it with the patience, diligence, and sophistication that the private markets demand.

Because at the ultra-affluent level, real wealth isn't just preserved — it's strategically amplified through access to the right opportunities, managed by the right people, at the right time.

Ultra Affluent is your permission slip to move beyond the noise of the public markets — to think, act, and invest like an institution, securing not just returns, but influence, legacy, and impact.

Chapter 25: Direct Investing: Accessing Co-Investment Opportunities

When your wealth reaches a certain echelon, the traditional avenues of investing — public equities, bonds, mutual funds — no longer offer the same thrill or strategic edge. You are no longer just seeking growth; you are seeking control, alignment, and access to deals that most investors never see. This is where direct investing and co-investment opportunities become central to the conversation. Direct investing — participating alongside private equity or venture capital firms in individual deals — offers the ultra-affluent a seat at the table and a chance to be closer to the real drivers of wealth creation. But it requires a different mindset, greater sophistication, and an appetite for complexity.

Imagine you are sitting across from me. You're a highly accomplished entrepreneur, executive, or investor who has already succeeded in public markets and private funds. You've seen friends or colleagues participate directly in company buyouts or fund growth-stage startups and reap outsized returns — all while avoiding the double fees charged by traditional fund structures. You wonder: how do they find these opportunities? How are they structured? And most importantly, should you be adding direct deals to your portfolio? The answer is nuanced. Direct investing isn't for everyone, but for those who can access it and manage it well, it can be an unparalleled wealth multiplier.

At its core, direct investing involves placing capital directly into a company or alongside a lead investor (such as a private equity or venture firm) in a deal. Co-investments occur when a fund manager invites limited partners (LPs) to invest additional capital in a specific deal outside of the main fund, often without paying additional management fees or carried interest. This structure can significantly enhance net returns, giving investors more control over individual exposures and improving portfolio customization. It also offers the rare chance to cherry-pick opportunities rather than accept the blind-pool risk inherent in traditional funds.

The pros of direct investing and co-investments are compelling. First, cost savings: co-investments typically waive management fees and carried interest, dramatically improving the economics of the investment. Second, control and transparency: you can conduct your own due diligence on the deal, understand the business in detail, and potentially influence governance decisions. Third, customization: direct deals allow you to tilt your portfolio toward sectors, geographies, or themes you believe in, rather than being beholden to a fund manager's strategy. Finally, direct investments can provide learning opportunities and deeper relationships with management teams and lead investors, which can be leveraged for future deals.

But the cons must not be overlooked. Direct investing demands rigorous due diligence — legal, financial, operational — far beyond what is required for traditional fund investing. The deals are often highly illiquid, locking up capital for five to ten years. Concentration risk is real: unlike diversified funds, direct investments place significant capital into a single company, amplifying both upside and downside potential. Access is another barrier; top-tier co-investment opportunities are typically invitation-only, offered to LPs with substantial existing relationships. Finally, successful direct investing requires significant internal resources — investment professionals, legal counsel, tax advisors — to source, vet, negotiate, and monitor deals effectively.

Real-world examples make these dynamics tangible. Consider a family office that participated in a co-investment alongside a leading private equity firm in a healthcare technology company. With no management fees and no carry, their returns were substantially higher than the fund's overall IRR. Moreover, by doing their own due diligence, they were able to understand the company's growth trajectory and risks at a level not typically available to LPs. Contrast this with another investor who lacked the infrastructure to properly vet a co-investment opportunity, resulting in a disastrous investment in a failing retail chain. The lesson: access alone is not enough — discipline and expertise are critical.

The action steps for incorporating direct investments and co-investments into your portfolio begin with an honest assessment of readiness. Do you have the team or access to a team that can perform private equity-grade due diligence? Are you prepared for the illiquidity and potential volatility of individual deals? If the answer is yes, the next step is to build relationships with top-tier fund managers known for offering co-investments. Express your interest early and be prepared to move quickly when opportunities arise; the best deals are often oversubscribed within days. Consider joining an investment consortium or family office network to expand your deal flow. And always allocate prudently — a good rule of thumb is to limit any single direct investment to no more than 5% of your overall portfolio to manage concentration risk.

Set clear goals: Are you looking to enhance returns by lowering fees? Gain exposure to specific industries or geographies? Build deeper relationships within the private markets ecosystem? Support companies aligned with your values or strategic interests? Your goals will dictate not just which co-investments to pursue, but how much time and resource allocation they justify. Importantly, treat co-investments as an extension of your broader asset allocation — not a separate playground. They should complement, not disrupt, the overall risk-return profile of your portfolio.

Now, the inevitable question: Can you do this on your own? The honest answer is probably not — at least not well. Successful direct investing and co-investing require expertise across multiple domains: finance, law, operations, industry-specific insights, and relationship management. A dedicated investment team or an experienced advisor is essential to navigate this complex terrain, avoid pitfalls, and maximize opportunity. Without that support, you risk turning what could be a powerful wealth generator into a costly learning experience.

Here's your bold call to action: Within the next 90 days, assess your readiness for direct investing. Review your current network for access points to high-quality co-investments. Identify gaps in your internal team's capabilities and explore partnerships or advisory relationships to fill them. Commit to a disciplined strategy: define your investment criteria, set allocation limits, and ensure every deal aligns with your overall wealth plan.

Because at the ultra-affluent level, wealth isn't just about growing — it's about growing with precision, control, and intention.

Ultra Affluent is your permission slip to move beyond passive wealth accumulation — to become an active architect of your financial future, one direct investment at a time.

Chapter 26: Real Estate Syndications and Private Funds

As you move deeper into the ultra-affluent space, the way you think about real estate evolves. Gone are the days of buying individual rental properties or investing passively in REITs. At this level, real estate becomes a strategic lever — a way to balance a portfolio with hard assets, generate stable cash flow, and access tax-advantaged growth. One of the most powerful yet underutilized tools for the ultra-wealthy is real estate syndications and private real estate funds. These vehicles provide a way to invest in large-scale commercial properties, development projects, and niche opportunities without the burdens of direct ownership — but with the potential for significant returns and diversification benefits.

Imagine you are seated across from me. You've built a substantial investment portfolio and are looking to expand into real estate without the day-to-day headaches of being a landlord or asset manager. You've heard whispers of friends participating in deals to acquire large apartment complexes, industrial parks, or boutique hotels. They talk about impressive returns and tax advantages, but also about the complexity and risk of such deals. You wonder: is this the next step for my portfolio? How do syndications and private funds work? More importantly, how do I select the right opportunities and partners? The reality is, real estate syndications and private funds are the ultra-affluent's gateway to scalable, institutional-grade real estate investing — but they require careful navigation.

A real estate syndication is a structure where multiple investors pool their capital to purchase or develop a property. Typically, a sponsor (or syndicator) manages the deal — finding the property, negotiating terms, arranging financing, managing the asset, and executing the business plan. Investors provide capital and, in return, receive a share of the profits. Private real estate funds operate similarly but on a larger, pooled basis — investors commit capital to a fund that will invest in multiple properties according to a stated strategy. The difference lies in diversification: syndications are typically single-asset plays, while private funds spread risk across a portfolio of assets.

The pros of real estate syndications and private funds are significant. They offer access to high-quality, institutional-grade real estate that would be difficult to acquire individually. They are passive — you invest your capital and the sponsor does the work. They provide tax benefits: depreciation, cost segregation studies, and 1031 exchange options can defer or even eliminate taxes on gains. They generate cash flow, often distributed quarterly, providing a steady income stream. Finally, they offer portfolio diversification, reducing dependence on public equities and bonds and offering a hedge against inflation.

Yet, the cons must be understood and respected. These investments are illiquid, often locking up capital for five to ten years. There is sponsor risk — the deal's success largely depends on the sponsor's expertise, alignment of interests, and execution. Fees can be high: acquisition fees, asset management fees, disposition fees, and a share of profits (the "promote") can erode returns if not carefully managed. Due diligence is essential, but many investors lack the time or expertise to properly vet sponsors and deals. Real estate markets are cyclical, and leverage — while enhancing returns in good times — can amplify losses in downturns.

Real-world scenarios bring these dynamics to life. A family office invested $10 million across several syndications focusing on multifamily housing in fast-growing Sunbelt cities. Through careful sponsor selection and diversification across markets, they achieved an internal rate of return (IRR) north of 15% annually, with strong cash flow along the way. Conversely, another investor put a large sum into a speculative office development project right before the pandemic — a single-asset bet with an inexperienced sponsor. The project faltered, and the investor faced significant capital losses and extended illiquidity.

Action steps for integrating real estate syndications and private funds into your portfolio begin with education and access. Understand the typical deal structures: preferred returns, waterfall distributions, promote arrangements, and key performance indicators. Build relationships with reputable sponsors and fund managers — often through networks of ultra-high-net-worth individuals, family offices, or specialized advisors. Conduct rigorous due diligence: vet the sponsor's track record, review underwriting assumptions, inspect legal documents, and understand the market dynamics of the target properties. Avoid overconcentration — limit any single deal to a manageable percentage of your portfolio.

Set clear goals: Are you seeking stable income, capital appreciation, or tax efficiency? Are you more comfortable with core-plus or value-add strategies, or are you willing to embrace opportunistic, higher-risk deals? Your objectives will dictate your selection of syndications or funds. Define your risk tolerance and time horizon clearly — real estate is not a place for impatient capital.

And now, the inevitable question: Can you do this alone? While it's possible to source and vet deals independently, the best opportunities often require access to private networks, insider relationships, and deep expertise in real estate underwriting and legal structuring. Partnering with a trusted advisor, consultant, or family office investment team experienced in private real estate can mean the difference between generating steady, tax-advantaged returns and exposing yourself to unnecessary risks.

Here's your bold call to action: Within the next 90 days, commit to evaluating your real estate exposure. If under-allocated, begin exploring real estate syndications and private funds that align with your wealth objectives. Focus on building relationships with top sponsors and learning the nuances of deal structures. Set a disciplined allocation strategy and ensure it integrates seamlessly with your broader portfolio.

Because at the ultra-affluent level, wealth is not just grown — it is curated, protected, and enhanced through strategic, thoughtful access to asset classes that others cannot easily reach.

Ultra Affluent is your permission slip to move beyond simple real estate investing — to harness the power of institutional-quality real estate without the burdens of active management.

Beyond the more common multifamily and office deals, there is a burgeoning world of niche real estate strategies that offer compelling returns and diversification for the ultra-affluent. One such niche is industrial real estate. Distribution centers, logistics hubs, cold storage facilities, and last-mile delivery warehouses have become critical infrastructure for the digital economy. As e-commerce continues its global dominance, demand for industrial space has skyrocketed. Savvy investors are leveraging syndications and funds that specialize in acquiring and managing industrial assets in strategic locations near major urban centers. These properties often offer long-term leases with creditworthy tenants and require less intensive management than multifamily or office properties, providing stable income streams and lower operational risk.

The pros of investing in industrial real estate are substantial. These assets often experience lower vacancy rates, longer lease terms, and less tenant turnover compared to other property types. Furthermore, industrial tenants typically invest significant capital into customizing their space, making them less likely to relocate. However, industrial real estate is not without risks. Market saturation, shifting logistics trends, or changes in tenant demand — especially with the rise of automation — can impact asset values. Careful market selection and tenant analysis are paramount, and aligning with sponsors who have deep sector expertise becomes even more critical.

Opportunity Zone funds offer another niche strategy, especially for those facing large capital gains tax liabilities. Created under the 2017 Tax Cuts and Jobs Act, Opportunity Zones are designated areas that encourage long-term investments in economically distressed communities. By investing capital gains into qualified Opportunity Zone funds, investors can defer their original tax liability, reduce it if the investment is held for a certain period, and ultimately eliminate taxes on any appreciation if the investment is held for at least ten years. For the ultra-affluent, this trifecta — tax deferral, reduction, and elimination — is extraordinarily attractive.

The pros of Opportunity Zone investing include the potential for substantial tax benefits, the ability to generate attractive returns through value-add development projects, and the social impact of investing in underserved communities. However, the cons are significant: Opportunity Zone projects are often development-heavy, bringing with them higher risk, longer timelines, and complex compliance requirements. Not all Opportunity Zones are created equal; some have genuine growth potential, while others lack the fundamentals for sustained economic development. Thorough due diligence on the project, sponsor, and underlying market is non-negotiable.

International private real estate funds represent yet another frontier. For ultra-affluent investors seeking geographic diversification and exposure to emerging markets, these funds can be particularly appealing. They invest in a range of property types — residential, commercial, hospitality, industrial — across countries with different growth trajectories, currency exposures, and economic cycles. Regions like Southeast Asia, Latin America, and parts of Europe offer opportunities to capitalize on urbanization trends, rising middle classes, and attractive yields compared to more saturated U.S. markets.

The pros of international real estate include diversification across markets and currencies, potentially higher yields, and the ability to tap into growth in developing economies. The cons involve political risk, currency risk, regulatory complexity, and a higher barrier to effective due diligence. Additionally, managing real estate abroad requires a deep understanding of local market dynamics, legal structures, and cultural nuances — which can be formidable even for seasoned investors.

Real-world examples abound. A group of investors participated in a real estate syndication targeting last-mile distribution centers near major European cities, achieving double-digit IRRs driven by the explosive growth of e-commerce. Another family office allocated to an Opportunity Zone fund focused on revitalizing downtown areas in secondary U.S. cities, benefiting from both attractive returns and significant tax advantages. Yet another investor partnered with a private fund specializing in high-end residential developments in Southeast Asia, capitalizing on the growing demand from the region's expanding affluent class.

The action steps for exploring these niche strategies start with self-education and strategic networking. Seek sponsors and fund managers with a proven track record in the specific niche you are considering. Don't merely rely on glossy pitch decks; dig deep into past performance, market selection criteria, underwriting assumptions, and exit strategies. Engage advisors who understand the nuances of each niche and can guide you through the complexities of legal structures, tax implications, and risk management. Start small — perhaps through a feeder fund or co-investment vehicle — to gain exposure and build familiarity before making larger allocations.

Set clear goals: Are you looking to enhance yield, achieve geographic diversification, optimize for tax efficiency, or invest with social impact in mind? Each niche strategy serves a different purpose, and clarity of intent will ensure you choose the right opportunities and allocate appropriately within your broader portfolio. Importantly, establish an internal process for monitoring and managing these investments over time — syndications and funds are not set-and-forget vehicles; they require periodic review and active oversight.

Again, the inevitable question: Can you navigate this alone? Real estate at this level of complexity is not a solo sport. Effective investment in niche real estate requires a team of experts — legal counsel, tax advisors, experienced asset managers, and real estate specialists. Building a network of trusted partners, or aligning with a multifamily office or boutique investment firm with niche real estate capabilities, can significantly improve your odds of success and mitigate risks.

Here's your bold call to action: Over the next 90 days, assess your real estate portfolio for concentration risk and opportunity gaps. Identify whether niche strategies — industrial, Opportunity Zones, or international real estate — align with your current investment objectives. Begin cultivating relationships with leading sponsors and fund managers in these areas. Develop a disciplined allocation plan that integrates these niche strategies into your overall wealth architecture.

Because at the ultra-affluent level, wealth is not just about accumulating assets — it's about strategically expanding access to differentiated, high-conviction opportunities that others overlook.

Ultra Affluent is your permission slip to move beyond traditional real estate — to become a global, sophisticated investor capable of harnessing the full power of private markets.

Chapter 27: Hedge Fund Selection and Due Diligence 101

When you reach the ultra-affluent level, traditional investment vehicles no longer satisfy your appetite for diversification, alpha, or tailored risk management. You begin to realize that true wealth preservation and growth requires access to investment strategies that are not available on the public shelf. Hedge funds enter the conversation not as speculative gambles, but as sophisticated, bespoke strategies designed to capture inefficiencies, manage volatility, and deliver returns that are uncorrelated to traditional markets. But the world of hedge funds is nuanced, opaque, and not without significant pitfalls — making hedge fund selection and due diligence one of the most critical skills an ultra-high-net-worth investor must master.

Imagine you are sitting across from me. You've built a substantial portfolio of traditional assets — equities, bonds, real estate — and you understand the importance of diversification. But you are looking for more: a way to smooth returns, reduce drawdowns, and possibly access strategies that benefit from market dislocations. You've heard of hedge funds that consistently outperform, that hedge risk effectively, that have a unique edge. But you've also heard the horror stories: high fees, poor transparency, disappointing returns. You wonder: how do I find the right hedge fund? How do I evaluate whether a manager is truly skilled or merely lucky? How can I ensure that I'm aligning myself with the best and protecting myself from hidden risks? These questions are the foundation of sophisticated hedge fund investing.

At its core, a hedge fund is a pooled investment vehicle that can invest flexibly across asset classes and strategies. Hedge funds might engage in long/short equity investing, global macro strategies, event-driven opportunities, or multi-strategy approaches that seek to generate absolute returns in any market environment. Their freedom from benchmark constraints allows them to seek alpha in ways that traditional managers cannot. However, this flexibility also introduces complexity and the need for rigorous manager selection and monitoring.

The pros of investing in hedge funds are compelling. They offer diversification benefits — many hedge fund strategies have low correlation to public markets. They can provide downside protection during bear markets through hedging techniques. Skilled managers can deliver alpha — returns above what can be explained by market exposures alone. Hedge funds also allow access to niche strategies, such as merger arbitrage, distressed credit, or volatility trading, that are difficult for individual investors to replicate. For the ultra-affluent, hedge funds can be an essential tool for enhancing risk-adjusted returns and achieving portfolio objectives not possible with long-only investing.

But the cons must be taken seriously. Hedge funds are expensive — the traditional "2 and 20" fee structure (2% management fee and 20% performance fee) is still common, although some managers offer more investor-friendly terms today. Transparency can be limited, with many hedge funds providing only quarterly reporting and little insight into underlying positions. Liquidity can also be an issue; many hedge funds impose lock-up periods or redemption gates that restrict when investors can access their capital. And perhaps most importantly, skill is rare — many hedge funds underperform after fees, and separating true skill from luck requires deep due diligence and ongoing monitoring.

Real-world scenarios highlight the importance of proper hedge fund selection and due diligence. Consider an ultra-affluent family that allocated a portion of their portfolio to a long/short equity fund with a strong track record and a disciplined investment process. During a market downturn, the fund's hedging strategies protected capital, providing a positive return while equities fell sharply. This allowed the family to maintain liquidity and capitalize on market dislocations. Contrast this with another investor who chased the high returns of a global macro fund without fully understanding its risk exposures; when the fund's aggressive currency bets unraveled, they suffered significant losses and faced restricted redemptions.

The action steps for effective hedge fund selection and due diligence begin with defining your investment objectives. Are you seeking absolute returns, downside protection, exposure to niche strategies, or diversification? Your goals will dictate the type of hedge fund strategies that are appropriate. Next, conduct a comprehensive screening process: examine the manager's track record, investment philosophy, risk management practices, and operational infrastructure. Perform quantitative analysis — Sharpe ratio, maximum drawdown, correlation metrics — but also qualitative analysis: who is the manager, what is their edge, how have they performed across different market cycles?

Due diligence must go beyond the glossy marketing materials. Conduct background checks on the manager and key team members. Evaluate the fund's service providers — auditors, administrators, legal counsel — for quality and independence. Scrutinize the fund's liquidity terms, valuation policies, and fee structure. Request transparency into portfolio holdings and risk exposures. If possible, perform on-site visits to the manager's office to assess culture, compliance practices, and investment process firsthand. Many ultra-affluent investors engage specialized consultants or advisory firms to assist in this rigorous due diligence process, leveraging their expertise and databases of manager information.

Set clear goals: How much of your portfolio do you want to allocate to hedge funds? Which strategies align with your overall asset allocation and risk profile? Are you comfortable with less liquidity in exchange for the potential of higher, more consistent returns? Do you have the internal expertise to conduct manager due diligence and ongoing monitoring, or do you need to partner with external experts? Defining these parameters upfront will guide your hedge fund selection process and prevent common pitfalls.

And now, the inevitable question: Can you navigate hedge fund investing alone? The candid answer is: only with great difficulty. The hedge fund universe is vast and opaque; identifying top-quartile managers and avoiding the landmines requires specialized knowledge, access, and a disciplined process. Even seasoned institutional investors often rely on dedicated teams to manage their hedge fund allocations. For the ultra-affluent individual or family, working with experienced advisors, consultants, or multifamily offices can provide the necessary infrastructure for effective hedge fund investing.

Here's your bold call to action: Over the next 90 days, assess your portfolio's current exposure to hedge funds and alternative strategies. If appropriate, define a hedge fund allocation target based on your goals and risk tolerance. Begin the process of identifying potential managers through trusted networks, consultants, or platforms that specialize in institutional-quality hedge fund access. Commit to a disciplined, rigorous due diligence process that includes both quantitative and qualitative analysis. Don't chase past returns; seek managers with a clear, repeatable edge and a demonstrated commitment to risk management and transparency.

Because at the ultra-affluent level, wealth is not just preserved — it is stewarded with precision, insight, and the humility to recognize that skill in manager selection is as critical as skill in markets.

Ultra Affluent is your permission slip to elevate your investment game — to move beyond passive allocations and into the realm where risk is sculpted, opportunities are seized, and capital is deployed with the care and confidence that true wealth demands.

Chapter 28: Impact Investing: Aligning Values with Capital

When you reach the level of wealth where you are no longer focused solely on accumulation but on legacy, the conversation inevitably shifts. No longer are you content with returns alone. You want your capital to mean something more—to reflect your values, to influence change, to leave the world a better place for your children and grandchildren. Impact investing emerges not as a trend or a fad, but as a natural evolution of wealth stewardship. At the ultra-affluent level, aligning capital with values becomes not only possible but imperative. The question isn't just, "What can my money do for me?"—it's, "What can my money do for the world, and how can I be part of that transformation?"

Imagine you are sitting across from me. You've built wealth through decades of focus, determination, and intelligent risk-taking. You've supported causes philanthropically, donated to foundations, perhaps even established your own donor-advised fund. But you realize that while your philanthropy is making a difference, the majority of your assets—your investment portfolio—are still deployed without regard to impact. You've heard about ESG (Environmental, Social, Governance) investing, about sustainable funds, about opportunities to invest in ways that align with your beliefs without sacrificing returns. You wonder: Is this real? Can you truly align values and capital? Will I be giving up returns if I shift toward impact investing?

Impact investing, at its core, seeks to generate positive, measurable social and environmental impact alongside a financial return. It goes beyond ESG screening or socially responsible investing (SRI), which typically focus on avoiding harm by excluding certain industries like tobacco or weapons. Impact investing actively seeks out investments that do good—funding renewable energy projects, affordable housing, education technology, sustainable agriculture, and healthcare access, among many others. The beauty of impact investing is that it doesn't require sacrificing financial rigor. In fact, many impact-focused companies and funds are among the most innovative and resilient, capturing secular growth trends that traditional investments often miss.

The pros of impact investing are compelling. First, alignment: your portfolio reflects your personal values and beliefs, creating a deeper sense of purpose in wealth management. Second, performance: numerous studies have shown that impact investments can deliver competitive, even superior, returns compared to traditional investments, especially as consumer and regulatory trends favor sustainable and ethical business practices. Third, influence: impact investors can drive change at scale by providing capital to underserved sectors and influencing corporate behavior. And finally, legacy: impact investing offers a way to engage the next generation of your family in wealth stewardship by connecting financial literacy with values-based decision-making.

But the cons must be acknowledged. Impact investing requires greater due diligence. Impact metrics are still evolving, and assessing the true social or environmental benefit of an investment can be complex. There is the risk of "greenwashing," where funds or companies overstate their impact credentials to attract capital without delivering real results. Liquidity can be an issue, especially for private impact investments such as direct investments in social enterprises or impact private equity funds. Additionally, impact investing requires a clear articulation of values and goals—what causes matter most to you? How do you balance financial return with impact objectives? Without this clarity, impact investing can become fragmented and ineffective.

Real-world scenarios make these trade-offs tangible. Consider an ultra-high-net-worth family that reallocated 25% of their private equity exposure to impact funds focused on renewable energy infrastructure. Over ten years, not only did they achieve strong double-digit returns, but they also contributed to the deployment of solar and wind projects that powered millions of homes. Another family foundation invested directly in early-stage education technology companies, aligning with their belief in access to quality education. These investments not only scaled innovative solutions but also provided attractive exits through acquisitions by larger tech firms. Contrast this with an investor who rushed into an impact fund without thorough due diligence, only to find later that the fund's impact claims were superficial and the financial returns disappointing.

The action steps for engaging in impact investing are deliberate and strategic. Start by clarifying your values. What issues resonate most with you—climate change, gender equity, healthcare access, education, sustainable agriculture? Define your impact objectives and determine how you will measure success. Then, review your existing portfolio through an impact lens: which holdings already align with your values, and where are the gaps? Engage with impact investment managers who have proven track records not only in financial performance but also in delivering measurable impact. Evaluate investment opportunities rigorously, assessing both traditional financial metrics and impact metrics such as carbon reduction, lives improved, jobs created, or communities served.

Set clear goals: Are you seeking market-rate returns with measurable impact, or are you willing to accept below-market returns for high-impact investments in areas like microfinance or affordable housing? What percentage of your portfolio do you want to allocate to impact strategies? How will you engage the next generation in these decisions to ensure continuity of your impact legacy? Answering these questions will create a framework for disciplined impact investing and prevent mission drift.

And now, the inevitable question: Can you navigate impact investing alone? While it is possible to start independently, the complexity and nuance of impact investing suggest that partnering with experienced advisors, impact consultants, or specialized family offices can significantly enhance results. These partners can help you access best-in-class impact funds, conduct rigorous due diligence, avoid greenwashing traps, and design a comprehensive impact strategy that integrates seamlessly with your overall wealth plan.

Here's your bold call to action: Within the next 90 days, initiate an impact audit of your portfolio. Identify the causes and issues that matter most to you. Set a target allocation for impact investments and begin sourcing opportunities that align with your financial and social goals. Engage advisors who understand the dual mandate of impact and financial performance. Commit to measuring and reporting on your impact annually, just as you would your financial returns.

Because at the ultra-affluent level, wealth is not just about accumulation — it is about intention, influence, and legacy.

Ultra Affluent is your permission slip to move beyond passive investing — to transform your capital into a force for good, creating returns that matter financially and existentially.

Beyond the foundational understanding of impact investing, the sophistication required at the ultra-affluent level involves knowing *how* to access these investments effectively and *how* to measure the results meaningfully. This is where impact investment vehicles become critical. No two impact investments are alike, and the structure you choose can greatly influence both financial and social outcomes.

Green bonds represent one of the most accessible impact investment vehicles. Issued by governments, corporations, and supranational organizations, green bonds raise capital specifically for projects with environmental benefits — think renewable energy, energy efficiency, clean transportation, and sustainable agriculture. For investors seeking fixed income exposure aligned with environmental goals, green bonds can be a compelling addition. They are typically investment-grade, liquid, and offer yields comparable to traditional bonds, making them an elegant solution for aligning a portion of a conservative portfolio with sustainability objectives. However, while the use of proceeds is earmarked for green projects, not all green bonds are created equal. Some issuers may adopt broad definitions of "green," and diligent evaluation is required to ensure alignment with your impact goals.

Impact private equity funds are another vital vehicle. These funds invest directly into mission-driven companies at various stages — from early-stage startups developing clean technologies to later-stage companies scaling affordable healthcare solutions. Impact private equity offers the potential for outsized returns and significant impact, but it comes with the illiquidity and longer time horizons typical of private markets. Managers of top-tier impact funds typically have deep sector expertise and relationships that allow them to source proprietary deals, influence company strategy, and ensure robust measurement of social and environmental outcomes. The key for ultra-affluent investors is to access best-in-class managers with proven track records in both impact creation and financial returns.

Sustainable infrastructure funds present another frontier. Investing in assets like renewable energy facilities, water treatment plants, or sustainable transportation networks not only provides critical services to society but also offers investors steady, long-term cash flows often indexed to inflation. Infrastructure investments can be particularly attractive in an era of low interest rates and heightened market volatility. However, the scale, complexity, and regulatory environment surrounding infrastructure projects require sophisticated underwriting and long-term commitment — this is not a short-term play, but a strategic allocation to resilience and stability.

Real-world examples bring these vehicles to life. A family office allocated $20 million to a sustainable infrastructure fund focused on solar and wind energy projects in emerging markets. Over a decade, not only did the investments generate stable, inflation-linked cash flows, but they also brought clean energy to millions who previously lacked reliable electricity. Another ultra-affluent individual invested through an impact private equity fund into a portfolio of healthcare technology companies targeting underserved populations. Several portfolio companies achieved successful exits through acquisitions by larger healthcare players, delivering attractive financial returns while expanding healthcare access across developing regions.

Of course, none of this matters if you can't measure the impact. Unlike financial returns, which are standardized and easily quantifiable, impact requires a different approach. The best impact investors adopt a framework that begins with *intentionality* — the conscious goal to generate social or environmental benefit — and follows with *measurement* and *verification*. Standardized tools are emerging. The Global Impact Investing Network (GIIN) offers IRIS+ metrics, and frameworks like the UN Sustainable Development Goals (SDGs) are often used to map investments to globally recognized objectives. The most sophisticated impact investors go further, commissioning third-party audits, integrating impact KPIs into investment memorandums, and requiring quarterly impact reports alongside financial performance.

An effective impact measurement framework often starts by identifying the *theory of change* — how exactly the investment leads to the desired outcomes. Then, specific indicators are selected — for example, metric tons of CO2 avoided, number of low-income individuals gaining access to financial services, or percentage of portfolio companies with diverse leadership teams. Finally, regular reporting and independent verification ensure accountability and prevent "impact washing," where the impact is overstated or misrepresented.

Action steps for building an impact measurement strategy are clear. First, articulate your impact thesis: what change do you want to see in the world? Next, select investments or funds that align closely with this thesis and demand transparency about how they measure and report impact. Establish your own impact dashboard — just as you would have a financial performance dashboard — and track key metrics over time. If necessary, engage specialized impact consultants who can help design and implement a robust impact measurement and management (IMM) system.

Set clear goals: Do you want to allocate a specific percentage of your portfolio to green bonds, impact private equity, or sustainable infrastructure? Are you more interested in environmental outcomes, social justice, or governance improvements? What is your desired balance between financial return and impact depth? Knowing these goals allows for disciplined portfolio construction and prevents emotional decision-making.

Now for the question that every sophisticated ultra-affluent investor must ask: Can you truly do all this alone? The reality is that impact investing at scale requires a specialized ecosystem. You need experienced fund managers, legal experts familiar with impact clauses and ESG regulations, consultants who understand how to design and monitor impact strategies, and wealth advisors who can integrate impact investing into your broader portfolio and estate plan. Trying to build and manage this alone risks inefficiencies and missed opportunities. The best outcomes come from leveraging expertise and building a collaborative impact investing infrastructure around your capital.

Here's your bold call to action: Over the next 90 days, go beyond intention. Commit to allocating a portion of your portfolio — 5%, 10%, 20% — to impact investments aligned with your values. Build a team, if you don't already have one, that can source, vet, and monitor these opportunities. Establish a set of impact KPIs that you will measure as rigorously as you measure financial returns. And most importantly, embed impact into your overall wealth strategy, ensuring that your legacy is not just financial, but transformational.

Because at the ultra-affluent level, wealth is not just about what you accumulate — it's about what you enable.

Ultra Affluent is your permission slip to elevate your investing from transactional to transformational — to turn your capital into a force for good that outlasts you, influences generations, and shapes the future you want to see.

Chapter 29: Investing in Art, Wine, and Collectibles: Passion Investments

At a certain level of wealth, the conversation around investments evolves beyond stocks, bonds, and private equity. It begins to include something more intimate, more tangible, and often more personally meaningful—passion investments. Fine art, rare wines, classic cars, vintage watches, rare manuscripts, luxury handbags, and sports memorabilia — these are not just objects of beauty and culture; they are alternative assets that, when approached with diligence and strategy, can become important parts of an ultra-affluent portfolio. Passion investments represent the intersection of wealth, culture, and personal expression, allowing you to align your financial strategy with your aesthetic and intellectual interests.

Imagine you are sitting across from me. You have spent decades building financial security and growing your investment portfolio. Traditional assets have treated you well. Yet, increasingly, you find yourself drawn to the idea of owning assets that you can see, touch, appreciate—assets that are unique and finite. You've admired friends who have assembled impressive art collections or curated wine cellars and seen them realize not only financial gains but also deep personal satisfaction. You wonder: Should I diversify into passion investments? Can they deliver real returns, or are they merely expensive hobbies? How do I approach these markets intelligently and without getting caught in the traps of speculation or sentimentality?

At their core, passion investments offer the ultra-affluent investor an opportunity to diversify into non-correlated assets. Unlike public equities, whose values can be buffeted by market cycles, interest rates, and geopolitical events, the value of a Basquiat painting, a magnum of 1945 Château Mouton Rothschild, or a Ferrari 250 GTO is driven by scarcity, provenance, condition, and cultural relevance. These markets operate on different dynamics, and while they can be volatile in their own right, they often provide a hedge against broader financial system risks.

The pros of passion investing are alluring. First, emotional return: passion assets provide enjoyment and personal engagement in a way that no index fund ever could. Second, diversification: passion assets typically have low correlation to stocks and bonds, enhancing portfolio resilience. Third, scarcity: the finite supply of a Rothko painting or a first-edition James Joyce novel confers a built-in rarity value that can appreciate over time, particularly as global wealth expands and demand for unique assets rises. Fourth, potential tax advantages: in some jurisdictions, collectibles are taxed differently from financial assets, and proper structuring through trusts or foundations can optimize tax outcomes.

But the cons must be acknowledged soberly. Passion investments are illiquid; selling a multimillion-dollar painting or a case of Romanée-Conti wine takes time, expertise, and access to the right buyers. Valuations can be opaque and subjective, influenced by trends, tastes, and auction dynamics. Transaction costs — auction house fees, dealer commissions, insurance, storage — can be high. Additionally, expertise matters enormously; the risk of overpaying, buying fakes, or investing in assets with dubious provenance is real and substantial. For these reasons, entering these markets without guidance is fraught with risk.

Real-world scenarios provide a rich tapestry of lessons. A private collector who amassed a significant post-war art collection by purchasing works directly from emerging artists saw exponential growth in the value of his collection as those artists gained critical acclaim. Another collector of rare Patek Philippe watches enjoyed not only decades of aesthetic pleasure but also impressive capital appreciation as vintage watches became a global phenomenon. Conversely, an investor who hastily purchased "investment-grade" wine at inflated prices during a speculative boom later discovered that storage conditions had compromised the wine's value, leading to disappointing returns at auction.

The action steps for engaging in passion investing are disciplined and strategic. First, invest time before capital. Educate yourself deeply in the asset class that speaks to you — whether that's contemporary art, Bordeaux wines, vintage cars, or rare books. Attend auctions, visit galleries and fairs, talk to dealers, read industry publications. Second, build relationships with reputable experts — art advisors, wine merchants, watch specialists, classic car consultants. Third, insist on provenance and authenticity. A passion asset without verifiable history and documentation is a risk not worth taking. Fourth, consider third-party appraisals and condition reports before any significant purchase. Finally, plan for storage, maintenance, insurance, and eventual sale—owning a Picasso requires different stewardship than owning shares of Berkshire Hathaway.

Set clear goals: Are you collecting for passion, profit, or both? What percentage of your net worth are you willing to allocate to passion investments? Are you seeking assets with long-term appreciation potential or personal satisfaction with potential upside? How will you evaluate success — by financial return, personal enjoyment, cultural impact, or family legacy? Your goals will guide your strategy and prevent the emotional pitfalls that can cloud judgment in these deeply personal markets.

And now, the inevitable question: Can you navigate passion investing alone? While it is possible to build knowledge and expertise over time, the complexity, opacity, and nuance of these markets suggest that partnering with seasoned advisors is prudent. Art advisors can negotiate better prices and provide access to off-market works. Wine consultants can verify provenance and advise on optimal storage. Legal experts can assist with contracts, export regulations, and tax planning. A well-structured team can turn passion investing from a risky adventure into a strategic, rewarding component of your wealth management plan.

Here's your bold call to action: Over the next 90 days, identify one area of passion investing that truly resonates with you. Immerse yourself in learning — attend an auction, visit a major art fair, tour a vineyard, or consult with a specialist. Define a preliminary budget and strategic objectives for entering this space. Begin building relationships with experts who can guide you. Most importantly, commit to approaching passion investments with the same rigor and discipline that you apply to your financial investments.

Because at the ultra-affluent level, wealth is not just about numbers on a balance sheet — it's about curating a life of meaning, beauty, and enduring value.

Ultra Affluent is your permission slip to move beyond transactional wealth — to craft a legacy that is not only financially significant but culturally and personally profound.

Evaluating Art as an Asset Class

Fine art is often considered the pinnacle of passion investments. Historically, top-tier art has demonstrated long-term appreciation, often outperforming public equities during specific periods. However, investing in art is not simply about picking what is beautiful or trendy. It is about understanding an intricate, opaque market driven by provenance, rarity, critical acclaim, exhibition history, and cultural relevance.

When evaluating art as an asset class, several key dimensions must be assessed. First is the artist's market — is the artist emerging, mid-career, or blue-chip? Emerging artists can deliver explosive returns but carry higher risk. Blue-chip names — Picasso, Basquiat, Warhol — offer more stability but at higher entry points and often with lower relative appreciation rates. Second is provenance — the chain of ownership. A painting once owned by a notable collector or exhibited at a major museum will command a premium. Third is liquidity — while some artworks have ready secondary markets, others may languish in private collections or auction catalogues for years. Fourth is authenticity — an ironclad guarantee that the work is genuine is non-negotiable.

The pros of art investing include potential high returns, portfolio diversification, inflation protection, and the aesthetic and intellectual joy of living with beautiful objects. The cons include illiquidity, high transaction costs, volatility tied to changing tastes and trends, and the necessity of costly storage and insurance. A prudent strategy might involve focusing on artists with growing institutional interest, seeking artworks with strong provenance and exhibition history, and partnering with a reputable art advisor who can access off-market opportunities and advise on the timing of acquisitions and sales.

Understanding Wine Investment Structures

Wine investing carries a timeless allure — the romance of vineyards, the craftsmanship of winemaking, the appreciation of terroir and vintage. Yet, behind the romance lies a highly specialized market. Fine wine has become an established alternative asset class, with indices such as the Liv-ex Fine Wine 100 tracking prices. Investing in wine can take several forms: direct purchase of bottles or cases for long-term holding, participation in wine funds, or fractional ownership through wine investment platforms.

Direct purchase gives the investor control but requires substantial knowledge of vintages, producers, storage standards, and market liquidity. Fine wines must be stored professionally, often in bonded warehouses, to preserve provenance and condition — any deviation can significantly diminish value. Wine funds pool capital to invest in diversified portfolios of investment-grade wine. The benefits include professional management, diversification, and scalability. However, fees can be significant, and transparency varies. Emerging platforms now offer fractional ownership, allowing investors to buy shares in high-value bottles or collections, democratizing access but also introducing platform risk.

The pros of wine investing are notable: steady long-term returns, low correlation to traditional markets, and inflation hedging characteristics. Additionally, wine tends to be resilient during market downturns as the wealthy continue to indulge in luxury consumption. The cons include storage costs, insurance, limited secondary market liquidity, and the risk of counterfeiting or provenance issues. Whether through direct purchase or managed funds, due diligence, and an understanding of the wine market's nuances are essential for success.

Due Diligence for Collectibles

Beyond art and wine, collectibles span a vast landscape — classic cars, rare watches, vintage handbags, rare books, historical manuscripts, sports memorabilia, and even luxury sneakers. Each category has its own market dynamics, authenticity standards, valuation methodologies, and risks. Yet the principles of due diligence remain remarkably consistent.

First, authenticity and provenance are paramount. Documentation verifying origin, ownership history, and condition is non-negotiable. In markets such as watches and handbags, the difference between a verified original and a counterfeit can be nearly impossible to detect without expert assistance. Second, market knowledge is crucial. Understanding trends — such as the recent surge in demand for 1980s Patek Philippe Nautilus watches or Hermès Birkin bags — can inform strategic acquisitions. Third, liquidity varies widely. Some collectibles, like rare baseball cards or vintage cars, have vibrant auction markets. Others may require extensive private networking to find qualified buyers.

Fourth, maintenance and storage are often overlooked but critical. A classic car requires proper climate-controlled storage and regular mechanical upkeep. A rare watch benefits from careful servicing by authorized specialists. Ignoring these details can erode value significantly. Fifth, insurance must be tailored to the asset type, covering not just theft but damage, loss in transit, and depreciation due to improper handling.

The pros of collectible investing include potential outsized returns, diversification, personal enjoyment, and legacy value. The cons are high transaction costs, opaque markets, illiquidity, and the need for constant vigilance against market fads and fraud.

Real-Life Passion Investing Scenarios

Consider the collector who focused on acquiring museum-quality photography prints when the category was still emerging. Over two decades, as institutions and private collectors increasingly valued photography as fine art, prices for key works rose dramatically, offering returns rivaling blue-chip paintings. Another example is a family office that methodically built a wine cellar featuring only the top vintages of first-growth Bordeaux and

Burgundy. When the market for fine wine soared, they realized significant returns — all while enjoying the personal prestige of hosting tastings and events showcasing their collection.

Conversely, a cautionary tale involves an investor who, enamored by the vintage watch market boom, purchased several six-figure timepieces without independent authentication. Several turned out to have undisclosed aftermarket modifications, severely impairing their value and undermining their investment thesis.

Action Steps for Passion Investing

Begin with self-awareness: what categories genuinely resonate with you? Art, wine, watches, cars, manuscripts? Passion investing is most effective when it aligns with your personal interests and knowledge base. Educate yourself rigorously: attend auctions, join collecting societies, build relationships with industry insiders, and study historical price trends. Establish a clear budget and define what percentage of your net worth you are willing to allocate to passion assets.

Build a trusted team: an art advisor, a fine wine merchant, a vintage car consultant, a collectibles insurance specialist, a legal advisor familiar with art law. Insist on provenance, authenticity, and expert third-party appraisals before any significant purchase. Understand the holding costs: storage, maintenance, insurance, advisory fees, and liquidity timelines. Plan for eventual sale or transfer — whether through auction, private sale, or family legacy.

Goals and Considerations

Define whether your primary goal is capital appreciation, diversification, personal enjoyment, legacy creation, or all of the above. Determine your time horizon — are you building a collection to be liquidated in 10 years or a legacy to be passed down? Establish how you will measure success: financial returns, cultural impact, or personal satisfaction? Decide if you can manage this on your own or whether you need to hire expertise to navigate authentication, valuation, acquisition, storage, and sale.

A Simple but Bold Call to Action

Over the next 90 days, commit to an exploration phase. Pick one passion asset category and immerse yourself. Attend a major auction (even virtually), visit a gallery, tour a vineyard, or inspect a private collection. Engage at least one expert in your category of interest and begin the conversation about intelligent passion investing. Allocate a preliminary budget and set an intention: to approach this not just as a hobby but as a thoughtful extension of your broader wealth strategy.

Final Note

Because at the ultra-affluent level, wealth is not merely about growing numbers on a statement — it is about creating a life of richness, beauty, and enduring meaning. Passion investing allows you to merge capital with culture, wealth with wisdom, investments with identity.

Ultra Affluent is your permission slip to curate a life — and a legacy — where passion and prudence walk hand in hand.

Chapter 30: Direct Indexing: Tax Efficiency and Customization for Large Portfolios

When your portfolio exceeds seven figures and begins stretching into eight, nine, or even ten, traditional investment strategies start to reveal their limitations. Mutual funds and ETFs have served you well on the path to wealth creation, but as your financial landscape becomes more complex, you realize that standard solutions lack the precision, flexibility, and efficiency your situation now demands. You're not just managing assets—you're orchestrating a symphony of investments, taxes, estate considerations, philanthropy, and family legacy. This is where direct indexing enters the conversation—not as a new asset class, but as a smarter, more sophisticated way to manage public equities in a way that is customized for you.

Imagine you are sitting across from me. You have a substantial, diversified portfolio. But you're feeling the sting of embedded gains in your mutual funds, limited flexibility in your ETFs, and an increasingly significant tax drag on performance. You want a more tailored approach—something that gives you market exposure, yes, but also respects your individual tax situation, values, and legacy goals. You've heard of direct indexing but wonder if it's just a buzzword or if it can truly elevate your wealth management strategy.

At its core, direct indexing allows you to replicate the exposure of a broad market index—like the S&P 500 or the Russell 3000—by owning the individual securities directly rather than through a fund. This simple structural difference unlocks profound advantages. First, it gives you the ability to harvest tax losses at the individual security level—selling individual stocks at a loss to offset capital gains elsewhere in your portfolio, reducing your tax bill. Second, it allows you to customize your exposure. Want to avoid tobacco companies or invest more heavily in clean energy? Direct indexing lets you align your portfolio with your personal values without sacrificing diversification.

The pros of direct indexing are powerful. Tax efficiency is the headline advantage—by realizing losses throughout the year, you can significantly reduce your taxable gains, enhancing after-tax returns. Customization is another key benefit. Unlike a one-size-fits-all ETF, a direct index portfolio can be tailored to your risk profile, factor exposures (like value or momentum), and ESG preferences. You also gain control over capital gains realization—important if you anticipate future liquidity needs, estate planning transitions, or strategic philanthropic giving. Furthermore, because you own the underlying securities, you have more flexibility for charitable donations of appreciated stock, allowing you to reduce concentrated positions and capture tax benefits simultaneously.

But there are cons to consider. Direct indexing introduces complexity. Managing hundreds—or even thousands—of individual stocks requires sophisticated technology and expertise. Without careful management, transaction costs and tracking error (the deviation from the benchmark's performance) can erode the benefits. Direct indexing also requires a level of engagement and oversight that some investors may find burdensome. And while loss harvesting opportunities are plentiful in volatile markets, they diminish during strong bull markets when losses are scarce.

Real-world scenarios illustrate these dynamics clearly. A tech entrepreneur who sold a company for $100 million faced a significant capital gains tax burden. By deploying a direct indexing strategy, he was able to systematically harvest losses from his broad equity exposure, offsetting gains from the sale and saving millions in taxes. Another family with a long-standing commitment to ESG principles used direct indexing to eliminate exposure to fossil fuels, firearms, and other industries they wished to avoid, without sacrificing diversification or expected returns. On the flip side, an investor who jumped into direct indexing without understanding the operational complexity ended up with significant tracking error and underperformance relative to benchmarks, undermining confidence in the strategy.

Action steps for considering direct indexing are straightforward. First, assess whether your portfolio is large enough to benefit from the strategy—generally $500,000 or more in taxable equities is a reasonable threshold. Next, clarify your goals: Are you primarily seeking tax efficiency, customization, or both? Engage a wealth advisor or direct indexing platform that offers sophisticated loss-harvesting algorithms, customization capabilities, and transparent reporting. Carefully evaluate the cost structure—some providers charge asset-based fees, others a flat fee—and understand how transaction costs are managed. Finally, integrate your direct indexing strategy with your broader wealth plan, including estate planning and philanthropic strategies.

Set clear goals: Are you trying to maximize after-tax returns? Align your investments with personal values? Manage a concentrated stock position more tax-efficiently? How will you measure success—relative performance, after-tax alpha, alignment with ESG goals, or ease of liquidity for future needs? Determining these objectives will ensure that direct indexing is deployed as a strategic tool rather than a trendy tactic.

And now the inevitable question: Can you execute direct indexing alone? Technically, yes—you could open a brokerage account and buy a basket of hundreds of individual stocks. But practically, for portfolios of significant size and complexity, direct indexing requires professional management, sophisticated technology, and a disciplined process to harvest losses, monitor exposures, and maintain benchmark tracking. Most ultra-affluent investors find it more efficient and effective to engage specialized wealth managers or firms offering bespoke direct indexing solutions tailored to UHNW needs.

Here's your bold call to action: Over the next 90 days, conduct a tax-efficiency audit of your current investment portfolio. Identify embedded gains, loss harvesting opportunities missed, and any misalignments with your values or liquidity needs. If your audit reveals friction or inefficiency, commit to exploring direct indexing with a trusted advisor. Ask the tough questions: How does their platform handle tax-loss harvesting? What customization options are available? What is the expected tracking error, and how is it managed?

Because at the ultra-affluent level, wealth management isn't just about growth—it's about precision, alignment, and optimization.

Ultra Affluent is your permission slip to move beyond traditional investing—to harness the full power of your wealth with strategies that are not only smarter but tailored uniquely for you.

Direct Indexing vs. ETFs: A Deeper Dive on Tax-Loss Harvesting and Customization

While ETFs are efficient, low-cost vehicles that have democratized access to diversified investment strategies, they are blunt instruments compared to the scalpel of direct indexing. When you own an ETF, you hold a basket of securities through a single tradable instrument. You get diversification and liquidity, but you forfeit control over the underlying assets. This limits your ability to harvest tax losses because you can't sell the individual underperformers within the ETF without selling the entire holding.

Direct indexing dismantles this limitation. By owning the underlying stocks directly, you create an environment ripe for tax-loss harvesting. Imagine holding a basket of 500 stocks replicating the S&P 500. Over time, while the index may rise overall, individual stocks will inevitably fall below your purchase price. Direct indexing enables the harvesting of these losses without disturbing the overall market exposure of the portfolio.

For example, let's say the S&P 500 gains 8% in a year, but within it, 40% of the stocks suffer losses. A traditional ETF holder sees only the net 8% gain. A direct indexer can harvest losses from the underperformers, offsetting gains elsewhere and creating a more favorable after-tax return. Over time, these incremental tax benefits compound significantly, often generating what's known as *after-tax alpha*—returns not necessarily superior in pre-tax terms, but meaningfully enhanced after taxes are accounted for.

Customization is another key differentiator. ETFs are standardized products. Whether you like every company in the S&P 500 or not, buying an S&P 500 ETF means owning them all. Direct indexing allows you to exclude companies or sectors that don't align with your values or strategic goals. Want to tilt toward companies with low carbon footprints? Exclude companies embroiled in ESG controversies? Overweight female-led enterprises? Direct indexing allows you to tailor your portfolio while still maintaining broad market exposure.

The trade-off is complexity. Managing hundreds or thousands of individual securities requires robust technology and daily oversight. Tracking error—the deviation between your customized portfolio and the index—must be carefully monitored. Too many exclusions or tilts can compromise the benefits of diversification.

Advanced Tax Strategies with Direct Indexing

Beyond routine tax-loss harvesting, direct indexing unlocks a suite of advanced tax strategies. One is *tax bracket management.* By selectively realizing gains and losses, you can engineer your income to stay within favorable tax brackets year to year, smoothing taxable income over time.

Another is *charitable gifting optimization.* Appreciated individual securities can be donated directly to charitable organizations or donor-advised funds (DAFs). By gifting appreciated securities, you avoid realizing capital gains and secure a full fair-market-value deduction for the donation, maximizing the tax benefit of your philanthropy. Direct indexing provides a plentiful inventory of appreciated securities for such gifts, allowing you to be strategic about which assets to donate and when.

Legacy planning is another frontier. By holding appreciated assets until death, you can pass them to heirs with a step-up in basis, eliminating capital gains tax liability. A direct indexing portfolio gives you the flexibility to designate which assets are held for legacy transfer and which are harvested or gifted during life.

Real-Life Scenarios in Direct Indexing

Consider a family office managing a $50 million taxable portfolio. By transitioning from ETFs to direct indexing, they generated more than $1 million in tax savings annually through loss harvesting and strategic charitable gifting. Over a decade, these incremental savings compounded to create an after-tax return several percentage points higher than a comparable ETF-based strategy, effectively enhancing their legacy while maintaining their market exposure.

Or take a tech executive whose compensation heavily involved company stock options. She used direct indexing to diversify her portfolio while maintaining control over taxable events, harvesting losses systematically to offset gains from exercising options, and aligning her non-company holdings with ESG principles important to her family.

Contrast this with an investor who tried to manage a direct indexing strategy manually, without technology or professional oversight. Unable to effectively monitor tax-loss harvesting or control tracking error, the portfolio underperformed the market, and the administrative burden became overwhelming.

Action Steps: Building a Direct Indexing Strategy

Start with a *tax audit* of your current portfolio. Identify embedded gains, unrealized losses, and potential sources of taxable events. Next, define your customization goals. Are there sectors, industries, or companies you wish to avoid? Are there ESG factors you want to integrate?

Then, select a direct indexing platform or partner. Look for technology that provides daily loss harvesting, tax-optimized rebalancing, and customizable index construction. Evaluate the platform's ability to minimize tracking error while honoring your customization preferences. Understand the fee structure—what portion is fixed, what portion is asset-based, and what additional costs (like transaction fees) may apply.

Finally, integrate your direct indexing strategy into your broader wealth management plan. Align it with charitable giving strategies, estate planning goals, and liquidity needs. Commit to regular reviews to ensure that your direct indexing strategy evolves with your life, tax situation, and market conditions.

Checklist for Vetting Direct Indexing Providers

- Do they provide daily, automated tax-loss harvesting?
- How do they manage tracking error relative to your chosen benchmark?
- Can they accommodate ESG or values-based customizations?
- What is their process for selecting replacement securities when harvesting losses (avoiding wash sales)?
- Are there minimum account sizes or customization thresholds?
- How transparent are their fees?
- Do they offer integration with broader financial planning and wealth management services?
- Is their platform technology-driven with human oversight?
- How do they assist with charitable gifting strategies?
- Can they coordinate with your CPA, estate attorney, and family office team?

Goals to Set for Direct Indexing

- Minimize current and future tax liability.
- Customize portfolio exposure to align with personal values.
- Manage concentrated stock positions tax-efficiently.
- Integrate with legacy and philanthropic planning.
- Enhance after-tax returns over the long term.
- Maintain liquidity for future life events or business ventures.

A Simple but Bold Call to Action

Within the next 90 days, commit to elevating your investment strategy. Conduct a tax and efficiency audit of your existing holdings. If inefficiencies are found—and they likely will be—initiate a dialogue with a wealth manager or platform that specializes in direct indexing for ultra-affluent individuals. Insist on clarity around tax-loss harvesting, customization, and integration with your total wealth picture. Don't settle for generic solutions at this level of wealth. Demand precision.

Final Note

Because at the ultra-affluent level, managing wealth is not about replicating what everyone else is doing—it's about tailoring a strategy that reflects your complexity, your values, and your goals. Direct indexing is not just another investment tactic. It's a rethinking of how you engage with public markets—on your terms, with your objectives in focus.

Ultra Affluent is your permission slip to leave behind off-the-shelf investing and embrace a bespoke, tax-efficient, values-aligned approach to growing and protecting your wealth.

Chapter 31: Private Placements and Alternatives: Expanding Beyond Public Markets

When you cross into the realm of ultra-high-net-worth, the investment conversations you have—and should be having—change. Public markets, while efficient and essential, represent only a sliver of the opportunity set available to you. Your scale and access unlock a broader toolkit: private equity, private credit, hedge funds, venture capital, real estate syndications, private placements, and other alternative investments. These are not fringe ideas; they are integral to how serious wealth is grown, preserved, and diversified at the highest levels.

Imagine you're seated across from me. You've built a portfolio that has served you well—broad exposure to equities, a measured allocation to bonds, maybe even a passive ETF strategy. But now, as you think more about legacy, long-term risk, and opportunity, you sense a shift. You recognize that real wealth stability comes not from chasing the next hot stock but from owning assets that move differently—assets that operate on longer time horizons, that are less correlated to public market swings, and that can unlock unique returns. You're ready to expand your investment philosophy beyond the familiar. This is where private placements and alternatives become not just interesting but essential.

Private placements refer broadly to investment opportunities not offered through public exchanges—direct investments in companies, real estate projects, credit facilities, or specialty funds that are typically accessible only to accredited or qualified purchasers. These investments can be illiquid, opaque, and complex. But they can also offer outsized returns, uncorrelated risk, and differentiated exposure unavailable to traditional investors. For the ultra-affluent, they represent a way to truly tailor a portfolio—to go beyond what's available off the shelf and design something built for endurance and impact.

The pros of private placements and alternatives are compelling. First, diversification. Private assets generally have lower correlation to traditional stocks and bonds, providing ballast during public market volatility. Second, alpha generation. Private markets, less efficient and more opaque, offer skilled managers the chance to generate excess returns by exploiting informational or structural inefficiencies. Third, access to innovation and growth. Venture capital opens doors to the next generation of technology or healthcare breakthroughs before they reach public markets. Fourth, predictable cash flows. Private credit or real estate syndications can deliver steady, contractual income streams, appealing in low-interest environments.

Yet these advantages come with real trade-offs. Private placements are illiquid—you can't sell easily, and you're often committed for years. They typically involve higher fees—management and performance charges can erode returns if not justified by true outperformance. There's also complexity: due diligence is labor-intensive, information is less transparent, and investment structures can be intricate. Manager selection is paramount. In private markets, the spread between top-quartile and bottom-quartile managers is vast, and mediocre managers destroy wealth as easily as great ones grow it.

Real-world examples clarify both the upside and the pitfalls. A family office that allocated 30% of its assets to top-tier private equity funds saw compounded returns significantly outpacing public equities over 20 years. Their wealth grew not just through market exposure but through active ownership, innovation, and strategic exits. In contrast, an investor who blindly committed capital to a "hot" venture fund without proper vetting found herself locked into a portfolio of overvalued startups, few of which exited successfully, resulting in significant underperformance relative to the public markets she could have easily accessed.

Private credit offers another instructive example. By investing in senior secured loans to mid-market companies, one investor achieved steady 8-10% annualized returns with low volatility. Yet another, chasing yield without proper risk assessment, ended up overexposed to distressed borrowers during a downturn, suffering material capital impairment.

Action steps for expanding into private placements are deliberate. First, conduct a portfolio diagnostic. How much of your current allocation is exposed to public market risk? Where might you benefit from less correlation and more differentiated return streams? Second, establish your liquidity budget. Alternatives are illiquid by design; ensure you have sufficient liquid assets to cover living expenses, opportunistic investments, and unforeseen needs without touching your private allocation. Third, source deals carefully. Work with advisors, family office networks, or boutique firms that can deliver access to top-quartile managers and vetted opportunities. Fourth, conduct rigorous due diligence. Scrutinize manager track records, fees, investment theses, and alignment of interests. Remember: in private markets, access and selection determine outcomes.

Set clear goals. Are you seeking higher returns, lower volatility, or inflation protection? Are you more interested in venture capital's asymmetric upside or private credit's steady income? What is your tolerance for illiquidity and complexity? Are you looking to express values—through impact investing or ESG-aligned alternatives—or purely to optimize financial outcomes? Clear goals will inform allocation decisions and help you avoid chasing fads or overcommitting to high-risk sectors.

And now the inevitable question: Can you build a private placement and alternatives portfolio alone? Technically, yes—but practically, no. Access to top funds and deals is gated and relationship-driven. Due diligence requires time, expertise, and often a specialized skill set. Negotiating favorable terms, understanding fee structures, and building a diversified alternatives allocation demands a level of focus that few individuals can maintain while also running businesses, families, and lives. The best outcomes come from leveraging experienced advisors, institutional-quality research, and peer networks that can deliver both access and insight.

Here's your bold call to action: Over the next 90 days, review your current portfolio and identify the gaps—where public markets dominate and where private alternatives could add meaningful diversification and return enhancement. Set an alternatives target—perhaps 20%, 30%, or 40% depending on your liquidity needs and risk tolerance—and begin building relationships with advisors and platforms that can source top-tier opportunities. Commit to one deep diligence process on a private investment opportunity—whether that's a venture fund, private credit facility, or real estate partnership. Learn the process. Engage seriously.

Because at the ultra-affluent level, wealth is not merely preserved—it is curated, cultivated, and constructed with a mindset that transcends the traditional.

Ultra Affluent is your permission slip to leave behind generic investment strategies and embrace the full spectrum of wealth-building tools available to you.

Private Equity: Owning the Engines of Growth

Private equity represents ownership stakes in private companies—companies not listed on public stock exchanges. It includes leveraged buyouts, growth equity, and restructuring plays. For the ultra-affluent, private equity is a core asset class, delivering access to entrepreneurial dynamism and wealth creation engines well before companies go public or are acquired.

The pros of private equity include high potential returns, hands-on governance to drive value creation, and exposure to companies at various growth stages. Skilled private equity managers, or General Partners (GPs), apply strategic, operational, and financial expertise to unlock value, generating returns that have historically outpaced public equities over long periods.

However, the cons are real. Capital is typically locked up for 7–10 years, liquidity is minimal, and performance dispersion is vast. A top-quartile private equity fund may generate double-digit annualized returns; a bottom-quartile fund may deliver losses or paltry returns barely beating inflation. Fees are high—2% management fees and 20% carried interest are standard—and only top-tier GPs truly justify these costs.

Real-world examples abound. A family office that partnered early with a seasoned private equity firm gained access to high-performing deals and co-investment opportunities, compounding wealth across two decades. Another investor, lured by the glamour of private equity, committed capital to an unproven GP and experienced disappointing returns and impaired capital.

Venture Capital: Betting on the Future

Venture capital (VC) is a subset of private equity focused on early-stage companies—startups with high growth potential but also high risk. For the ultra-affluent, VC offers asymmetric return profiles: most portfolio companies may fail, but a few home runs can generate outsized gains.

The pros of venture capital include access to innovation, market disruption, and transformational business models. A successful VC-backed investment can deliver returns in multiples—not percentages—of original capital. For investors seeking excitement, influence, and the possibility of creating the next market leader, VC is unparalleled.

The cons? Venture capital is risky. Most startups fail. Capital is tied up for 7–10 years. Due diligence is challenging, as early-stage companies often lack extensive financial histories. Performance is highly skewed, and manager selection is critical. Additionally, venture valuations can be volatile and susceptible to changing market sentiments.

Successful investors in VC, like those who backed early rounds of companies like Airbnb, Uber, or Stripe, saw exponential wealth creation. However, for every headline-making unicorn, countless startups quietly disappear, taking invested capital with them.

Private Credit: Steady Yields in a Low-Interest World

Private credit refers to non-bank lending to businesses, often through senior secured loans, mezzanine debt, or distressed debt strategies. For the ultra-affluent, private credit offers attractive yields, strong downside protection through collateralization, and diversification away from public bond markets.

The pros are compelling: predictable cash flows, lower correlation to equity markets, and seniority in capital structures. In an era of low yields on public bonds, private credit provides a powerful income engine.

The cons include illiquidity, default risk, and complexity in underwriting. Borrowers are typically mid-sized companies that might lack access to public debt markets. Understanding their financial health, collateral quality, and macroeconomic sensitivity is critical.

Investors who align with skilled private credit managers can enjoy stable, high-single-digit to low-double-digit returns with relatively low volatility. Those who chase yield without careful diligence may find themselves overexposed to credit events and loss of capital.

Real Estate: Tangible Wealth Anchors

Private real estate investments—through direct ownership, syndications, or private funds—provide exposure to tangible assets with intrinsic value. Core strategies include multifamily housing, commercial office, industrial properties, and niche sectors like senior living or data centers.

The pros of private real estate include income through rents, capital appreciation, inflation hedging, and portfolio diversification. Real estate is tangible—you can see it, touch it, and leverage it.

The cons involve illiquidity, management intensity, and cyclicality. Property values and rental incomes can suffer during economic downturns. Real estate syndications or funds also carry fees and require careful vetting of operators.

Families who have compounded wealth through patient, strategic real estate investing often enjoy multi-generational benefits. Others who rushed into overheated markets or partnered with inexperienced operators have learned hard lessons about capital loss and illiquidity.

Private Placements: Niche Opportunities with High Upside

Private placements can include investments in private companies, special purpose vehicles (SPVs), private funds, or even direct project financing. They are bespoke and often highly tailored to specific investor needs.

Pros include customization, direct access to management teams, and potential for above-market returns. Private placements also offer opportunities to participate in unique asset classes—like litigation finance, music royalties, or intellectual property rights.

Cons include complexity, higher risk profiles, limited transparency, and significant due diligence requirements. Deals are often syndicated to a limited number of investors, and access is typically relationship-driven.

Action Steps for Engaging in Private Markets

First, build a clear *alternatives policy statement* as part of your broader investment plan. Define allocation targets, liquidity budgets, return objectives, and acceptable risk parameters.

Second, assemble a team. This may include alternative investment consultants, fund of funds managers, legal counsel for reviewing subscription documents, and tax advisors for structuring.

Third, source deals through multiple channels: private banks, independent advisors, family office networks, and direct relationships with GPs and syndicators.

Fourth, commit to rigorous, ongoing due diligence. Evaluate manager track records, terms and fees, governance structures, and alignment of interests. Scrutinize the investment thesis, downside scenarios, and exit strategies.

Finally, monitor and manage. Private investments require oversight. Regularly review fund reports, performance updates, capital call schedules, and liquidity windows.

Checklist for Evaluating a Private Investment

- Who are the principals, and what is their track record?
- What is the investment thesis and competitive edge?
- How are returns generated—income, appreciation, or both?
- What are the key risks, and how are they mitigated?
- What is the fee structure—management fees, performance fees, hidden costs?
- What is the liquidity profile—lock-up periods, redemption windows?

- How transparent is reporting?
- Are investor interests aligned with the managers'?
- What is the legal structure—LLC, LP, SPV?
- What are the tax implications—U.S. sourced income, foreign investments, K-1s?

Goals for Alternative Investing

- Enhance portfolio returns through access to top-quartile private market managers.
- Reduce public market correlation to build resilience.
- Generate steady cash flows for income needs.
- Gain exposure to innovation and long-term growth.
- Hedge against inflation and market volatility.
- Align investments with personal values (e.g., impact investing, ESG themes).

A Simple but Bold Call to Action

Within the next 90 days, commit to expanding your investment opportunity set. Allocate time and resources to understanding and accessing private markets. Initiate a conversation with your wealth advisor about setting up an alternatives allocation. Attend an industry event focused on private markets. Evaluate at least one private investment opportunity with rigor. Take the first step beyond public markets into the sophisticated, rewarding world of private alternatives.

Final Note

Because at the ultra-affluent level, wealth is not about chasing what everyone else can buy—it's about harnessing your access, scale, and sophistication to curate a portfolio that's resilient, diversified, and uniquely yours.

Ultra Affluent is your permission slip to build a portfolio not bound by market headlines, but driven by thoughtful, strategic, long-term private investing.

Chapter 32: Working with Traders: Execution Matters When You're Ultra Affluent

At a certain level of wealth, how you buy and sell securities becomes just as important as what you buy and sell. For ultra-high-net-worth individuals, the stakes are higher, the dollar amounts larger, and the cost of inefficiency more profound. A mistimed order, poorly executed trade, or misunderstood market nuance can cost hundreds of thousands—or even millions—of dollars in slippage, market impact, or opportunity cost. Execution is no longer an afterthought; it is a critical element of wealth management strategy.

Imagine you're sitting across from me. You've spent your career building a successful business, scaling it, and ultimately achieving a liquidity event that placed you among the ultra-affluent. Now, with tens—or hundreds—of millions of dollars to deploy, you assume that trading is straightforward: click, trade, done. But it's not. At this level, markets react to size, timing matters, and precision in execution can be the difference between incremental wealth and costly mistakes. Welcome to the world where trading strategy is not a technical footnote—it's a lever of value creation and preservation.

Let's start by understanding the basic dynamic: markets are not perfectly liquid or frictionless, especially at scale. When you place a large order to buy or sell a security, the market notices. Prices move against you—this is called market impact. Additionally, spreads widen, and opportunities to execute at favorable prices diminish. Retail investors may ignore these nuances, but for you, they are unavoidable realities. Whether buying $10 million in a single equity or rebalancing a $100 million portfolio, execution efficiency directly affects your returns.

The pros of working with experienced traders are clear. First, price improvement. Sophisticated traders understand how to break up large orders, use algorithmic trading tools, and work with liquidity providers to minimize market impact. Second, risk management. Traders help you avoid adverse selection, limit slippage, and time trades to optimize outcomes. Third, anonymity and discretion. Traders know how to mask your intentions in the marketplace, protecting you from being front-run or unduly influencing the price of securities. Fourth, access. Experienced traders often have relationships with multiple liquidity venues—dark pools, alternative trading systems (ATSs), and institutional desks—that can source better execution opportunities than what appears on the screen.

The cons of poor trading practices are equally significant. Inefficient execution leads to slippage—the difference between the expected price of a trade and the actual price. It exposes you to unnecessary market risk, especially if trades take too long to fill or if orders signal your intentions to the market. It creates tax inefficiencies if trades are not executed with careful tax-lot considerations. And poor execution can undermine portfolio strategies, distorting allocations and introducing unintended risks.

Real-world scenarios underscore these points. A family office rebalancing a $250 million portfolio without professional trading support experienced over $2 million in slippage and realized unnecessary short-term capital gains due to poor execution strategies. Conversely, a UHNW individual working with a dedicated trading desk saved $1 million in a single year through smart execution tactics—algorithmic trading, block trades through dark pools, and precise tax-lot harvesting to manage gains.

Action steps for improving trade execution start with acknowledging the need for specialized expertise. First, assess your current execution framework. Are you relying on retail brokerage platforms not designed for UHNW needs? Are trades executed in bulk, indiscriminately, without attention to size, timing, or market conditions? Second, build a relationship with a trading desk—whether through a private bank, multi-family office, or independent wealth manager—that understands institutional-grade execution. Third, insist on transparency. Request execution quality reports. Analyze price improvement statistics. Understand how your trades are routed and at what cost.

Fourth, integrate trading strategy with tax strategy. Sophisticated trading includes not just minimizing slippage but also optimizing tax outcomes. Traders who understand tax-lot accounting can execute trades in a way that realizes losses to offset gains or selectively realizes gains to manage tax brackets.

Set clear goals for your trading strategy. Are you optimizing for cost, speed, discretion, or tax efficiency? What is your tolerance for market impact? Do you want to incorporate ESG screens or custom portfolio tilts? Are you rebalancing periodically, opportunistically, or tactically based on market conditions? Clear trading goals will inform how your execution strategy is designed and managed.

Now, can you manage sophisticated trade execution on your own? Technically, perhaps—but practically, no. The complexity of market microstructure, the need for algorithmic tools, access to multiple liquidity venues, and the importance of discretion make this a specialized discipline. Just as you wouldn't attempt to perform surgery without a surgeon, you shouldn't attempt to execute ultra-high-net-worth trades without a professional trader.

Here's your bold call to action: Over the next 30 days, review your current trading practices. Analyze your execution costs, market impact, and tax consequences. If you're not working with a professional trading desk, initiate a dialogue with one. Ask about their approach to minimizing slippage, accessing liquidity, and integrating with tax and portfolio strategy. Don't leave this critical lever of wealth preservation to chance.

Because at the ultra-affluent level, every basis point matters. Every dollar saved or lost in execution compounds over time. Precision is not a luxury; it's a necessity.

Ultra Affluent is your permission slip to treat trading not as an afterthought but as an essential element of strategic wealth management.

Advanced Trading Techniques for the Ultra Affluent

Once you understand that execution matters, the natural next step is to ask: how exactly do professional traders achieve better outcomes? It starts with mastering advanced trading techniques that go far beyond simply placing a market order. Techniques like VWAP, TWAP, dark pool trading, and algorithmic slicing are critical tools for minimizing market impact and achieving best execution.

Let's begin with VWAP—Volume Weighted Average Price. This algorithmic strategy seeks to execute orders in line with the average price of a security over the course of the trading day, weighted by volume. Why is this important? Because it ensures that your large order doesn't unduly move the market; instead, it rides along with natural liquidity, minimizing disruption and slippage. VWAP is ideal for liquid securities where price stability is desired, and it helps benchmark execution quality against market norms.

TWAP—Time Weighted Average Price—is another algorithmic tool. It focuses on executing a large order evenly over a specified time period, regardless of volume spikes. TWAP is useful in less liquid securities where volume may be unpredictable or where spreading the order over time reduces visibility to the market. By executing incrementally, TWAP minimizes market signaling risk—the chance that others notice your activity and move prices against you.

Dark pools are another essential tool in the UHNW trading arsenal. Dark pools are private exchanges where large blocks of securities can be traded anonymously without revealing trade size or intent to the public markets. For the ultra-affluent investor dealing with multi-million-dollar orders, dark pools provide a critical advantage: they allow you to transact without broadcasting your presence, preserving price integrity and protecting against front-running by high-frequency traders or opportunistic market participants.

Algorithmic slicing refers to breaking a large order into smaller, random-sized pieces executed at random time intervals. This technique masks the size and intent of the order, reducing market impact. Sophisticated trading desks use proprietary algorithms to slice and route orders dynamically based on real-time market conditions, adapting to shifts in liquidity, volatility, and spread.

Real-world examples demonstrate the power of these strategies. A UHNW investor looking to liquidate a $50 million equity position over a week worked with a trading desk using a combination of VWAP and dark pool execution. The result: execution prices better than the average market price, minimal market impact, and savings of over $500,000 compared to naïve market orders. Another investor, attempting to rebalance a $200 million portfolio without professional trading support, executed large block trades on the open market, moving prices against himself and incurring millions in slippage—entirely avoidable with the right strategy.

The Cost of Poor Execution

Quantifying the cost of poor execution is eye-opening. Consider slippage—the difference between the expected and actual execution price. Even a modest 20 basis points (0.20%) of slippage on a $100 million portfolio is $200,000 lost—not to taxes, not to market losses, but purely to inefficient trading. Over time, repeated slippage compounds into significant wealth erosion.

Market impact, too, can be costly. A poorly timed large order can move the price of a security, leading to a worse average execution price and ripple effects on portfolio performance. Trading too aggressively can trigger alarms in the market, causing others to anticipate your moves and exploit them.

Taxes are another hidden cost. Executing without attention to tax lots—selling low-basis securities first, for instance—can accelerate capital gains unnecessarily. Strategic execution prioritizes high-basis securities for sale to minimize tax liabilities or realizes losses to offset gains.

Working with Professional Traders

Professional trading desks designed for UHNW clients do more than execute orders—they provide strategic advice. They help design trade schedules, choose execution venues, select algorithms, and coordinate trading with tax strategy. They monitor market conditions and adjust tactics dynamically. They understand the nuances of liquidity, volatility, spreads, and market psychology.

When engaging with a professional trading desk, insist on transparency and alignment. How are they compensated? Are they incentivized to achieve best execution or simply complete orders? Ask for trade execution reports showing fill prices, benchmarks (like VWAP comparisons), and market impact analysis. Sophisticated trading desks provide this data routinely and use it to refine execution strategies over time.

Checklist for Evaluating a Trading Partner

- What execution algorithms do they offer (VWAP, TWAP, implementation shortfall, dark pool access)?
- How do they minimize market impact and slippage?
- Do they offer real-time monitoring and dynamic adjustment of trade strategies?
- What reporting and transparency are provided post-trade?
- How are they compensated—flat fee, per share, basis points of execution value?
- What is their experience with UHNW and institutional clients?
- Do they integrate trading strategy with tax and portfolio strategy?
- How do they source liquidity—public exchanges, dark pools, internal crossing networks?

Goals for Optimizing Execution

- Minimize trading costs, slippage, and market impact.
- Achieve price improvement over standard benchmarks.
- Preserve anonymity and discretion.
- Integrate trading with tax-loss harvesting and broader tax strategy.
- Align execution with portfolio objectives and rebalancing needs.

- Create a scalable execution framework for ongoing portfolio management.

A Simple but Bold Call to Action

Over the next 60 days, conduct an execution audit. Review your trade history: How much slippage have you experienced? Were trades executed at favorable prices relative to benchmarks? If you are not currently using advanced execution strategies—VWAP, TWAP, dark pool routing—commit to engaging a professional trading desk that can deliver institutional-quality execution tailored to UHNW needs.

Final Note

At the ultra-affluent level, every detail matters. Trading isn't just about moving money—it's about moving money wisely. Precision in execution protects wealth, enhances returns, and preserves the legacy you've worked so hard to build.

Ultra Affluent is your permission slip to elevate trading from a mechanical task to a strategic advantage.

Chapter 33: Building a Core-Satellite Portfolio: Traditional and Alternative Blends

At a certain point in wealth building, you realize that diversification isn't just a textbook concept—it becomes a lived experience. When you've crossed into the realm of tens or hundreds of millions of dollars in assets, the volatility of the market is not an abstraction; it is a direct risk to your lifestyle, your future, and your legacy. Managing that risk smartly, while still growing wealth meaningfully, is not about chasing hot stocks or swinging for the fences. It's about structure—thoughtful, deliberate, strategic structure. And one of the most powerful frameworks for doing this is building a core-satellite portfolio that intelligently blends traditional and alternative investments.

Imagine you're seated across from me. You've succeeded beyond expectations. You have the means to build an investment portfolio that can withstand market storms, capture new opportunities, and reflect your values and long-term goals. Yet you're frustrated by the noise of financial markets—the endless news cycles, the temptation to chase returns, the fear of missing out on the next big thing. You know you need a plan, not a patchwork of ideas. That plan starts with thinking about your portfolio as a core surrounded by satellites.

The "core" of your portfolio is designed for stability, efficiency, and predictability. It's the bedrock—typically made up of low-cost, diversified public equities, high-quality bonds, and perhaps a sprinkle of global exposure. Think broad index funds, direct indexing strategies, and municipal or investment-grade fixed income. These are the reliable, tested instruments that drive long-term, steady returns without requiring constant tinkering. Your core provides the ballast that keeps the ship upright when markets get rough.

The "satellites," by contrast, are designed to generate alpha—excess returns above market benchmarks—or to hedge specific risks. These are the more specialized, less correlated, and often less liquid investments: private equity, venture capital, hedge funds, private real estate, private credit, infrastructure, commodities, and more. Satellites are where you take advantage of your access, scale, and ability to invest patiently. They are where you tilt your portfolio toward opportunities that are not available to average investors.

The pros of a core-satellite structure are compelling. First, it creates clarity: the core gives you reliable, low-cost market exposure, while the satellites give you targeted, high-conviction exposure to alternative strategies. Second, it optimizes risk and return: the core reduces volatility and keeps costs low; the satellites pursue differentiated sources of return. Third, it gives you flexibility: you can dial up or down your satellite exposure based on market conditions, liquidity needs, and personal preferences. Fourth, it aligns with behavioral finance principles: by having a strong core, you reduce the temptation to react emotionally to market swings, knowing that a portion of your portfolio is already safely anchored.

Of course, there are cons to consider. The biggest is complexity. Managing a diversified set of satellite investments—private funds with different capital call schedules, liquidity windows, fee structures, and tax implications—requires expertise and administrative support. There's also the risk of over-allocating to satellites and losing the benefits of simplicity and liquidity. Illiquidity is another challenge; many alternative investments lock up capital for 7–10 years, which must be carefully balanced against your broader cash flow and liquidity needs. Finally, manager selection risk looms large: in private markets, the spread between top-quartile and bottom-quartile managers is vast, and access to top performers is often restricted.

Let's consider a real-world example. A seasoned entrepreneur sold her business and netted $200 million in proceeds. She constructed a core-satellite portfolio with 50% in a diversified core: direct indexing of U.S. equities, municipal bonds, and international exposure. The other 50% was allocated to satellites: 20% private equity, 10% venture capital, 10% private credit, and 10% private real estate. Over a decade, the core delivered steady 6–7% annualized returns, providing liquidity and predictability. The satellites, despite some volatility and illiquidity, delivered higher returns—12%+ in private equity, 15% in venture capital—and contributed materially to overall portfolio growth. Importantly, the structure allowed her to weather market downturns calmly, knowing that liquidity and stability were built into the plan.

Contrast this with another investor who placed 80% of his wealth into illiquid private equity and venture funds without considering cash flow needs or liquidity timing. When unexpected expenses arose—a major philanthropic commitment and an opportunity to invest in a family member's startup—he found himself selling public market holdings at an inopportune time and borrowing against his portfolio, incurring unnecessary costs and stress. Structure matters.

Action steps for building a core-satellite portfolio are clear. First, conduct a portfolio audit. Assess current allocations, risk exposures, and liquidity profiles. Second, define your core: what portion of your wealth should be in stable, liquid, low-cost investments designed for long-term growth and liquidity? Typically, 40–60% is a good starting point, but this varies based on your specific needs, age, risk tolerance, and legacy goals.

Third, map your satellites. Identify the alternative asset classes that align with your return goals, risk appetite, and time horizon. Decide how much illiquidity you can tolerate—remembering that alternative investments often require 7–10 years before full realization of value. Build a disciplined pipeline of commitments, staggering vintages across years to manage liquidity risk.

Fourth, select managers with care. In private markets, manager skill is everything. Focus on track records, operational expertise, alignment of interests (e.g., GP commitments), and transparency. Work with advisors who have access to top-quartile managers and who can perform deep due diligence.

Set clear goals. Are you aiming to enhance returns beyond public markets? Hedge against public market volatility? Gain access to innovation or real assets? Generate predictable income streams? Goals will dictate structure.

Now, ask yourself honestly: can you build and manage a core-satellite portfolio at the ultra-affluent level on your own? Maybe. But the complexities of sourcing, diligence, monitoring, tax management, and risk control often demand a team: a seasoned wealth manager, an alternatives specialist, a tax strategist, and legal counsel to structure investments appropriately.

Here's your bold call to action: Over the next 60 days, audit your portfolio. Identify the current core and satellites. If your portfolio is all core—pure public market exposure—consider how satellites could enhance returns and diversification. If your portfolio is too heavily tilted toward satellites, assess liquidity risks. Build or refine your core-satellite map and set an implementation plan for the next 12 months.

Because at the ultra-affluent level, random diversification is not enough. Strategic, intentional portfolio architecture is what preserves and grows wealth across generations.

Ultra Affluent is your permission slip to move beyond generic investment plans and build a portfolio as sophisticated and enduring as the wealth it's designed to serve.

Core-Satellite Portfolio Allocations for Different Ultra-Affluent Profiles

Now that you understand the framework of the core-satellite portfolio, let's translate theory into action with real-world, tailored allocation models based on different UHNW profiles. Because the truth is, there is no one-size-fits-all portfolio at this level. Your wealth didn't come from a cookie-cutter path, and neither should your portfolio construction.

Profile 1: The Tech Founder – Recently Liquid, Still Growth-Oriented

Imagine a 42-year-old tech entrepreneur who has just sold a major stake in her company, netting $100 million in liquid wealth. She's still entrepreneurial at heart, focused on growth, relatively young, and has a high risk tolerance. Liquidity is less important because she has modest lifestyle needs relative to her wealth, and she's thinking long-term.

- Core: 40%
- 20% Direct indexing U.S. equities
- 10% Global equities
- 10% Municipal bonds for tax-free income
- Satellites: 60%
- 20% Venture capital (early and growth stage funds)
- 20% Private equity (buyout and growth funds)
- 10% Private credit (senior loans, opportunistic credit)
- 10% Real estate (opportunistic or value-add)

Why This Works: The core ensures long-term growth exposure and liquidity. The satellites aggressively pursue higher returns through private markets, consistent with the founder's entrepreneurial DNA. Private credit adds a yield component and diversifies risk, while real estate offers inflation hedging and tangible assets.

Profile 2: The Real Estate Entrepreneur – Cash Flow Focused, Tax Sensitive

Now imagine a 55-year-old real estate entrepreneur who has amassed wealth through decades of direct real estate investments and now seeks to diversify. With $250 million in net worth, the priority is predictable cash flow, tax efficiency, and preserving wealth for his children and grandchildren.

- Core: 50%
- 20% Direct indexing U.S. equities (tax-loss harvesting)

- 10% Dividend-paying global equities
- 20% Municipal bonds and tax-free fixed income
- Satellites: 50%
- 20% Private real estate funds (core/core-plus)
- 15% Private credit (asset-backed lending, real estate credit)
- 10% Infrastructure (income-generating projects)
- 5% Hedge funds (market-neutral strategies)

Why This Works: The portfolio focuses on cash flow generation and tax efficiency. Private real estate and credit provide steady income streams, and infrastructure offers long-term inflation-protected returns. The core supports liquidity needs and provides public market diversification.

Profile 3: The Multigenerational Family – Preservation and Philanthropy Driven

Consider a family with $500 million in net assets, spread across trusts and foundations. Their priorities are wealth preservation, prudent growth, intergenerational transfer, and philanthropy. They are sophisticated investors, focused on risk management and legacy.

- Core: 60%
- 30% Global direct indexing (U.S., developed, and emerging markets)
- 20% Municipal and high-quality corporate bonds
- 10% Short-duration bonds and cash equivalents (liquidity buffer)
- Satellites: 40%
- 15% Private equity (diversified across vintages and strategies)
- 10% Private real estate (core-plus, income-driven)
- 10% Impact investments (aligned with philanthropic goals)
- 5% Hedge funds (long/short equity, global macro)

Why This Works: The core is intentionally conservative and liquidity-focused, supporting both spending needs and stability. Satellites are carefully selected for their ability to generate incremental returns and reflect the family's philanthropic mission through impact investing strategies.

Common Mistakes in Core-Satellite Construction

Even among sophisticated investors, there are common mistakes to avoid when building a core-satellite portfolio:

1. **Neglecting Liquidity Needs:** Over-allocating to illiquid satellites can create a cash crunch during unexpected life events or market downturns.
2. **Chasing Yield:** Stretching for yield in private credit or real estate without proper underwriting increases risk without commensurate reward.
3. **Overpaying for Alternatives:** Not all private investments are created equal. High fees and mediocre managers can erode returns dramatically.
4. **Ignoring Taxes:** Poorly coordinated satellite investments can trigger unnecessary tax liabilities, particularly if gains are not managed across entities or generations.
5. **Lack of Integration:** Alternatives must be integrated into a comprehensive wealth plan, including estate planning, risk management, and philanthropy—not managed in isolation.

Action Steps for Core-Satellite Success

- **Liquidity Planning:** Conduct a thorough liquidity analysis. How much cash or near-cash do you need to cover three years of lifestyle expenses, taxes, and opportunistic investments?
- **Satellite Budgeting:** Determine the maximum percentage you are comfortable committing to illiquid investments. Common targets are 30–50%, but this should be tailored.
- **Manager Diligence:** Partner with advisors who have access to top-quartile managers and perform robust due diligence. Manager selection drives 80–90% of the return variance in private markets.
- **Fee Scrutiny:** Negotiate fees wherever possible. Favor managers with transparent fee structures and meaningful GP commitments (skin in

the game).

- **Risk Monitoring:** Establish a cadence for monitoring alternative investments. Private markets don't have daily price feeds, but quarterly reports and annual valuations are critical.

A Sample 10-Year Projection: Core-Satellite vs. Traditional 60/40 Portfolio

Consider two portfolios:

- **Traditional 60/40:** 60% equities, 40% bonds, net 6% annual return, high liquidity.
- **Core-Satellite:** 50% core (public markets, bonds), 50% satellites (private equity, credit, real estate), net 9% annual return (with higher illiquidity but higher expected alpha).

On $100 million over 10 years:

- **60/40 Portfolio:** $179 million (compounded at 6%)
- **Core-Satellite Portfolio:** $237 million (compounded at 9%)

That's a $58 million difference over a decade, just by optimizing structure and tapping into private markets carefully.

Goals for Building Your Core-Satellite Structure

- Achieve durable wealth growth with lower correlation to public markets.
- Balance liquidity needs with return aspirations.
- Capture unique opportunities available only to UHNW investors.
- Optimize after-tax, after-fee returns through smarter allocation.
- Build a portfolio resilient to market, economic, and political shocks.
- Create a legacy portfolio that can support not just your needs, but those of multiple future generations.

A Simple but Bold Call to Action

Within the next 60 days, map your portfolio using the core-satellite framework. Assess whether your current allocation supports your liquidity, return, and legacy goals. If it doesn't, design a new structure—one that uses your wealth's scale to its fullest advantage. Set a timeline to reallocate thoughtfully over the next 12–24 months. Commit to this higher standard of portfolio construction.

Final Note

At the ultra-affluent level, random diversification is not enough. Careful architecture—balancing liquidity, growth, risk, and legacy—is what transforms wealth from transient fortune to enduring dynasty.

Ultra Affluent is your permission slip to move beyond simplistic models and build a resilient, purpose-driven portfolio worthy of the legacy you're creating.

Part V: Family Office & Legacy Planning

When wealth reaches a level where it spans generations, the conversation must shift from accumulation to stewardship. Part V of *Ultra Affluent* is devoted to the critical transition from individual wealth management to family office leadership and legacy architecture. This section offers a blueprint for building a family office that doesn't just preserve wealth but amplifies its purpose, protects against risk, and strengthens family cohesion across generations.

You'll learn how modern family offices operate—balancing investment management, risk mitigation, tax efficiency, estate planning, and philanthropic initiatives under one integrated structure. We unpack how to design governance frameworks that foster healthy communication and accountability, reducing the common pitfalls of wealth erosion and family discord.

We explore the pillars of legacy planning: multigenerational wealth transfer strategies, the role of trusts and private foundations, and how to craft family constitutions and mission statements that align wealth with shared values. This section emphasizes the importance of educating heirs, instilling financial literacy, and preparing them not just to inherit assets but to inherit purpose and responsibility.

Through real-world case studies, we reveal how well-designed family offices evolve over time and why successful legacy planning is as much about emotional intelligence and leadership as it is about tax codes and legal structures.

Part V challenges ultra-affluent families to think beyond the balance sheet—to design enduring legacies, foster unity, and steward wealth with intention and clarity.

Because true wealth isn't just measured by what you accumulate—it's measured by what you sustain, nurture, and pass forward.

Chapter 34: Single-Family Office vs. Multi-Family Office Structures

At a certain point in the journey of wealth accumulation, the complexity of managing it all exceeds the capabilities of even the best personal advisors working individually. You don't just need a great CPA, attorney, or investment advisor; you need an entire ecosystem working cohesively under one roof. This is where the concept of a family office becomes not just attractive but necessary. But as you sit here, considering the next evolution of your wealth management strategy, a key decision looms: Should you build a Single-Family Office (SFO) tailored exclusively to your family's needs, or should you leverage the infrastructure and scale of a Multi-Family Office (MFO)?

Imagine you're seated across from me. Your net worth has climbed north of $150 million. Your financial affairs have grown complicated: multiple investment accounts, trusts, private equity deals, philanthropic endeavors, insurance structures, and a budding interest in legacy planning for your children and grandchildren. You feel the strain of trying to coordinate advisors, monitor risks, and ensure nothing slips through the cracks. You sense that you've outgrown the traditional wealth management model, and it's time to institutionalize your wealth—just as you institutionalized your business back when it scaled from a startup into a market leader.

The first model to consider is the Single-Family Office (SFO). An SFO is a private company, fully dedicated to managing the financial and personal affairs of one wealthy family. It provides investment management, estate planning, philanthropy management, tax optimization, family education, concierge services, and more—all in one custom-built operation. The beauty of the SFO is control. You design the structure, hire the staff, set the policies, and tailor the services to exactly what your family needs and values. If you want a CIO to manage a custom-built portfolio strategy, a CFO to oversee cash flows, a general counsel to coordinate estate planning, and a concierge team to handle travel and lifestyle needs—you can have it.

The pros of an SFO are immense. First, privacy: you control all the data, personnel, and decision-making, reducing the risk of information leakage. Second, alignment: your family's interests are the only interests being served. Third, customization: the services are precisely tailored to your family's values, priorities, and ambitions. Fourth, holistic integration: investment, tax, legal, and legacy planning work seamlessly together under your oversight.

But there are cons. SFOs are expensive. Operating a fully staffed SFO can cost \$1–\$5 million per year depending on size and complexity—representing roughly 0.5% to 1.5% of assets under management. Recruiting, training, and retaining talented professionals is another challenge; the best CFOs, CIOs, and estate attorneys command high salaries and expect to work with sophisticated, well-structured organizations. Moreover, governance can be tricky. Without clear structures and boundaries, family dynamics can seep into operational decisions, creating friction and undermining professionalism.

On the other hand, a Multi-Family Office (MFO) offers many of the same services but across multiple families, sharing resources and infrastructure. MFOs typically offer investment management, estate planning coordination, tax advisory, philanthropic consulting, and even family governance support. The primary advantage of an MFO is scale. Because resources are shared, costs are lower—often a fraction of an SFO's cost. You also benefit from access to broader investment opportunities, better technology, and a deeper bench of specialists that would be difficult to assemble and afford on your own.

The pros of an MFO are compelling. First, cost efficiency: you access institutional-grade services without having to bear the full cost of building the infrastructure. Second, access: many MFOs have relationships and access to top-tier private equity, venture capital, and hedge fund opportunities typically reserved for the largest institutions. Third, specialization: MFOs often employ seasoned professionals across multiple disciplines, offering a depth of expertise difficult for a single family to replicate internally.

Yet there are cons here as well. With an MFO, you give up some control. While reputable MFOs customize services to client families, you're still one of many clients—and there's a risk that service levels may not always meet your expectations. Privacy can also be a concern; while client confidentiality is paramount, your data is still part of a larger ecosystem. Finally, conflicts of interest can arise if the MFO is compensated for investment products or services they recommend.

A real-world scenario illustrates the choice. A family who exited a $500 million business decided to build a SFO. They hired a CIO, tax counsel, and philanthropic advisor, designing a custom investment strategy blending direct investments, private equity, and impact funds aligned with their values. Family governance was a major priority, so they also employed a family dynamics coach and developed a family constitution to prepare the next generation for stewardship. While the costs were significant—over $3 million annually—they valued the control and bespoke service.

Conversely, another family with $200 million opted for an MFO model. They accessed a full suite of investment, estate, and philanthropic services for less than $400,000 per year. Their MFO gave them access to private investments, coordinated estate planning, and helped them launch a donor-advised fund. They were satisfied with the service and appreciated not having to deal with the HR and operational burdens of running an SFO.

Action Steps for Deciding Between SFO and MFO

First, conduct a needs assessment. What services do you require—investment management, estate planning, philanthropy, family governance, concierge? How complex are your investments, trusts, and entities?

Second, evaluate scale. Many experts suggest that $250 million+ is the threshold where an SFO becomes financially justifiable, though smaller families sometimes build "light" SFOs with fewer staff and outsource certain functions.

Third, consider control vs. cost. Are you willing to pay a premium for full control and privacy, or do you prefer cost-efficient access to institutional-grade services even if it means some compromises?

Fourth, define your family's governance philosophy. Families who prioritize governance, education, and legacy-building often lean toward SFOs because they can tailor initiatives exactly to their values and succession plans.

Goals for Making Your Family Office Decision

- Determine the full scope of services your family needs.
- Understand your cost tolerance for building and operating a family office.
- Define your priorities: control, privacy, access, governance, cost efficiency.
- Evaluate the available MFOs or service providers if choosing the multi-family office route.
- If building an SFO, design a governance structure, hiring plan, and operational blueprint.

A Simple but Bold Call to Action

Over the next 90 days, conduct a family office feasibility study. Interview SFO executives and MFO representatives. Understand what each structure entails—costs, services, risks, and benefits. Map your needs against these offerings. Make an informed decision based not just on where you are today, but on where your family will be 10, 20, or 50 years from now.

Final Note

At the ultra-affluent level, wealth management is no longer about beating the market—it's about building institutions. Whether you construct a bespoke SFO or leverage the power of an MFO, the goal is the same: to institutionalize your wealth management, safeguard your legacy, and create a platform for enduring prosperity across generations.

Ultra Affluent is your permission slip to move beyond ad hoc management and architect a family enterprise as sophisticated and lasting as the wealth it is designed to steward.

Chapter 35: Creating Family Governance Structures That Last

There is a moment every ultra-affluent family faces, sooner or later, where the reality sets in: the wealth you have built can either unify or divide the generations that follow you. It is one thing to accumulate wealth. It is another to preserve it — not just the assets, but the values, the relationships, the vision — across generations. And that preservation doesn't happen by accident. It requires intentional structure. It requires governance.

Imagine you are seated across from me, considering the future of your wealth, not in terms of investment returns or tax efficiencies, but in terms of family. You are thinking about your children, perhaps their children. You wonder: Will this wealth be a blessing or a burden? Will it empower them or erode them? These are the right questions. And the answer lies in building a family governance structure designed not just for today's challenges, but for tomorrow's inevitable transitions.

Family governance is the system by which a family makes collective decisions, manages conflict, articulates its shared values, and stewards its wealth over time. It involves family constitutions, mission statements, councils, assemblies, and often formalized processes for communication, education, and decision-making. It is the bridge between family and enterprise — whether that enterprise is a family business, a portfolio of investments, a family foundation, or a legacy of philanthropy.

The core of lasting family governance begins with a family mission statement. This isn't just a feel-good exercise. It's the foundational document that defines why the family's wealth exists, what the family believes, and how it intends to use its resources. A strong mission statement provides clarity and unity, especially as the family grows more complex with each generation. It anchors decision-making in shared purpose rather than personal preference or generational drift.

Once the mission is clear, the next step is structuring a family constitution. Think of it as the operating manual for the family. It outlines the family's core values, rules for membership (Who is in the family? How are in-laws involved?), governance structures (Do you have a family council? What are its powers?), and procedures for decision-making (How do you elect leaders? How are disputes resolved?). A well-drafted constitution provides predictability and fairness — two pillars of long-term family harmony.

Pros of formal family governance structures are significant. First, they prevent disputes before they arise by creating clear rules and expectations. Second, they foster a sense of belonging and responsibility among family members. Third, they create an environment for ongoing education, preparing the next generation not just to inherit wealth, but to manage it wisely and purposefully. Fourth, they reinforce shared values and identity, reducing the risks of fragmentation and entitlement.

Of course, there are cons — or better said, challenges. Creating governance structures takes time, patience, and skilled facilitation. Families are emotional systems, not corporations, and imposing rigid structures without buy-in can create resentment. Furthermore, governance is not a "set it and forget it" process. Constitutions and councils must evolve as the family grows and changes. And governance requires leadership — often a difficult transition from founder-centric authority to shared leadership among siblings, cousins, and beyond.

Let's look at a real-world scenario. A third-generation family with a diversified investment portfolio and multiple family branches was facing increasing tensions over how wealth should be managed and distributed. They engaged a family governance consultant to facilitate a series of family meetings, ultimately drafting a mission statement and a constitution. They created a family council with representatives from each branch, established clear rules for governance, and built an educational curriculum for younger generations. The result: conflict decreased, participation increased, and the family's wealth and relationships flourished.

Contrast this with another family that ignored governance. As the founder passed wealth to the next generation, lack of clarity led to disputes over investment decisions, philanthropic priorities, and family business succession. Lawsuits ensued, relationships fractured, and the family fortune was divided — and diminished — within two decades.

Action Steps for Building Family Governance

First, convene family meetings — not just ad hoc gatherings, but structured meetings with agendas and skilled facilitation. Begin the conversation about values, mission, and shared vision. Document these discussions carefully.

Second, draft a family mission statement. What does the family stand for? What is its purpose? What role does wealth play in the family's vision of a successful life?

Third, develop a family constitution. Include governance structures (family council, family assembly), membership definitions, leadership roles, decision-making processes, and conflict resolution mechanisms. Keep it flexible enough to evolve but structured enough to provide clarity.

Fourth, establish governance bodies. A family council (an elected group tasked with leadership and decision-making) is often the heart of family governance. Some families also have family assemblies (annual gatherings of the broader family) and committees focused on philanthropy, education, or investment oversight.

Fifth, invest in family education. Governance without preparation is hollow. Create programs for financial literacy, leadership development, and family history. Teach not just the "what" but the "why" behind the family's wealth and values.

Goals for Family Governance

- Foster unity and shared purpose across generations.

- Prevent and manage conflicts through structured communication.
- Prepare heirs not just to inherit wealth, but to steward it wisely.
- Preserve and transmit family values alongside financial assets.
- Institutionalize decision-making processes to avoid founder dependency.
- Create a family culture of engagement, responsibility, and service.

A Simple but Bold Call to Action

Within the next 90 days, initiate your first structured family meeting. Engage a facilitator if necessary. Begin drafting your family's mission statement. Set a one-year goal to have a working draft of your family constitution. This is not a "someday" project — it is the foundation for enduring family success.

Final Note

At the ultra-affluent level, wealth without governance is a recipe for division and decline. Family governance isn't about control — it's about stewardship. It's about giving your family the tools, clarity, and culture to manage wealth not just for today, but for generations to come.

Ultra Affluent is your permission slip to move beyond wealth accumulation and build a legacy of leadership, unity, and purpose.

Chapter 36: Preparing the Next Generation: Financial Literacy for Heirs

As wealth grows, so too does the responsibility to ensure that the next generation is prepared to inherit it—not just the money, but the wisdom, stewardship, and discipline that will keep it intact and impactful. Picture yourself sitting across from me, reflecting on what you've built: the business ventures, the investments, the estate plan, the legacy. You've worked tirelessly to reach this point. But quietly, a more profound question lingers: Are your heirs ready? Are they equipped to understand, manage, and multiply what they are about to receive?

Financial literacy for heirs is not optional. It's the foundation upon which successful wealth transfer is built. Statistics are sobering: 70% of wealthy families lose their wealth by the second generation, and 90% lose it by the third. The reasons are not poor investments or tax policy shifts. The reasons are lack of preparation, lack of communication, and lack of education. In short, financial literacy gaps.

Financial literacy for heirs goes beyond teaching them how to balance a checkbook or manage a portfolio. It's about instilling a framework for understanding wealth, risk, responsibility, and purpose. It's about shaping mindsets, not just skill sets. It's about helping them view wealth not as an entitlement, but as a tool—one that requires skillful handling and a clear sense of mission.

Start with the basics, but don't stop there. Yes, they must understand financial statements, budgeting, and investment principles. But they must also grasp more complex topics: risk management, asset allocation, estate planning basics, the mechanics of trusts, philanthropic strategy, and even the human dynamics of wealth—entitlement, guilt, ambition, and stewardship. Knowledge is power, but wisdom is resilience.

The pros of investing in heir financial education are many. First, it empowers the next generation to make informed decisions rather than becoming passive recipients dependent on advisors. Second, it builds confidence. Many heirs quietly fear not knowing enough, which can lead to poor decisions or avoidance altogether. Third, it promotes responsible stewardship—aligning wealth with purpose rather than allowing it to drift toward consumption and decline. Fourth, it creates a culture of communication and transparency, which is the bedrock of successful multigenerational wealth.

There are challenges, too. Not all heirs are equally motivated. Some may resist education efforts, seeing them as tedious or unnecessary. Others may feel overwhelmed by the complexity. Still others may bring different values or visions for the wealth, sparking intergenerational tension. This is where patience and customization come in—tailoring education to different learning styles, ages, and levels of maturity.

Consider a real-world scenario. A family with a $500 million estate created a structured educational program for their heirs, starting at age 12 with basic financial literacy and progressively advancing to investing, philanthropy, and leadership development by the time they were in their twenties. They held annual family retreats focused not just on balance sheets but on family mission, values, and the responsibilities of wealth. The result? By the time the wealth transitioned, the heirs were not only competent but confident, carrying the family's legacy forward with intention.

Contrast that with a different family who assumed that private school education and access to top-tier advisors would be enough preparation. When the estate transitioned, heirs were unprepared for the complexity of their inheritance, leading to mismanagement, infighting, and eventual financial loss. The difference was not the quality of the wealth, but the preparation of the recipients.

Action Steps for Preparing the Next Generation

First, assess your heirs' current level of financial literacy. Have open conversations. What do they understand about budgeting, investing, risk, taxes, and philanthropy? Where are the knowledge gaps?

Second, design an education plan. This may involve formal courses, workshops, mentoring with trusted advisors, or structured family meetings focused on financial topics. Use a progressive approach, starting with foundational knowledge and building toward advanced concepts.

Third, create opportunities for practice. Consider giving heirs small investment portfolios to manage under supervision, encouraging philanthropic initiatives they can lead, or involving them in family governance discussions.

Fourth, focus on values as much as technical knowledge. Wealth without values is a house built on sand. Discuss the family's mission, the role of wealth, the responsibilities of stewardship, and the importance of service.

Fifth, model financial literacy yourself. Actions speak louder than words. Demonstrate prudent financial management, disciplined decision-making, and values-based leadership. Heirs learn as much by observing as by studying.

Goals for Heir Financial Literacy

- Equip heirs with the knowledge and skills to manage wealth responsibly.
- Build confidence and competence to reduce dependence on external advisors.
- Foster a mindset of stewardship rather than entitlement.
- Strengthen family communication and transparency around wealth.
- Ensure the family's legacy endures across generations, not just assets.

A Simple but Bold Call to Action

Within the next 90 days, launch a financial literacy initiative for your heirs. Start small if necessary—a family book club on financial topics, a weekend retreat with financial education sessions, or one-on-one coaching.

Make a commitment that your wealth will come with a manual, not just a check.

Final Note

At the ultra-affluent level, preparing heirs is not a luxury—it's a necessity. Wealth without wisdom is a burden, not a blessing. Financial literacy is the key that unlocks confident stewardship, enduring legacy, and family harmony.

Ultra Affluent is your permission slip to move beyond wealth accumulation and focus on wealth cultivation—planting the seeds of knowledge, discipline, and values that will bear fruit for generations to come.

Chapter 37: Succession Planning for Family-Owned Businesses

As an ultra-affluent individual who has spent decades building not just wealth but a business empire, you sit across from me today with a new set of challenges. Your business is thriving, your legacy is secure — for now. But there's an uneasiness underneath your confidence. The question is no longer how to grow the business. It's how to ensure it endures. How do you pass on not just assets, but leadership, vision, and stewardship to the next generation? This is the essence of succession planning for family-owned businesses. And it's one of the most complex, emotionally charged, yet critically important processes you will ever undertake.

Family business succession is not merely a financial transaction or a legal restructuring. It's a transition of leadership, culture, values, and control. It requires a different playbook than traditional corporate succession because the lines between family and business are deeply intertwined. Loyalty, legacy, and emotion often outweigh pure economics — but that doesn't make the stakes any less real. In fact, family business succession is where fortunes are most often made — or lost.

At its core, succession planning asks three questions. First: Who will lead? Second: How will ownership be structured? Third: How will the family continue to work together (or not) once leadership transitions? These questions seem simple, but the answers are often anything but.

Let's start with leadership. Identifying the next leader requires more than choosing the oldest child or the one who "likes business the most." It demands an honest assessment of skills, passion, vision, and readiness. Leadership succession should be based on merit, not birth order. Many successful families develop leadership grooming programs early, involving next-generation family members in internships, rotational assignments, external work experiences, and formal education — MBA programs, leadership academies, or direct mentorship under the current CEO.

The pros of internal succession are obvious: continuity, cultural preservation, and the ability to embed family values into the business's DNA. But the cons are significant: family dynamics can cloud judgment; promoting an unqualified heir can erode morale among non-family executives; and conflict between siblings or cousins can paralyze decision-making. Some families decide to appoint non-family executives to leadership roles, keeping the family in ownership and governance positions. This hybrid model often ensures professional management while preserving family control.

Ownership structure is the next critical frontier. Will the business be passed down equally among all heirs? Will only active family members receive ownership shares? How will liquidity be handled if some family members want out? These decisions must be codified through buy-sell agreements, shareholder agreements, and governance documents. Without clarity, family disputes can easily turn into litigation — and litigation into liquidation.

Consider the real-life example of a manufacturing family who failed to plan. The founder assumed his children would "figure it out" after his passing. When he died unexpectedly, the three siblings disagreed bitterly over the company's future. One wanted to grow aggressively, another wanted to sell, and the third wanted to take dividends and maintain status quo. Without clear succession documents or a leadership plan, the dispute escalated to court. The business was ultimately sold to a private equity firm for less than it was worth in a fire-sale environment. Generations of effort evaporated in months.

Now contrast that with another family who handled succession well. Over a 10-year period, they created a Family Council, developed a next-generation leadership training program, and implemented a detailed succession plan. The heir apparent spent time working outside the business before entering at a junior level. As his competence grew, he took on progressively larger roles. Simultaneously, the family established a shareholder agreement defining who could own shares, how shares could be sold, and how dividends would be distributed. When the founder stepped back, the transition was smooth, the business continued to thrive, and the family harmony was preserved.

Action Steps for Family Business Succession

First, start early. Succession is a process, not an event. Ideally, succession planning begins 10 to 15 years before the founder expects to exit.

Second, assess leadership objectively. Use external consultants if needed to evaluate family members' leadership potential. Define what success looks like in the CEO role — skills, values, vision — and match candidates against that profile.

Third, educate and prepare heirs. Provide opportunities for formal education, external work experience, and progressive responsibility within the business. Leadership readiness is earned, not inherited.

Fourth, clarify ownership structures. Draft shareholder agreements, buy-sell agreements, and governance documents that define how ownership transitions will occur, how disputes will be resolved, and what rights and responsibilities shareholders will have.

Fifth, institutionalize family governance. Create Family Councils, Boards of Directors with independent members, and Family Constitutions to guide family decision-making beyond the founder's tenure.

Sixth, plan for liquidity. Consider whether the business will fund buyouts for heirs who wish to exit or how external capital might be used without diluting family control.

Goals for Family Business Succession

- Identify and prepare future leadership.
- Establish ownership structures that promote unity and fairness.
- Separate business leadership from family politics.

- Institutionalize governance to outlast individual personalities.
- Protect the business's strategic vision and values.
- Minimize family conflict and maximize generational continuity.

A Simple but Bold Call to Action

Within the next 90 days, conduct a family business succession audit. Identify whether you have a written succession plan. If not, begin the process. If you do, review it critically: Is it up to date? Is it fair? Is it strategic? This is not a task to postpone — the future of your family enterprise depends on it.

Final Note

At the ultra-affluent level, succession planning is not just about avoiding taxes or ensuring smooth management transitions. It's about preserving a legacy that took a lifetime to build. It's about securing not just financial wealth, but relational wealth — the trust, unity, and shared purpose that turn a family business into a family institution.

Ultra Affluent is your permission slip to approach succession not as a reluctant necessity but as a strategic opportunity to architect the future — thoughtfully, deliberately, and boldly.

Chapter 38: Foundations vs. Donor-Advised Funds for Strategic Philanthropy

When you reach a level of wealth where financial security is no longer a question and legacy becomes the focus, philanthropy often shifts from charitable giving to strategic giving. You sit across from me now, not wondering whether to give, but how to give wisely, effectively, and with enduring impact. Two powerful vehicles enter the conversation: private foundations and donor-advised funds (DAFs). Both offer pathways to structure your philanthropy thoughtfully, but each carries different implications for control, complexity, tax benefits, and legacy.

A private foundation is a nonprofit organization you create, fund, and control. It requires legal establishment, typically as a 501(c)(3) entity, and must operate within regulatory frameworks designed for tax-exempt organizations. A donor-advised fund, by contrast, is a giving account housed within a public charity — think of it as a charitable investment account where you can recommend grants but don't own or directly control the assets once they're contributed.

Foundations appeal to ultra-affluent families because they offer total control. You determine the mission, the grantmaking priorities, the board members (often family), and the investment strategy. You can even hire staff, open offices, and create a public philanthropic identity. Foundations are excellent vehicles for those who see philanthropy as an extension of their entrepreneurial spirit — an enterprise that requires vision, strategy, and long-term stewardship.

The pros of a foundation are significant: control over operations and investments, ability to compensate family members for their service, capacity for legacy-building through named grants or initiatives, and flexibility to operate grantmaking programs, scholarship funds, or even direct charitable activities. Foundations also offer powerful estate planning benefits: contributions are deductible up to 30% of adjusted gross income (AGI) for cash gifts and 20% for appreciated assets, and they remove assets from your taxable estate.

But there are cons. Foundations come with regulatory burdens: annual tax filings (Form 990-PF), minimum distribution requirements (5% of assets annually), and excise taxes on net investment income. They require administrative infrastructure — legal, accounting, and governance support — and carry reputational risk if mismanaged. Foundations are highly visible; grants and financial details are matters of public record. For some families, this level of complexity and exposure is unwelcome.

Donor-advised funds offer a simpler path. They require no separate legal entity. You contribute assets to a DAF sponsor (such as a community foundation, a financial institution's charitable arm, or an independent DAF provider) and recommend grants over time. The DAF sponsor legally controls the funds, but you retain advisory privileges. Contributions to a DAF are immediately tax-deductible up to 60% of AGI for cash gifts and 30% for appreciated securities — more generous than foundation limits.

The pros of a DAF are clear: simplicity, cost-effectiveness, anonymity (DAF grants can be made without public disclosure of donor identity), and flexibility in timing. You can contribute in a high-income year for the tax deduction but spread out your grantmaking over many years. DAFs require no tax filings, no board meetings, and minimal administration. They are ideal for families who want philanthropic impact without the burden of running an organization.

The cons? Less control. You must make grant recommendations, but the sponsoring organization has ultimate authority to approve them (although in practice, this is rarely a barrier). You cannot hire staff or run direct charitable programs through a DAF. There is also a philosophical debate about perpetuity: DAFs do not have distribution requirements, leading to criticism that they can become vehicles for indefinite tax-advantaged capital accumulation without meaningful giving.

Consider a real-world scenario: a family with $200 million in net worth, passionate about education, decides to create a private foundation. Over time, the foundation funds scholarships, builds relationships with universities, and establishes an annual family service day. Family members sit on the board, cultivating a tradition of philanthropy and leadership. The foundation's name becomes synonymous with educational opportunity in their community.

Contrast this with another ultra-affluent individual who experiences a significant liquidity event — a $50 million exit from a tech company. Wanting immediate tax benefits and flexibility, she sets up a DAF. She makes a large contribution in the year of the sale, offsetting capital gains taxes, and then thoughtfully disburses grants to a wide array of causes over the next decade. She values the anonymity and ease, choosing to focus on impact rather than administration.

Action Steps for Strategic Philanthropy

First, define your philanthropic goals. Are you seeking to create a legacy institution, engage family members in governance, or maximize simplicity and efficiency? Are you motivated by control or convenience? Public recognition or privacy?

Second, consult with legal and tax advisors. Foundations and DAFs have distinct tax implications. Model different contribution scenarios to understand their impact on your tax position and estate plan.

Third, consider scale. Foundations are typically more appropriate for families planning to give $5 million or more and who want an enduring institution. DAFs are ideal for those giving smaller amounts or wanting to test the waters of strategic philanthropy before committing to a foundation.

Fourth, assess your tolerance for complexity. Foundations require significant administrative effort; DAFs do not. Be honest about the time, expertise, and resources you are willing to devote.

Fifth, revisit and revise your strategy. Philanthropy evolves as families grow, passions shift, and societal needs change. Build flexibility into your structures — foundations can sunset or morph; DAFs can be transferred to a foundation if your ambitions expand.

Goals for Strategic Philanthropy

- Align charitable giving with personal or family values and missions.
- Optimize tax benefits while ensuring meaningful societal impact.
- Create structures that match your desired level of control and involvement.
- Foster family engagement and intergenerational legacy.
- Build flexibility to adapt to changing philanthropic priorities over time.

A Simple but Bold Call to Action

Within the next 90 days, articulate your philanthropic mission statement — even informally. Then, determine whether a foundation or a donor-advised fund best aligns with that mission. Take the first step toward building the giving structure that will define your legacy.

Final Note

At the ultra-affluent level, philanthropy is not about writing checks — it's about writing a story. A story of impact, purpose, and values. Whether you choose a foundation's enduring architecture or a DAF's flexible simplicity, the key is intentionality.

Ultra Affluent is your permission slip to elevate your giving from generous to strategic, from episodic to enduring.

Foundations vs. Donor-Advised Funds: A Strategic Decision Matrix

When evaluating whether a private foundation or a donor-advised fund (DAF) best suits your philanthropic goals, it's helpful to compare them across several key dimensions. Below is a detailed comparison, presented in a vertical, paragraph-based format — no tables or charts — just clean, structured flow for a thoughtful decision:

1. Control

- **Foundation:** Total control over mission, governance, grantmaking, and investment strategy. You set the rules. You decide the pace, priorities, and public profile. You can establish customized grant programs, scholarship funds, or operating charities.
- **DAF:** Limited control. You retain advisory privileges over grants, but the sponsoring organization holds legal ownership of the assets and final approval rights over disbursements. In practice, reputable DAF sponsors honor donor recommendations if the recipient is a qualified charity.

2. Complexity and Administration

- **Foundation:** High complexity. Requires creation of a legal entity (typically a 501(c)(3)), annual IRS filings (Form 990-PF), adherence to self-dealing and excess business holding rules, and ongoing administrative oversight. Requires either in-house staff or outside advisors.
- **DAF:** Minimal complexity. No separate legal entity. No tax filings by the donor. The sponsoring charity handles administration, legal compliance, and tax reporting. You focus solely on recommending grants.

3. Cost

- **Foundation:** Higher upfront and ongoing costs. Legal and accounting fees for formation, annual tax preparation, audit (for larger foundations), insurance, and staff compensation if applicable. Administrative costs are part of your responsibility.
- **DAF:** Low costs. Most DAF sponsors charge an administrative fee, typically ranging from 0.25% to 1% of assets annually, which covers all administrative services, compliance, and reporting.

4. Tax Benefits

- **Foundation:** Contributions of cash are deductible up to 30% of adjusted gross income (AGI); appreciated securities and real property up to 20% of AGI. Excise tax of 1.39% on net investment income applies. Less favorable deduction limits compared to DAFs.
- **DAF:** Contributions of cash are deductible up to 60% of AGI; appreciated securities up to 30% of AGI. No excise taxes on investment income. Generally more favorable deduction limits.

5. Privacy

- **Foundation:** Public disclosure required. IRS Form 990-PF is public, listing assets, board members, grants made, and other financial information. High transparency can be a reputational asset but also increases scrutiny.
- **DAF:** Greater privacy. Grants can be made anonymously. Donor identity is not disclosed on public tax filings. Useful for families who prefer discreet philanthropy or want to avoid public solicitations.

6. Legacy and Perpetuity

- **Foundation:** Strong legacy potential. Foundations can exist indefinitely, with family members serving on the board for generations. A powerful tool for building a lasting family legacy and engaging heirs.
- **DAF:** Some DAF sponsors offer multi-generational succession, but typically limited to one or two generations. DAFs are generally designed for efficient charitable giving rather than perpetual legacy-building.

7. Philanthropic Flexibility

- **Foundation:** Highly flexible. You can conduct direct charitable activities (e.g., operating programs, running a museum or a school), make program-related investments (PRIs), and set up scholarships. Complete flexibility in terms of grant recipients and mission focus.

- **DAF:** Grantmaking limited to IRS-qualified public charities. No ability to run direct charitable operations. Cannot make grants to individuals or conduct direct programs. Philanthropy is limited to grants and advisory work.

8. Staff and Compensation

- **Foundation:** Permits hiring and compensating family members and others for foundation work, subject to "reasonable compensation" rules. Can establish a professional staff to scale grantmaking and impact.
- **DAF:** No staff. The donor cannot hire or compensate individuals through a DAF structure. Administrative support is provided by the sponsoring charity.

9. Minimum Payout Requirements

- **Foundation:** Must distribute at least 5% of assets annually for charitable purposes.
- **DAF:** No mandatory distribution requirement. Grants can be made at any pace, although the donor is encouraged to be active in their philanthropy.

10. Timeline for Setup

- **Foundation:** Longer setup time — typically several months. Requires legal structuring, IRS application for tax-exempt status (Form 1023), and governance documents.
- **DAF:** Fast setup — often within days. Opening an account and making the initial contribution can be handled swiftly through the sponsoring organization.

Action Steps for Choosing Between a Foundation and a DAF

- Reflect on your philanthropic mission: Is this about legacy and building a public institution or about flexible, efficient giving?
- Evaluate your desire for control: Do you want full autonomy, or are you comfortable recommending grants without operational responsibility?
- Consider your appetite for complexity: Are you willing to manage staff, compliance, and reporting?
- Review your tax situation: Which structure provides the best deduction limits and estate planning leverage given your current wealth profile?
- Think about privacy: Would you prefer public recognition or quiet impact?

Real-Life Scenario: Strategic Decision-Making

Take the example of the Patel Family, with a net worth exceeding $500 million. Their goal was clear: to create a lasting philanthropic legacy in medical research and education. They opted for a private foundation, hired a professional staff, and engaged the next generation in board governance. Over 20 years, the Patel Foundation not only funded groundbreaking research but also embedded the family's name in institutions they supported — a legacy that will endure for generations.

Contrast this with Jordan, a tech entrepreneur who sold his company and wanted immediate impact without overhead. He placed $20 million into a DAF at a major financial institution's charitable affiliate. Over five years, he funded hundreds of projects — from clean water initiatives to scholarships — anonymously and flexibly, maintaining a low profile while maximizing reach.

A Simple but Bold Call to Action

Within the next 90 days, map out your top three philanthropic priorities. Decide whether you seek legacy, control, or efficiency. Use this matrix to choose the structure that will carry your mission forward — a foundation if you're building a dynasty of impact, a DAF if you want nimble, focused giving without complexity.

Final Note

At the ultra-affluent level, giving is not merely a financial transaction; it's a statement of purpose. Foundations and donor-advised funds are not interchangeable tools — they are distinct pathways to shaping your philanthropic legacy. Choose deliberately.

Ultra Affluent is your permission slip to architect your giving with the same precision you applied to building your wealth. Strategic philanthropy is the final frontier of wealth mastery.

Chapter 39: Structuring Family Meetings: Communication, Governance, and Legacy

When wealth reaches a level where it spans generations, what's at stake is no longer just financial. It's relational. It's cultural. It's the story you leave behind, not just the balance sheet. You're seated across from me today not to talk about rates of return or asset allocations, but something much more nuanced — how to communicate with your family about the wealth you've built and how to make sure it strengthens rather than splinters your legacy. Enter the family meeting — one of the most underutilized but powerful tools of ultra-affluent families who seek not only to preserve wealth but to preserve unity.

The family meeting is not a board meeting. It is not a shareholder call. It's a different animal entirely. It's where financial education, governance frameworks, family values, and long-term planning come together in a structured, intentional format. Well-run family meetings can prevent the misunderstandings, rivalries, and sense of entitlement that often destroy wealth faster than taxes or market downturns ever could.

The first question to answer is: Why meet at all? Some ultra-affluent parents worry that talking openly about wealth will create laziness or entitlement among their heirs. Others fear loss of control or surfacing of old family conflicts. But the alternative — silence — is far more dangerous. When wealth is a secret, it breeds suspicion. When it's revealed suddenly (often after the death of the wealth creator), it fosters confusion, resentment, and rash decisions. Family meetings create a forum where expectations are set early and revisited often, where financial literacy can be built gradually, and where the family can craft a shared narrative about what their wealth is for.

A well-structured family meeting starts with defining the purpose. Early meetings may focus on education — basic financial literacy, the family history, the origins of the wealth, the family values. Later meetings can evolve to governance discussions — introducing the family trust structures, explaining ownership roles in the family business, or reviewing the family's philanthropic mission. Mature family meetings may tackle more complex topics: leadership succession, governance elections, investment strategies, or even difficult conversations around prenuptial agreements and next-generation readiness.

There is a rhythm to effective family meetings. They are not ad hoc or thrown together casually. Ideally, they happen at regular intervals — annually, semi-annually, or quarterly depending on the family's size, complexity, and geographic dispersion. They are planned thoughtfully, often with an agenda circulated in advance. They may include external facilitators — wealth advisors, family governance experts, or family business consultants — particularly when addressing sensitive topics.

The pros of family meetings are profound: clarity, communication, trust-building, and early identification of issues before they become problems. Families that meet regularly are more likely to transition wealth successfully across generations. They are better at conflict resolution, more likely to engage heirs in philanthropy, and more capable of preserving not just financial capital, but human and intellectual capital — the talents, values, and leadership capabilities of family members.

The cons? Family meetings require effort and vulnerability. Scheduling can be challenging. Generational differences may surface, and not every conversation will be easy. There is also a risk that poorly structured meetings devolve into gripe sessions or that dominant personalities overshadow quieter voices. That's why facilitation and ground rules are crucial.

Action steps for structuring family meetings begin with preparation.

Define a mission statement for the meetings themselves: Is the goal education, communication, governance, or planning? Set ground rules — confidentiality, respect for all voices, no interruptions. Develop a clear agenda and assign pre-work if necessary — reading materials, financial statements, or discussion questions.

Create an inclusive atmosphere. Meetings should balance formal sessions with informal time — family dinners, recreational activities, and time for private conversations. This balance helps reinforce family bonds and builds the trust needed for honest dialogue.

Involve the next generation early. Waiting until children or grandchildren are "old enough" can backfire. Tailor education to the audience — younger family members may start with basic financial principles; older heirs may learn about trust structures, estate plans, or governance roles.

Document decisions. Good family meetings produce minutes or a summary document capturing key points, agreements, and action items. This creates accountability and continuity from meeting to meeting.

Real-life example: The Edwards Family, founders of a successful real estate development company, began annual family retreats when their children were in their twenties. The first meetings were casual — shared family history, values, and basic investment principles. Over time, they formalized a Family Constitution, established a Family Council, and created governance policies for their family foundation. When the time came for succession, there was no drama — leadership roles were filled smoothly, and family unity remained intact.

Contrast that with the Simmons Family, where no structured communication occurred. When the patriarch passed away, his children learned for the first time about complex trust structures, business ownership stakes, and philanthropic obligations. Lacking prior exposure or education, disagreements quickly escalated into legal disputes. The family fortune was fractured within a decade, and so were the family relationships.

Pros and Cons of Family Meetings

- **Pros:** Improved communication, alignment of values, conflict resolution, education, and succession planning.

- **Cons:** Time-consuming, emotionally charged discussions, potential for conflicts if poorly facilitated, logistical challenges.

Action Steps

1. Draft a Family Meeting Mission Statement.
2. Set a regular meeting schedule (annual or biannual).
3. Develop a standing agenda format (education, governance, open discussion, social time).
4. Assign a family member or advisor as meeting coordinator.
5. Document key outcomes and action items from each meeting.
6. Include all adult family members and develop age-appropriate sessions for younger heirs.

Goals for Family Meetings

- Educate family members about wealth, values, and responsibility.
- Develop a shared vision for family wealth and legacy.
- Build governance structures — Family Constitution, Family Council, Philanthropy Committees.
- Create a pipeline of leadership across generations.
- Ensure a smooth, values-driven transition of wealth and governance roles.

A Simple but Bold Call to Action

Within the next 90 days, schedule your first structured family meeting. Start small: a weekend retreat with an agenda focused on education and open conversation. Commit to making family meetings a tradition — not a one-time event — because legacy is not built in a moment. It's built through ongoing dialogue, trust, and shared purpose.

Final Note

At the ultra-affluent level, true wealth is measured not only in dollars but in relationships, values, and leadership. Structuring family meetings is not about imposing control; it's about inviting conversation. It's about crafting a legacy that is not just inherited but embraced.

Ultra Affluent is your permission slip to elevate your family communication from polite avoidance to courageous stewardship. The greatest inheritance you can leave is not just assets — it's a family united by purpose and prepared to lead.

Sample First Family Meeting Agenda: Setting the Foundation

For ultra-affluent families venturing into formal family meetings for the first time, the key is to start with intentionality but without overwhelming complexity. The first meeting sets the tone for future interactions. Below is a suggested agenda for your inaugural gathering:

1. Welcome and Purpose Statement

Begin the meeting with a clear articulation of *why* you are gathering. This isn't about money; it's about mission, legacy, and stewardship. The patriarch or matriarch — or the family leader — should offer a personal reflection on the family's history, values, and hopes for the future.

2. Family Story

Spend time revisiting the family's history. How was the wealth built? What sacrifices were made along the way? Sharing the origin story humanizes the wealth and connects family members, especially younger generations, to the broader narrative beyond numbers on a balance sheet.

3. Introduction to Financial Literacy

Offer a basic primer on the nature of family wealth. This is not a full financial seminar but an introduction — understanding the difference between income and assets, appreciating the role of investing, and recognizing the responsibilities that come with stewardship.

4. Family Values Discussion

Facilitate a discussion about core family values. What principles have guided decisions in the past? What values do the next generation believe are most important to carry forward? Capture these values openly — they form the bedrock of your future governance documents.

5. Introduction to Philanthropy

If your family engages in charitable giving, introduce this as a cornerstone of family culture. Discuss past philanthropic activities and invite input on future areas of interest. Philanthropy is often the gateway for younger family members to get involved meaningfully.

6. Governance Overview

Give a high-level introduction to family governance — what it means, why it matters, and how it will evolve over time. Explain the concept of a Family Council, Advisory Board, or Family Constitution, setting the stage for more detailed discussions in future meetings.

7. Social and Informal Time

Include time for non-business interaction: a shared meal, a family game, or an outdoor activity. Relationship-building is as critical as agenda topics. Families that laugh together are more likely to stay together when the conversations get harder.

8. Closing Reflections and Next Steps

End with a reflection round — what did each family member learn or appreciate about the meeting? Set the expectation for a follow-up meeting and begin to outline topics for future discussions.

Outline of a Family Constitution: Crafting the Family's Guiding Document

A Family Constitution is not a legal contract. It's a moral compass. It defines how the family will make decisions, resolve disputes, steward wealth, and engage future generations. Here's how you might structure yours:

1. Preamble

An introduction to the family's history, mission, and purpose. Why does this Constitution exist? What legacy does the family hope to preserve?

2. Statement of Values

A clear articulation of the family's core values. Integrity, stewardship, philanthropy, entrepreneurship, education — whatever your family stands for, this is where it's enshrined.

3. Vision and Mission

Where does the family see itself 10, 20, or 50 years from now? What is the family's mission beyond wealth — what is the "why" behind all the planning?

4. Governance Structure

Explanation of formal governance roles:

- Family Council: Who serves? What is the process for selection and tenure?
- Family Meetings: Frequency, format, and leadership.
- Advisory Boards or Investment Committees: Their role and authority.

5. Communication Framework

How does the family commit to communicating? What are the expectations for honesty, confidentiality, respect, and inclusion?

6. Education and Development

Commitments around preparing the next generation: financial literacy programs, leadership training, and philanthropy engagement for heirs.

7. Conflict Resolution Process

Pre-agreed processes for resolving disputes: mediation protocols, voting procedures, and escalation pathways.

8. Philanthropy Policy

Guidelines for charitable giving, whether through a foundation, donor-advised fund, or other vehicles. How are philanthropic initiatives chosen and funded?

9. Wealth Stewardship Principles

Investment philosophies, risk tolerances, liquidity expectations, and views on entrepreneurship vs. wealth preservation.

10. Amendment Process

Families change; so should the Constitution. Define how and when it can be amended to reflect new circumstances, generational shifts, or evolved family goals.

Real-Life Scenario: The Mitchell Family Constitution

The Mitchells, a multi-generational family of entrepreneurs and investors, realized that as their family grew — with children and grandchildren entering adulthood — the risks of fragmentation increased. They hired a governance consultant to guide them through a two-year process of drafting a Family Constitution.

Today, their Constitution outlines clear roles: a Family Council that oversees family business interests, an Investment Committee that manages pooled investment vehicles, and a Philanthropy Board that educates next-gen family members about giving and social impact. Annual family meetings are structured around their Constitution, with agenda items like investment performance, philanthropic reviews, and next-generation leadership development.

The result? Not only has the family's wealth endured, but the family itself has remained cohesive, with a clear sense of shared identity and purpose.

A Simple but Bold Call to Action

Within the next 120 days, schedule your family's first formal meeting — and take the first step toward drafting a Family Constitution. Start by capturing your shared history and values. Legacy isn't automatic; it's architected, one conversation at a time.

Final Note

At the ultra-affluent level, wealth is not the hardest thing to build — but it's the hardest thing to preserve if families don't invest as much in communication as they do in portfolios. Structured family meetings and a living Family Constitution are not luxuries; they are necessities. They transform wealth from a point of vulnerability into a source of durable, multi-generational strength.

Ultra Affluent is your permission slip to move beyond hope and into structure, beyond silence and into dialogue, beyond division and into unity.

Your future self will thank you.

Your heirs will too.

And if you do it right, your great-great-grandchildren will know you not just by the wealth you passed down — but by the wisdom you embedded.

Part VI: Liquidity and Business Exit Planning

At the ultra-affluent level, liquidity isn't simply about having cash on hand — it's about engineering optionality. Business exits, liquidity events, and major asset sales are inflection points that can create immense opportunity — or immense disruption — depending on how they are planned. Part VI of *Ultra Affluent* focuses on helping wealth creators and inheritors prepare for, execute, and thrive through these critical transitions.

This section begins by demystifying liquidity itself — not just what it means to be "liquid," but why liquidity is strategic. It then moves into the highly specialized world of exit planning, showing why a business exit is not a transaction, but a process — one that can take years to optimize and must be deeply integrated with tax, estate, and investment planning.

We explore how to prepare a business for sale, when and how to engage investment bankers, attorneys, and valuation experts, and the crucial role of pre-exit tax strategies like qualified small business stock (QSBS) treatment or deferred sales trusts. We also discuss how liquidity events impact overall portfolio construction and risk management — because turning an illiquid asset into cash isn't the end; it's the beginning of a new phase of wealth stewardship.

Real-world case studies bring these topics to life: the founder who achieved a nine-figure exit by planning five years in advance, the family business that nearly unraveled due to poor succession planning, and the serial entrepreneur who learned the hard way that liquidity without structure leads to confusion, not freedom.

Throughout, we maintain the central theme: At the ultra-affluent level, liquidity is not just about freedom to spend — it's about freedom to design the next chapter of life intentionally. Whether you are nearing a business exit, contemplating selling a major asset, or simply seeking to increase financial flexibility, this section gives you the frameworks, tools, and strategic mindsets to do it wisely.

By the end of Part VI, you won't just understand liquidity. You'll have a playbook for engineering it — thoughtfully, deliberately, and with the future in mind.

Chapter 40: Pre-Liquidity Event Planning for Founders and Business Owners

Imagine you're sitting across from a founder on the cusp of a life-changing liquidity event. Their company, their life's work, is about to be acquired. The headlines will announce the transaction value with plenty of zeros, but behind that number is a complex web of opportunity and risk that requires precise pre-liquidity planning. Let's start with a concept: wealth isn't simply built by growing a business. True wealth — sustainable, generational, secure wealth — is built by intentionally navigating what happens before and after liquidity.

One of the first steps in pre-liquidity planning is to understand the structure of the deal. Is it cash, stock, or a combination? Each form of payment carries different tax implications and planning opportunities. Cash offers simplicity but may trigger significant income tax liabilities. Equity in the acquiring company might defer taxes but introduces concentration risk. Action Step: Sit down with your CPA and transaction attorney early to map out the deal's structure, the estimated tax bill, and the opportunities to optimize both.

Consider a founder, Alex, who built a software firm over fifteen years. When a private equity firm approached with a generous offer, Alex's first instinct was relief. But under the surface, questions lingered. What would the taxes look like? How much of the sale proceeds would Alex actually keep? Could this event jeopardize Alex's financial security rather than guarantee it? The realization set in that a plan was needed — not after the deal closed, but now.

Next comes entity structuring. Before liquidity, many founders overlook the benefit of restructuring their ownership. Grantor Retained Annuity Trusts (GRATs), Spousal Lifetime Access Trusts (SLATs), and other estate planning vehicles can move future appreciation out of the taxable estate. The catch? These structures must be established before the deal closes, before the IRS views the transaction as 'imminent.' Procrastination could cost millions in avoidable taxes. Pros: Significant estate tax savings, legacy preservation. Cons: Complexity, legal costs, and potential loss of control. Action Step: Engage a sophisticated estate attorney months in advance to explore whether advanced trust planning makes sense.

Another vital pre-liquidity strategy is charitable planning. Donor-Advised Funds (DAFs) and Charitable Remainder Trusts (CRTs) allow founders to fulfill philanthropic goals while receiving immediate tax deductions. Critically, contributions must be made with pre-liquidity shares, not post-sale cash. Otherwise, the founder misses the capital gains avoidance. Real-Life Scenario: Jordan, another founder, set up a DAF six months before closing. By donating $5 million in appreciated stock, Jordan avoided nearly $1.2 million in capital gains taxes while setting up a family giving legacy. Action Step: Clarify your philanthropic goals early and discuss DAF or CRT strategies with your advisor.

Liquidity events also trigger a shift in investment philosophy. Pre-sale, founders are typically 'all-in' on their businesses. Post-sale, diversification becomes critical. But diversification isn't a knee-jerk reaction — it requires a roadmap. How will proceeds be allocated among asset classes? What's the appropriate risk tolerance given the founder's new financial reality? Will the founder maintain some exposure to private equity or venture capital? Action Step: Work with a wealth manager who has experience guiding ultra-affluent clients through this transition. Build an investment policy statement that aligns with the founder's goals and risk appetite.

Insurance planning deserves attention too. Life insurance may have been an afterthought during the high-growth years, but post-liquidity it becomes a key estate planning tool. Large estates face significant tax liabilities upon death. Permanent life insurance can provide liquidity to cover estate taxes, ensuring that heirs don't have to fire-sale assets. Also consider umbrella liability insurance — as wealth increases, so does visibility and litigation risk. Pros: Asset protection, estate liquidity. Cons: Cost, underwriting complexity. Action Step: Conduct a full risk management review before the deal closes.

Debt planning often gets overlooked in pre-liquidity conversations. Some founders benefit from pre-event financing strategies, such as monetizing shares through private bank lending. This can provide liquidity for planning strategies without triggering a taxable event. However, leveraging must be done carefully. The goal is strategic liquidity, not lifestyle inflation. Action Step: Explore lending options with private banks and compare terms well before the deal's final stages.

Beyond dollars and cents, there's an emotional side to liquidity events. Founders often experience an identity shift. For years, the business was their passion and purpose. After the sale, a void may appear. This psychological transition can impact financial decisions if not proactively managed. Some founders jump into new ventures too quickly; others become paralyzed by fear of losing their newfound wealth. Real-Life Scenario: When Melissa sold her healthcare company, she quickly launched two startups within a year. Neither matched the original success, and she confessed later that she hadn't truly processed the first exit. Action Step: Assemble a personal advisory board — mentors, coaches, and advisors — who can provide guidance not just on finances but on life after liquidity.

Another subtle but crucial aspect is family governance. Sudden wealth can strain family dynamics. Discussions about values, inheritance, and financial education should start before the liquidity event occurs. The goal is to turn wealth into an opportunity for cohesion rather than conflict. Action Step: Initiate family meetings to discuss the coming changes. Consider a family mission statement or even a formal family office structure if the wealth level justifies it.

Finally, remember that time is the most valuable asset. Many planning strategies lose their effectiveness or become unavailable once the deal is signed. Early, proactive planning turns a good exit into a legacy-defining event. The ultimate goal isn't just a big payday — it's financial independence, legacy preservation, and peace of mind.

So, as you sit here now, the deal still on the horizon, the call to action is clear: Assemble your team — a sophisticated CPA, an estate planning attorney, a wealth manager who understands UHNW complexity, and a private banker. Begin the conversations today. Build a plan that addresses taxes, trusts, philanthropy, investments, insurance, debt, emotional well-being, and family governance. Don't leave your future — or your family's future — to chance or last-minute scrambling.

The goals you want to accomplish — maximizing after-tax proceeds, safeguarding your legacy, protecting your family, achieving personal fulfillment — are within reach. The question is whether you can accomplish them alone or whether you need a carefully curated team of experts. For almost every ultra-affluent founder and business owner, the answer is clear: Hire the right team, and start early.

Chapter 41: Deferred Compensation, Executive Comp Plans, and Stock Options

Executive compensation is a sophisticated mosaic of base salary, annual bonuses, deferred compensation, stock options, and long-term incentive plans. The numbers may appear impressive on paper, but complexity often obscures clarity. Future wealth may seem within reach, yet the details create a fog. Managing executive compensation is not simply about maximizing a payout; it is about orchestrating a multi-dimensional strategy that reduces risk, minimizes taxes, and preserves wealth.

Deferred compensation plans are often the first critical element to master. Nonqualified Deferred Compensation (NQDC) plans offer the ability to defer a portion of income, typically until retirement, allowing deferred amounts to grow without immediate taxation. While tax deferral is attractive, the reality is that NQDC plans are unsecured promises from the employer. In the event of bankruptcy, deferred assets become no more than unsecured claims. A high-level executive who deferred $1 million annually for five years faced exactly this fate—standing in line with creditors after the company collapsed, forfeiting years of deferred earnings. The pros are clear: tax deferral and income smoothing. The cons: credit risk and liquidity constraints. A prudent strategy involves evaluating the financial health of the employer and balancing deferred amounts with other, more secure retirement savings vehicles.

Stock options, whether Incentive Stock Options (ISOs) or Non-Qualified Stock Options (NSOs), form another major pillar. ISOs allow for favorable tax treatment if holding periods are met, qualifying gains for long-term capital gains rates rather than ordinary income rates. However, exercising ISOs can unexpectedly trigger Alternative Minimum Tax (AMT) liabilities. NSOs, on the other hand, are taxed as ordinary income upon exercise. Managing the exercise of options requires a carefully staged strategy—one that balances AMT exposure with market performance, minimizing tax spikes while capitalizing on growth. A staggered, multi-year exercise plan can protect against the market and regulatory surprises that erode wealth.

Restricted Stock Units (RSUs) appear straightforward but hide complexity beneath their surface. RSUs vest over time and are taxed as ordinary income when they do, regardless of whether shares are sold. Without a liquidity strategy in place, executives can find themselves with a hefty tax bill but no available cash. A CFO watched company stock double in a year, only to vest, owe hundreds of thousands in taxes, and experience a crushing 40% market correction before selling. Preparing for tax liabilities before vesting events through strategic selling plans is essential to preserving wealth during market downturns.

Bonuses tied to long-term performance metrics introduce another layer of complexity. Cash bonuses are simple—taxed as ordinary income—but equity-based bonuses, phantom stock, and performance shares invoke nuances in taxation and timing. Deferred compensation rules, especially Section 409A, must be navigated carefully to avoid punitive tax penalties. Missteps in structuring or electing bonus deferrals can be devastating. Early collaboration with a seasoned tax advisor ensures compliance and maximizes outcomes.

Golden parachutes—lucrative payouts triggered by change-of-control events—represent both security and risk. While they provide a financial cushion in the event of an acquisition or merger, large payouts exceeding IRS thresholds invite steep excise taxes under Section 280G. Planning ahead with 280G analyses and structuring "gross-up" provisions or alternative arrangements protects against unexpected tax burdens while preserving the benefits of these packages.

Supplemental Executive Retirement Plans (SERPs) offer additional retirement income but often carry the same credit risks as other unfunded deferred plans. Balancing SERPs with more secure and diversified retirement strategies mitigates the risk of overexposure to a single employer's fortunes.

Concentration risk is a persistent threat for executives, many of whom accumulate an outsized portion of their wealth in their employer\u2019s stock. Loyalty to the company is commendable but financially dangerous. Discipline is critical: using 10b5-1 trading plans allows for systematic, pre-arranged selling that complies with insider trading regulations while reducing single-stock risk.

Timing is another dimension often overlooked. The coordination of deferred comp distributions, stock option exercises, and RSU vesting with broader life and tax planning goals cannot be left to chance. Spreading income events across multiple tax years rather than bunching them in one can mean the difference between an optimized tax outcome and an unnecessarily inflated tax bill. One COO successfully structured distributions over a decade, reducing his tax bracket and preserving liquidity well into retirement.

Charitable giving strategies provide yet another lever. Gifting appreciated employer stock to Donor-Advised Funds (DAFs) or private foundations not only fulfills philanthropic goals but also eliminates capital gains taxes and yields immediate deductions. High-income years, particularly during liquidity events or windfalls, are ideal times to integrate philanthropy into the financial strategy.

At this level, executive compensation planning cannot be a do-it-yourself endeavor. Mistakes carry extraordinary costs—lost wealth, penalties, and excess taxation. The necessary foundation is a team: a financial advisor with deep executive comp expertise, a tax strategist adept at navigating complex structures, and an estate attorney who can ensure long-term preservation. The goal transcends mere accumulation; it is about sustainable wealth that enables personal freedom, generational legacy, and purposeful living.

The call to action is precise: Get organized. Get educated. Get the right help. Executive compensation, with all its moving parts, represents both opportunity and risk. Mastery here lays the foundation for mastering wealth at large.

The goals—financial independence, tax efficiency, legacy building, and personal freedom—are well within reach. Whether these outcomes can be achieved independently or require the expertise of seasoned advisors is a pivotal decision. For most ultra-affluent executives, the prudent course is clear: build a trusted team and proceed with deliberate, structured precision.

Chapter 42: Exit Planning: IPO, M&A, SPACs, and Strategic Business Sales

Exit planning is one of the most critical, yet most misunderstood, stages of building wealth. For ultra-high-net-worth individuals who have invested years, if not decades, in growing a business, the exit is not simply a transaction—it is the culmination of vision, strategy, and perseverance. Choosing the right exit path—whether through an IPO, M&A transaction, SPAC merger, or strategic sale—requires a nuanced understanding of each route's risks, benefits, and long-term implications.

An Initial Public Offering (IPO) is often seen as the crown jewel of exits. It offers liquidity, prestige, and the potential for substantial valuation. Yet the IPO journey is grueling. Regulatory requirements, including detailed financial disclosures, SEC scrutiny, and Sarbanes-Oxley compliance, create significant burdens. Moreover, post-IPO executives must answer to a board and shareholders, shifting from entrepreneurial autonomy to public company rigor. Pros: Access to public capital markets, increased valuation, enhanced brand visibility. Cons: Loss of control, regulatory burden, stock price volatility. Action Step: Engage an experienced IPO advisory team — investment bankers, legal counsel, auditors — at least 18-24 months in advance to assess readiness and navigate pre-IPO grooming.

Mergers and acquisitions (M&A) offer another compelling path. In a sale to a strategic or financial buyer, the transaction may involve a premium on valuation without the compliance costs of going public. Strategic buyers seek synergies, while private equity firms look for growth and exit potential.

However, M&A negotiations are intense. Due diligence is invasive. Cultural alignment can be overlooked in favor of economics, sometimes leading to integration challenges post-sale. Real-Life Scenario: A tech founder sold to a strategic competitor at a significant premium, only to watch the culture he built slowly dissolve under new management. Pros: Immediate liquidity, reduced compliance, strategic partnerships. Cons: Potential cultural erosion, complex deal terms, earn-outs tied to performance. Action Step: Conduct a readiness assessment and consider a "sell-side" quality of earnings report to preempt buyer concerns and streamline the process.

Special Purpose Acquisition Companies (SPACs) have surged in popularity. They offer a faster, less cumbersome route to public markets. A SPAC raises capital through an IPO and then merges with a private company, essentially taking it public without the traditional IPO rigors. However, SPAC transactions can involve significant dilution for original owners and heightened scrutiny from both the SEC and investors in the wake of recent regulatory tightening. Pros: Speed to market, negotiated valuations. Cons: Dilution risk, post-merger performance pressures. Action Step: If considering a SPAC, engage advisors who specialize in these transactions to navigate the evolving regulatory landscape and mitigate dilution risk.

Strategic business sales, often to private entities or family offices, offer a more bespoke exit option. These transactions can be tailored to meet personal goals—retaining some ownership, ensuring legacy preservation, or safeguarding employees' futures. Negotiations are more private, timelines more flexible. Yet strategic sales may fetch lower multiples compared to frothy public market valuations. Real-Life Scenario: A manufacturing entrepreneur sold a majority stake to a family office, maintaining minority ownership and board influence. This structure allowed him to de-risk while continuing to shape the company's future. Pros: Customization, privacy, ongoing involvement. Cons: Lower valuations, potential for slower liquidity. Action Step: Define clear personal and financial goals upfront to identify buyers whose vision aligns with yours.

Beyond selecting the exit path, timing is paramount. Market conditions, interest rates, geopolitical stability—all influence deal valuations and investor appetite. Internal readiness is equally critical: audited financials, clean cap tables, clear intellectual property ownership, and management depth signal to buyers or investors that a company is truly "exit-ready." Action Step: Conduct a comprehensive readiness audit two to three years prior to the target exit date.

Tax planning cannot be overstated. Different exit routes carry distinct tax consequences. An IPO triggers capital gains on the sale of shares; M&A deals can involve cash, stock, or a mix, each with different tax treatments. SPACs may offer tax deferral opportunities if structured properly. Trust planning before the liquidity event can shift future appreciation out of the taxable estate. Real-Life Scenario: A founder who pre-funded Grantor Retained Annuity Trusts (GRATs) before selling shares in a SPAC transaction saved tens of millions in estate taxes. Action Step: Begin tax planning years in advance, leveraging strategies like QSBS exclusions, GRATs, SLATs, and philanthropic structures to optimize outcomes.

Estate planning must be integrated. Post-exit wealth can balloon rapidly, and without careful planning, estate taxes could claim 40% or more upon death. Structures such as dynasty trusts, family limited partnerships (FLPs), and charitable lead trusts (CLTs) protect and direct wealth efficiently. Pros: Generational wealth transfer, asset protection, charitable legacy. Cons: Complexity, upfront legal and administrative costs. Action Step: Coordinate estate planning strategies alongside exit negotiations to align timing and asset valuations.

Post-exit life deserves thoughtful preparation. Many business owners find their identity intertwined with their company. A sudden exit, even a lucrative one, can leave a void. Investing time in defining post-exit purpose—philanthropy, new ventures, family engagement—can ease the psychological transition. Real-Life Scenario: After exiting via an M&A transaction, a healthcare entrepreneur shifted focus to venture philanthropy, channeling energy and expertise into funding innovative health startups.

Liquidity management post-exit is another key pillar. Windfalls require disciplined investment strategies to avoid erosion through taxes, market volatility, and lifestyle inflation. Action Step: Partner with a wealth manager adept at stewarding large liquidity events to design an investment policy statement, create tax-efficient portfolios, and manage risk.

Exit planning is not a one-size-fits-all formula. Each route—IPO, M&A, SPAC, or strategic sale—has distinct dynamics. Each founder or business owner has unique personal, financial, and legacy goals. The most successful exits are not accidents; they are engineered through deliberate, proactive planning.

The call to action is clear: start early, engage the right advisors, and plan across every dimension—legal, financial, tax, estate, and personal. Maximizing the value of an exit while preserving personal peace and legacy requires sophistication, foresight, and expertise.

The goals are significant: financial freedom, family security, philanthropy, new ventures, legacy creation. Achieving them is possible, but not without guidance. Assess whether these complex undertakings can be navigated alone or whether a team of elite advisors is necessary to execute flawlessly. For most ultra-affluent entrepreneurs and business owners, surrounding themselves with seasoned experts is the smartest investment they will ever make.

Chapter 43: 1042 Rollovers: Selling C-Corp Stock to ESOPs

A 1042 rollover represents one of the most elegant yet underutilized strategies available to ultra-affluent business owners holding C-Corporation stock. When the time comes to consider an exit strategy, selling to an Employee Stock Ownership Plan (ESOP) can achieve several critical objectives simultaneously: liquidity, legacy preservation, employee reward, and substantial tax deferral. Yet, despite its benefits, the 1042 rollover requires a level of precision and forethought that only the most discerning and well-advised sellers can appreciate and execute.

At its core, the 1042 rollover allows a C-Corp shareholder to sell their shares to an ESOP and defer capital gains taxes indefinitely, provided they reinvest the proceeds into Qualified Replacement Property (QRP) within a 12-month window. Qualified Replacement Property typically includes domestic operating company stocks and bonds, specifically designed to encourage reinvestment into the broader U.S. economy. Unlike traditional sales to third parties, where gains are taxed immediately, this deferral can preserve and enhance wealth in ways few other transactions allow.

The benefits are compelling. First and foremost is the tax deferral itself. By reinvesting into QRP, the capital gains tax—often a seven-figure liability—is postponed indefinitely. For many ultra-high-net-worth individuals, the ability to keep that capital compounding without an immediate tax haircut can translate into millions in preserved wealth. Second, selling to an ESOP fosters legacy. Employees become owners.

The culture and ethos built over decades are more likely to endure under employee ownership than under a private equity buyer or strategic acquirer. Finally, ESOP transactions can often be structured more flexibly than third-party sales, giving the seller influence over timing, transition, and leadership succession.

However, 1042 rollovers are not without complexity or risk. The universe of eligible QRP investments is narrow and nuanced. The IRS has strict guidelines, and a misstep can disqualify the entire deferral. The shares sold to the ESOP must be common stock with the highest voting and dividend rights, and the ESOP must own at least 30% of the company's outstanding stock post-transaction. Moreover, the seller must have held the stock for at least three years. Failure to meet any of these technical requirements jeopardizes the entire tax strategy. Action Step: Engage a team of specialists well-versed in ESOP structuring, 1042 rollovers, and QRP portfolio design—an interdisciplinary team including tax advisors, legal counsel, and investment specialists.

There are real-life scenarios that illuminate both the potential and the pitfalls. Consider an industrial services company owned by a second-generation founder. A sale to private equity would have netted a high valuation but dismantled the company's culture and resulted in layoffs. Instead, the founder sold 70% of the company to an ESOP, deferred nearly $50 million in capital gains taxes, and reinvested the proceeds into a laddered portfolio of corporate bonds and blue-chip stocks structured as QRP. Today, the founder enjoys significant cash flow from the bond interest and dividends, the employees own the company, and the founder's wealth continues to grow tax-deferred.

Conversely, another entrepreneur attempted a 1042 rollover but selected an investment advisor unfamiliar with QRP requirements. Several investments were later deemed non-compliant. When the IRS audited the transaction, the entire gain became immediately taxable, resulting in an unanticipated tax bill and penalties. The lesson: precision and expertise are non-negotiable in executing this strategy.

Liquidity considerations also play a role. QRP investments are not as liquid as cash, and certain investments may carry higher risks or reduced marketability. A well-constructed QRP portfolio must balance income generation, preservation of principal, and liquidity needs, tailored to the seller's future lifestyle and estate planning goals.

Additionally, estate planning must be integrated into the 1042 strategy. The QRP portfolio will eventually form a significant part of the seller's estate. Without proper planning, heirs could inherit highly appreciated assets with no step-up in basis, resulting in a sizeable future tax liability. Charitable remainder trusts (CRTs), grantor retained annuity trusts (GRATs), and other advanced strategies can be layered to mitigate these issues and further enhance legacy goals.

Beyond financial mechanics, there is the human element. Selling to an ESOP aligns the financial interests of employees with the success of the company. It creates an ownership culture that can drive productivity, loyalty, and long-term company health. For business owners who view their companies as more than just financial assets—as communities of people and ideas—an ESOP sale can be the most emotionally satisfying exit available.

Yet, timing matters. Market conditions, interest rates, and company performance influence the valuation and feasibility of an ESOP transaction. ESOPs are financed through debt, and high-interest environments can complicate financing structures. Early planning, ideally beginning three to five years before an anticipated exit, provides the runway necessary to optimize conditions and groom the company for sale.

A 1042 rollover, executed flawlessly, is not merely a tax strategy. It is a wealth preservation strategy, a legacy strategy, and a values strategy. It aligns the seller's financial goals with their human and societal goals in a way that few other exit paths can achieve.

The call to action is unmistakable: If holding C-Corp stock in a thriving company, take the time now to evaluate whether a 1042 rollover ESOP sale aligns with broader wealth, legacy, and life goals. Assemble a team—specialized attorneys, tax advisors, investment experts, and ESOP consultants. Precision is essential. Planning is non-negotiable. The rewards for executing well are measured not just in dollars saved but in lives touched and legacies preserved.

The goals are ambitious: tax efficiency, wealth preservation, legacy fulfillment, and human impact. They are achievable. But they demand sophistication, strategy, and elite advisory support. For most ultra-affluent owners, the path forward is clear: Surround yourself with expertise and engineer an exit that honors both wealth and purpose.

Chapter 44: Post-Liquidity Planning: Managing the Influx of Capital

The closing of a major liquidity event—the sale of a business, an IPO, a strategic acquisition—marks a significant milestone. But in many ways, it is just the beginning. For the ultra-affluent, managing a sudden influx of capital is a complex, nuanced endeavor that demands more than traditional wealth management. The stakes are higher, the tools more sophisticated, and the consequences of missteps more profound. Post-liquidity planning is not about reacting to wealth; it is about orchestrating it deliberately, with precision, vision, and discipline.

The first principle of post-liquidity planning is intentionality. Capital at this scale needs a purpose. Without clarity of intent, money has a way of dissipating — not necessarily through extravagance, but through drift. Defining the "why" behind the wealth — be it legacy, philanthropy, entrepreneurial reinvention, or personal freedom — is the bedrock upon which the entire strategy must be built. Action Step: Begin with a personal wealth mission statement, crafted carefully to anchor every subsequent financial decision.

Liquidity management itself is the first technical pillar. A sudden windfall often tempts immediate allocation, but wisdom counsels patience. Capital needs to be segmented into liquidity tiers: immediate cash needs, short-term reserves, and long-term investment capital. The immediate post-liquidity phase should focus on "parking" funds in ultra-safe, highly liquid vehicles — think Treasury bills, money market funds, or insured cash sweep accounts. This buys time to deliberate and design the long-term strategy without feeling rushed. Real-Life Scenario: An entrepreneur who sold a company for $200 million parked proceeds in a mix of Treasury ladders and high-yield savings accounts for six months, resisting the urge to rush into investments, and emerged with a clear, refined strategy that preserved both wealth and peace of mind.

Asset allocation is the next frontier. Traditional 60/40 portfolios are insufficient at the ultra-affluent level. Wealth of this magnitude demands sophisticated diversification across public equities, fixed income, private equity, venture capital, real estate, hedge funds, and direct investments. Strategic allocations must reflect both return aspirations and risk tolerances, rebalanced continually to adjust for market conditions and personal objectives. Pros: Diversification across multiple risk dimensions. Cons: Complexity, illiquidity in private markets. Action Step: Engage in the development of a customized Investment Policy Statement (IPS) — a living document guiding all portfolio management decisions.

Tax optimization is inseparable from investment strategy. Post-liquidity wealth faces multiple layers of taxation: income tax, capital gains tax, estate tax, even generation-skipping transfer taxes. Tactics such as asset location optimization, tax-loss harvesting, Qualified Opportunity Zone (QOZ) investments, and charitable planning (Donor-Advised Funds, private foundations, Charitable Lead Trusts) must be integrated seamlessly. Real-Life Scenario: A founder leveraged a QOZ investment to shelter $10 million of capital gains, marrying investment objectives with tax efficiency. Action Step: Assemble a tax planning team that collaborates with investment managers and estate planners to ensure no opportunity for mitigation is overlooked.

Risk management also evolves post-liquidity. Increased wealth brings heightened visibility, and with it, heightened risk. Umbrella insurance, directors and officers (D&O) coverage, private aviation insurance, and even kidnap and ransom insurance must be considered. Asset protection strategies — such as irrevocable trusts, family limited partnerships (FLPs), and offshore entities where appropriate — should be deployed thoughtfully.

Pros: Preservation of wealth against lawsuits and unforeseen liabilities. Cons: Cost, administrative complexity. Action Step: Conduct a comprehensive risk audit post-liquidity to identify vulnerabilities and implement protective structures.

Estate planning becomes an entirely different conversation. Federal estate taxes can confiscate up to 40% of a large estate without diligent planning. Structures like dynasty trusts, Spousal Lifetime Access Trusts (SLATs), Grantor Retained Annuity Trusts (GRATs), and Generation-Skipping Trusts (GSTs) can protect and preserve wealth across multiple generations. Real-Life Scenario: A family office structured a series of irrevocable trusts that successfully moved $75 million out of the taxable estate within five years, ensuring generational continuity and philanthropic endowments. Action Step: Begin estate planning immediately post-liquidity; leverage valuation discounts and exemptions before regulatory environments change.

Philanthropy often becomes a core focus after liquidity. Many ultra-affluent individuals view wealth not just as a personal asset but as a tool for broader societal impact. Structured giving vehicles — private foundations, Donor-Advised Funds, charitable trusts — can magnify the impact of philanthropy while also providing meaningful tax benefits. The most successful philanthropists approach giving with the same strategic rigor as they did their business endeavors. Action Step: Define a philanthropic mission and engage with advisors to build a structure that reflects both passion and prudence.

Lifestyle planning is an often-overlooked dimension. Post-liquidity wealth enables lifestyle expansion, but absent clear boundaries, lifestyle creep can erode even substantial fortunes over time. Private aviation, multiple residences, yachts — all come with carrying costs and complexities. Budgeting at the ultra-affluent level requires a different approach: a strategic allocation of capital to lifestyle assets that balances enjoyment with sustainability. Pros: Enhanced quality of life. Cons: Asset-heavy lifestyles can become financial and administrative burdens. Action Step: Develop a "lifestyle allocation" plan that sets clear boundaries on spending versus investing.

Family governance is crucial. Wealth without governance often leads to conflict, erosion, and entitlement in future generations. Establishing family councils, mission statements, education programs, and succession plans fosters cohesion and stewardship. Real-Life Scenario: A multigenerational family with a $500 million fortune instituted a formal family governance charter, quarterly family meetings, and a rising generation education program — sustaining wealth and unity for over three generations. Action Step: Treat family governance with the same seriousness and structure as corporate governance.

Post-liquidity planning is not a one-time event; it is an ongoing discipline. Markets shift. Laws evolve. Family dynamics change. The most successful ultra-affluent individuals treat their wealth like a dynamic enterprise, subject to continual review, adjustment, and refinement.

The call to action is unequivocal: Do not squander the once-in-a-lifetime opportunity that liquidity provides. Engage intentionally. Assemble an elite advisory team. Engineer a strategy that preserves wealth, enhances legacy, and aligns with purpose.

The goals are ambitious: financial security, generational continuity, meaningful impact, personal fulfillment. They are achievable — but only through deliberate, structured, sophisticated planning. For those who have achieved liquidity at scale, the journey has just begun. Surround yourself with the best minds, and approach this new phase with the vision, discipline, and rigor that built the fortune in the first place.

Part VII: Lifestyle and Global Legacy Enhancements

Part VII: Lifestyle and Global Legacy Enhancements explores how the ultra-affluent can elevate wealth beyond personal success, using it as a tool for lifestyle enrichment, global impact, and multigenerational influence. This section moves beyond traditional wealth management, diving into how to curate a life of purpose, sophistication, and significance on a global stage.

Topics include the strategic acquisition and management of luxury assets such as private aviation, art collections, and real estate across continents. It addresses building a lifestyle that balances indulgence with intention, ensuring that wealth enhances life rather than complicates it.

We further explore creating a global legacy — from international philanthropy and establishing family foundations to cross-border estate planning and global citizenship strategies. Special emphasis is placed on governance structures that sustain wealth, values, and influence across multiple generations and geographies.

The aim is clear: to move from wealth accumulation to wealth orchestration, crafting a life and legacy that transcend borders and endure for centuries. The focus is on engineering a life of impact, sophistication, and enduring meaning.

Chapter 45: Residency and Citizenship by Investment (Golden Visas, Second Passports)

Residency and citizenship by investment have become indispensable tools for the ultra-affluent seeking flexibility, security, and global mobility. Wealth has always opened doors, but today, in an increasingly complex geopolitical landscape, second passports and golden visas are more than conveniences—they are strategic assets. They offer not only personal freedom but also expanded opportunities for business, taxation, and legacy planning.

At the core, citizenship by investment (CBI) and residency by investment (RBI) programs allow individuals to acquire legal residency or citizenship in a foreign country by making qualifying investments—typically in real estate, government bonds, business development funds, or direct contributions to national development projects. These programs are available in a growing list of countries, each offering unique benefits and requirements. For the discerning ultra-high-net-worth individual, these programs must be approached not as transactions but as elements of a broader life and legacy strategy.

Golden visas, which grant residency rather than citizenship, offer the advantage of relatively quick access to the benefits of a new country—think education, healthcare, business opportunities, and the right to reside—without renouncing existing citizenships or dramatically altering tax obligations. Portugal's Golden Visa, for example, allows for minimal physical presence while paving the way toward citizenship after five years. Real-Life Scenario: A tech entrepreneur from California secured a Portuguese Golden Visa through a €500,000 real estate investment, gaining access to the EU while diversifying personal and business options without significant lifestyle disruption.

Second passports, on the other hand, offer deeper, sovereign benefits. Citizenship in countries like Malta, St. Kitts and Nevis, or Dominica can provide visa-free access to over 140 countries, asset protection advantages, and strategic relocation options in the event of political or economic instability at home. Pros: enhanced travel freedom, redundancy in personal security, potential tax optimization. Cons: substantial upfront costs, stringent due diligence, and varying degrees of reputational scrutiny.

Not all programs are created equal. Caribbean nations tend to offer the fastest and most affordable citizenship-by-investment options, with processing times as short as 3-6 months and investments starting around $100,000 to $150,000. European options, such as Malta's Individual Investor Program, are more expensive but carry the cachet of EU citizenship, offering freedom of movement throughout the Schengen Zone and broader global respectability.

Understanding the tax implications is essential. While some jurisdictions offer citizenship with no change in global tax obligations, others, particularly if residence is established, may impose tax liabilities. Portugal's Non-Habitual Resident (NHR) program, for example, provides generous tax breaks for the first ten years of residence, making it a strategic choice for those looking to reduce tax exposure. Action Step: Conduct a comprehensive cross-border tax analysis before acquiring new residency or citizenship status.

Residency and citizenship planning also plays a vital role in estate and legacy strategies. Certain jurisdictions provide more favorable laws for wealth transfer, asset protection, and succession planning. Real-Life Scenario: A family office diversified residency and citizenship holdings across three jurisdictions—Malta, the United States, and New Zealand—allowing them to optimize cross-border estate strategies, reduce geopolitical risk, and prepare the next generation for global citizenship.

It is equally critical to align investment choices with broader financial goals. For instance, investing in real estate for a golden visa should not only meet the minimum investment threshold but also serve as a sound financial investment. The last thing any ultra-affluent individual should want is a "passport property" that depreciates or becomes illiquid. Action Step: Vet investment options with the same rigor as any major real estate or private equity investment, considering yield, market trends, and exit strategies.

The reputational element cannot be ignored. Some programs, especially those in smaller Caribbean nations, have been scrutinized for perceived lax due diligence. High-profile individuals must weigh the potential reputational risks of associating with certain programs. European programs, although more expensive, often conduct extensive vetting, providing a measure of credibility. Action Step: Engage legal advisors specializing in CBI and RBI programs to ensure a clean, defensible acquisition process.

Beyond the technical and financial dimensions, there is a psychological component to global mobility. A second passport or foreign residency provides not just logistical benefits but peace of mind. It is an insurance policy against the unexpected—political upheaval, currency devaluation, tax regime changes. For families, it provides expanded educational and employment opportunities across borders, creating a truly global footprint.

However, it must be noted that some countries are tightening or even suspending their CBI and RBI programs under external pressure, often from the European Union or global regulatory bodies. Programs that were available five years ago may no longer exist, or their terms may have evolved significantly. Early action, based on informed, strategic analysis, is key.

Post-acquisition planning is crucial. Simply holding a second passport or residency permit is not enough; the benefits must be actively managed. Renewal requirements, physical presence mandates, tax filings, and continued compliance must be monitored diligently. Real-Life Scenario: An investor neglected to meet the minimum stay requirements under his golden visa, resulting in loss of residency rights and the need to reapply under stricter conditions.

Residency and citizenship by investment strategies are not just about personal security; they are about legacy. They are about handing down not just wealth, but options, resilience, and freedom to the next generation. They allow families to live, work, and invest globally, unhindered by the confines of a single jurisdiction.

The call to action is direct: View global mobility as an essential pillar of your wealth architecture. Approach it with the same level of diligence, rigor, and strategic foresight that governs all other aspects of your wealth.

The goals—enhanced freedom, global opportunity, strategic diversification, and intergenerational resilience—are attainable. But they demand a deliberate, expertly navigated process. For the ultra-affluent individual, investing in global mobility is no longer a luxury; it is a prudent, forward-looking necessity.

Chapter 46: Global Mobility and International Tax Optimization

Global mobility and international tax optimization are no longer luxuries reserved for a select few; they are imperatives for the ultra-affluent navigating an increasingly interconnected and regulatory-heavy world. Wealth at scale brings privilege, but it also brings scrutiny, complexity, and vulnerability. The ability to live, invest, and operate across borders must be matched with intelligent structuring to ensure that mobility is not only strategic but also tax-efficient.

At its essence, global mobility is about optionality—the ability to choose where to live, where to invest, where to educate children, and where to safeguard wealth. International tax optimization is about ensuring that these choices do not lead to unnecessary erosion of capital through avoidable taxation. These two concepts must work hand-in-hand; mobility without tax optimization can result in punitive tax exposure, while tax optimization without mobility can leave wealth vulnerable to geopolitical and economic shocks.

Residency and domicile are foundational concepts. Residency is where an individual lives for tax purposes; domicile is where an individual is legally tied, often by birth or long-term association. These definitions vary by country and can dramatically affect tax liability. For example, the United States taxes citizens on worldwide income regardless of residence, while countries like Portugal or Monaco offer favorable tax regimes to residents without imposing taxes on foreign income. Action Step: Conduct a residency and domicile audit to understand current exposures and identify jurisdictions that align better with lifestyle and tax objectives.

Real-life examples illustrate the strategic advantage of proper structuring. A British entrepreneur relocated to Monaco, reducing his tax exposure significantly while maintaining proximity to his European investments. A Silicon Valley executive obtained residency in Portugal under the Non-Habitual Resident (NHR) program, enjoying ten years of substantial tax reductions. Each strategy was tailored to personal goals—proximity, lifestyle, business opportunities—and tax efficiency.

The use of trusts and holding companies also plays a pivotal role. Trusts in jurisdictions like the Cayman Islands, the British Virgin Islands, or Guernsey can provide confidentiality, asset protection, and tax optimization. Similarly, international holding companies structured in places like Singapore, Luxembourg, or the Netherlands can facilitate efficient management of global investments and intellectual property. Pros: Asset protection, tax deferral, confidentiality. Cons: Complexity, costs of maintenance, and increasing regulatory scrutiny under global initiatives like the Common Reporting Standard (CRS). Action Step: Engage cross-border legal and tax advisors to design structures that balance protection, compliance, and tax efficiency.

Citizenship by investment and golden visa programs, discussed earlier, are not just about passports—they are essential tools in the mobility-tax optimization nexus. Strategic acquisition of a second passport can open doors to more favorable tax jurisdictions and provide leverage against shifting political climates. Real-Life Scenario: A family office with U.S. citizenship sought St. Kitts and Nevis citizenship for family members to facilitate a structured expatriation, ultimately reducing global tax obligations while maintaining travel flexibility.

Investment location matters profoundly. Different countries tax investment income, capital gains, and dividends differently. A portfolio heavily weighted toward U.S. equities can generate significant tax drag for non-resident investors due to withholding taxes, while investments routed through tax treaty-friendly jurisdictions can mitigate this exposure. Action

Step: Conduct an international investment audit to realign portfolios for optimal after-tax returns based on residency and citizenship status.

Tax treaties are another vital instrument. Bilateral tax treaties between countries can reduce or eliminate double taxation on income, dividends, interest, and royalties. They can also provide clarity on residency status and tax obligations. However, treaties must be applied meticulously—missteps can trigger audits, penalties, and loss of treaty benefits. Action Step: Work with international tax counsel to map applicable tax treaties and ensure all filings and residency tests are satisfied.

Global mobility also requires vigilance around exit taxes. Countries like the United States impose exit taxes on individuals renouncing citizenship or long-term residency, taxing unrealized gains as if assets were sold at the time of exit. Proactive planning—such as gifting assets to trusts, revaluing interests, or restructuring ownership—can reduce or defer these burdens. Real-Life Scenario: A tech founder structured a pre-expatriation gifting program to minimize exit tax liabilities, saving tens of millions in hypothetical tax costs.

Lifestyle choices must align with tax planning. Where days are spent—tracked meticulously through passport stamps, credit card receipts, mobile phone records—can trigger tax residency under "days tests." Many countries consider 183 days the threshold for tax residency, but others, like Spain, use economic center-of-interest tests. Action Step: Maintain detailed travel logs and work with advisors to ensure that residency tests are not inadvertently triggered.

Compliance is paramount. In the wake of FATCA, CRS, and other international initiatives, transparency is the new normal. Asset ownership, banking relationships, and income streams must be disclosed accurately and timely. The days of anonymous offshore accounts are gone; sophisticated strategies focus on legitimate, fully compliant structures. Action Step: Conduct a compliance audit to ensure all reporting obligations—FATCA, CRS, FBAR, Form 8938—are being met.

Philanthropy can also serve as a strategic lever in global tax optimization. Structured charitable giving through foundations, donor-advised funds, or charitable trusts can provide significant tax deductions while fulfilling personal missions. International giving, however, requires careful navigation of both home-country and recipient-country tax laws. Action Step: Incorporate philanthropy into the overall tax and mobility plan to maximize impact and minimize tax liabilities.

Family considerations must not be overlooked. Wealth planning for future generations must anticipate cross-border complexities. Different jurisdictions have varying inheritance tax laws, forced heirship rules, and probate requirements. Structuring wealth transfers through multi-jurisdictional trusts or family holding companies ensures smoother transitions and preserves capital. Real-Life Scenario: An ultra-affluent family established a Singapore-based private trust company to manage global assets and succession planning for three generations, achieving tax efficiency and continuity across multiple countries.

Ultimately, global mobility and international tax optimization are not one-time projects; they are ongoing disciplines requiring continuous adjustment as laws, circumstances, and goals evolve. The ultra-affluent who thrive globally do so not because they chase the lowest tax rates, but because they craft a life that blends opportunity, security, and efficiency across borders.

The call to action is clear: Approach global mobility and tax optimization not as defensive maneuvers, but as strategic pillars of wealth management. Plan deliberately. Act compliantly. Operate globally.

The goals—global freedom, tax efficiency, asset protection, multigenerational security—are within reach. But they require a carefully orchestrated plan, led by elite advisors with cross-border expertise. For those who have achieved substantial wealth, the mandate is unmistakable: invest in global infrastructure as meticulously as in financial markets, and elevate your legacy to one that transcends borders.

Chapter 47: Luxury Asset Management: Yachts, Jets, and Rare Collections

Luxury assets—yachts, jets, and rare collections—are not merely symbols of success. For the ultra-affluent, they represent a blend of lifestyle enhancement, investment diversification, and legacy building. Yet, without strategic management, these assets can become liabilities, draining capital and creating unnecessary complexity. Managing luxury assets requires the same level of discipline, precision, and foresight that governs core investment portfolios.

Yachts are often the first indulgence. A superyacht offers privacy, exclusivity, and the ability to explore the world on one's own terms. But yachts are complex financial instruments. Beyond the initial acquisition cost—which can range from tens to hundreds of millions—annual operating costs typically run between 10-15% of the yacht's value. Crewing, maintenance, docking, insurance, and regulatory compliance add layers of management complexity. Ownership structures must also be carefully designed—whether through offshore companies or yacht ownership trusts—to optimize for liability protection and tax efficiency. Real-Life Scenario: A family office structured its yacht ownership through a Maltese company, optimizing VAT exposure on European charters while enhancing asset protection. Action Step: Engage a maritime attorney and a yacht management firm to design ownership structures and manage day-to-day operations.

Private jets offer another level of autonomy and efficiency. Time, after all, is the ultimate luxury. A jet eliminates the constraints of commercial travel and enhances security and privacy. Yet, jets come with significant costs: acquisition, crew salaries, maintenance, hangar fees, insurance, and regulatory compliance with aviation authorities. Ownership models vary—full ownership, fractional ownership, or jet cards—each with trade-offs. Full ownership provides maximum flexibility but also maximum cost and responsibility. Fractional ownership reduces the burden but can introduce scheduling conflicts and restrictions. Pros: Time efficiency, privacy, security. Cons: High fixed and variable costs, regulatory complexity. Action Step: Conduct a detailed usage analysis and cost-benefit study to determine the optimal ownership structure, factoring in tax treatment of depreciation and deductions where applicable.

Rare collections—fine art, vintage automobiles, rare wines, collectible watches—serve both as passion projects and alternative investments. Properly curated, they can yield substantial returns while enhancing personal lifestyle. Yet, rare collections require meticulous management: provenance verification, insurance, storage, maintenance, and liquidity planning. The art world, for example, is rife with authenticity issues, and high-value collections are increasingly targets for theft and fraud. Real-Life Scenario: An investor's art collection, valued at $50 million, was restructured into a private foundation, providing tax benefits and facilitating succession planning. Action Step: Partner with specialists in valuation, authentication, and insurance, and consider structuring collections within legal entities to optimize tax and estate outcomes.

Taxation looms large over luxury assets. Many jurisdictions impose VAT or sales taxes on yacht and jet purchases. Annual property taxes, use taxes, and import duties can also apply. Savvy owners employ jurisdictional planning—registering yachts in favorable flag states like the Cayman Islands or jets under entities in Delaware or the Isle of Man—to mitigate these exposures. Action Step: Conduct a tax jurisdiction analysis before acquisition to optimize for operational and tax efficiency.

Asset protection must also be front of mind. Luxury assets are high-visibility targets in litigation. Structuring ownership through LLCs, trusts, or offshore entities can shield personal wealth from potential claims. However, courts and regulators scrutinize these structures, making compliance and substance—real management and decision-making—essential. Action Step: Design ownership structures that provide both legal protection and operational legitimacy.

Insurance is non-negotiable. High-value assets demand specialized coverage: blue-water insurance for yachts, aviation insurance for jets, fine art policies for collections. Standard homeowner policies are inadequate. Specialized brokers understand the nuances—such as coverage for international waters or for art in transit—and can tailor policies to the unique risk profile of each asset. Action Step: Conduct a comprehensive insurance review to ensure adequate coverage tailored to asset type and usage.

Liquidity planning is crucial. Luxury assets are often illiquid. Yachts and jets can take months or years to sell, often at a discount to asking price. Rare collections, while sometimes appreciating, can suffer from thin markets. Owners must plan for liquidity events—sales, loans against asset value, or structured gifting. Real-Life Scenario: A collector utilized a line of credit secured against a fine art collection to access liquidity without triggering a taxable sale. Action Step: Engage with private banks and specialty lenders to explore liquidity options secured by luxury assets.

Estate planning cannot be neglected. Succession of luxury assets can become contentious if not handled properly. Yachts, jets, and collections often carry sentimental value, but without clear instructions, they can become divisive among heirs. Structuring assets in trusts or LLCs, with clear succession directives, ensures smooth transitions. Action Step: Integrate luxury asset holdings into broader estate planning to prevent future disputes and preserve value.

Technology is transforming luxury asset management. Smart asset tracking, predictive maintenance software for jets and yachts, and blockchain verification for fine art authenticity are now integral to high-end asset management. Embracing these technologies enhances transparency, reduces risk, and preserves value. Action Step: Leverage emerging technologies to optimize asset management, documentation, and security.

Lifestyle integration must not be overlooked. These assets are not merely financial holdings—they are meant to be enjoyed. Yet, enjoyment must be balanced with stewardship. Proper staffing, usage scheduling, maintenance protocols, and budgeting ensure that luxury assets enrich life without becoming burdens. Action Step: Create a luxury asset use and maintenance plan that blends enjoyment with preservation.

Luxury asset management demands the same rigor as financial portfolio management. It requires intentionality, expertise, and proactive stewardship. Without this, what should be sources of joy and enrichment can quickly become sources of stress and erosion.

The call to action is clear: Approach yachts, jets, and rare collections not as trophies, but as integral parts of your wealth strategy. Manage them with the same discipline and sophistication that built your fortune.

The goals—enhanced lifestyle, preserved value, generational legacy—are attainable. But they require a curated team of advisors: maritime and aviation attorneys, tax experts, specialized insurers, appraisers, and estate planners. For the ultra-affluent, the true luxury is not ownership—it is mastery.

Chapter 48: Education Trusts: Leaving a Legacy Through Education

Education has always been one of the most enduring legacies a family can provide. For the ultra-affluent, ensuring that future generations have the resources to access premier educational opportunities is more than an act of generosity; it is a strategic imperative. Education trusts offer a powerful vehicle to structure this legacy, blending thoughtful estate planning with the timeless value of knowledge.

An education trust is a legal structure established to fund the educational expenses of designated beneficiaries. Unlike direct gifts or 529 plans, education trusts provide enhanced control, flexibility, and protection. They can specify the types of education covered—private primary and secondary schools, universities, graduate programs, even continuing education or specialized training. They can also articulate standards for disbursement, such as minimum academic performance, eligible fields of study, or participation in internships and community service.

The benefits are profound. A properly structured education trust removes the uncertainty around funding future tuition and related costs. It also insulates educational funding from potential mismanagement or outside claims against the family wealth. For families concerned with preserving legacy values, trusts allow grantors to embed purpose and guidance alongside capital. Real-Life Scenario: A family established an education trust that not only covered tuition but also mandated study abroad opportunities, fostering a global perspective for each successive generation. Action Step: Define the educational philosophy and goals you wish to embed in the trust document.

There are important distinctions between revocable and irrevocable education trusts. Revocable trusts allow flexibility but offer fewer asset protection and tax benefits. Irrevocable trusts, once funded, remove assets from the grantor's estate, providing both estate tax efficiencies and creditor protection. The trade-off is the loss of direct control once the trust is established. Pros: Asset protection, estate tax reduction, multi-generational impact. Cons: Reduced flexibility, administrative complexity. Action Step: Consult with an estate planning attorney to determine the optimal trust structure based on tax strategy, control preferences, and asset size.

Funding strategies vary. Trusts can be funded with cash, marketable securities, real estate, or even interests in family businesses. Some families endow education trusts with life insurance proceeds to magnify the funding capacity without depleting other estate assets. Funding should align with projected costs, taking into account tuition inflation, living expenses, and the possibility of beneficiaries pursuing advanced degrees. Action Step: Conduct a future cost analysis to ensure the trust corpus is sufficient to meet its objectives across multiple generations.

Tax considerations are crucial. Properly structured, education trusts can avoid generation-skipping transfer (GST) taxes, which would otherwise erode wealth intended for grandchildren and beyond. Income generated by trust assets may also qualify for preferential tax treatment if structured thoughtfully. Real-Life Scenario: A trust funded with a diversified portfolio of municipal bonds provided tax-free income to cover education expenses, reducing the overall tax burden on the trust and preserving principal. Action Step: Work with tax advisors to design a tax-efficient investment strategy within the trust.

Trustee selection is a pivotal decision. The trustee will administer the trust, interpret its terms, make distribution decisions, and ensure compliance with fiduciary duties. Families often appoint a professional trustee—such as a trust company—to ensure impartiality and administrative expertise. However, some opt for co-trusteeships, blending family members and professionals to retain a personal touch. Action Step: Select trustees who align with the educational values and financial sophistication required to steward the trust.

Flexibility clauses can future-proof the trust. Including provisions that allow for adaptation—such as broad definitions of "educational expenses," discretion to support non-traditional education paths, or powers of appointment for future generations—ensures the trust remains relevant as educational models and costs evolve. Real-Life Scenario: A trust originally established for traditional university expenses was adapted by successor trustees to fund entrepreneurial boot camps and online certifications for beneficiaries pursuing non-traditional careers. Action Step: Build in flexibility without compromising the trust's core mission.

Education trusts also serve as effective tools for instilling values. Grantors can include letters of wishes to articulate the "why" behind the trust, sharing personal stories, hopes, and expectations. This narrative guidance can be as impactful as the financial support itself, reinforcing family values and encouraging beneficiaries to view education as a privilege rather than an entitlement. Action Step: Draft a legacy letter to accompany the trust, ensuring the transfer of values alongside assets.

Beyond individual family benefit, education trusts can extend to broader philanthropic aims. Some families establish trusts that fund scholarships for descendants as well as charitable educational initiatives, blending personal legacy with public good. Real-Life Scenario: A family trust funded college scholarships for descendants while also endowing scholarships at the alma mater of the family patriarch, amplifying the family's legacy in both private and public spheres.

Education is a gift that compounds over time, not just financially but intellectually, culturally, and socially. Structuring that gift through an education trust ensures it is delivered with the care, precision, and strategic foresight worthy of a significant legacy.

The call to action is clear: Do not leave educational opportunity to chance or assumption. Engineer it deliberately, preserving and magnifying your family's most important assets—knowledge, character, and opportunity.

The goals—multi-generational empowerment, legacy preservation, value transmission—are within reach. But they demand careful planning, thoughtful structuring, and elite advisory collaboration. For the ultra-affluent, an education trust is more than a tool; it is a blueprint for a legacy that will echo through generations.

Chapter 49: Concierge Medicine and Healthcare Access for UHNW Families

In a world where time, privacy, and performance are paramount, healthcare for ultra-high-net-worth families must transcend the traditional. Concierge medicine has emerged as the gold standard, providing bespoke healthcare experiences that match the expectations and demands of the ultra-affluent. It is not simply about access to physicians—it is about orchestrating a proactive, personalized, and confidential healthcare strategy that protects one of the most valuable assets: personal and family well-being.

Concierge medicine, also known as boutique or retainer medicine, fundamentally redefines the doctor-patient relationship. Patients pay an annual fee, often ranging from $10,000 to over $100,000 per person, in exchange for highly personalized care. This typically includes 24/7 direct access to physicians, extended appointment times, same-day or next-day visits, comprehensive annual executive physicals, and enhanced coordination of specialist care. Real-Life Scenario: A global family office engaged a concierge physician group that coordinated all care—including on-site visits during international travel—ensuring seamless, uninterrupted healthcare regardless of location. Action Step: Assess healthcare needs and lifestyle patterns to select a concierge service model that matches family dynamics and travel schedules.

The benefits extend beyond convenience. Concierge medicine emphasizes preventive care. With fewer patients—often 100 to 600 versus the traditional 2,000 to 3,000—concierge physicians have the bandwidth to focus on proactive health management. Advanced genetic screening, early detection testing, personalized wellness plans, and lifestyle optimization are standard offerings. Pros: Enhanced preventive care, faster diagnosis, reduced hospitalization rates. Cons: High annual fees, potential duplication with traditional insurance costs. Action Step: Integrate concierge care with broader health insurance and risk management strategies to ensure comprehensive coverage without redundancy.

Privacy is a significant driver. High-profile individuals often face concerns about confidentiality and data security. Concierge practices typically offer heightened privacy protocols—limiting electronic medical record exposure and offering discreet consultation environments. Some services even provide in-home or on-yacht consultations, eliminating the need for clinic visits altogether. Action Step: Evaluate the privacy protocols of potential concierge providers to ensure they meet family security standards.

Access to top specialists is another critical advantage. Leading concierge providers often have established relationships with world-renowned specialists and medical centers. They facilitate expedited referrals and "VIP pathways" into institutions like Mayo Clinic, Cleveland Clinic, or international centers of excellence. Real-Life Scenario: A CEO facing a rare cardiac issue was navigated within 24 hours to a top surgeon at a premier medical center, bypassing the months-long waitlist. Action Step: Confirm that your concierge provider has established referral networks with the world's top specialists and institutions.

Global healthcare coordination is essential for families who live and operate internationally. Some concierge groups specialize in worldwide care—providing medical evacuation services, access to international hospitals, and even mobile medical teams. This ensures healthcare continuity regardless of geography. Action Step: Align concierge healthcare services with global mobility plans, ensuring that international travel and residency do not disrupt access to high-quality care.

Innovation and advanced technologies are hallmarks of top-tier concierge medicine. Services often include comprehensive genomics, personalized medicine approaches, advanced imaging, biomarker monitoring, and AI-assisted diagnostics. Annual assessments go beyond basic blood panels to encompass full-body MRIs, cardiovascular screening, cognitive function tests, and more. Action Step: Ensure that the selected concierge practice leverages the latest medical technologies and methodologies to provide cutting-edge care.

Wellness integration has become increasingly sophisticated. Concierge practices now incorporate nutritionists, fitness experts, mental health professionals, and even longevity specialists into their care teams. The result is a holistic, 360-degree approach to well-being, not merely the treatment of illness. Real-Life Scenario: A multigenerational family established a comprehensive wellness plan—covering diet, exercise, mental resilience training, and annual cognitive evaluations—tailored to each family member's needs and goals. Action Step: Choose a concierge provider that goes beyond traditional medicine to offer integrated wellness and longevity planning.

Insurance compatibility is another consideration. While concierge fees typically cover physician access and annual exams, they do not replace traditional health insurance for hospitalizations, surgeries, or catastrophic events. Integrating concierge medicine with a robust private insurance policy or international health plan ensures seamless coverage across all health events. Action Step: Coordinate with wealth advisors and insurance specialists to align concierge medicine with comprehensive risk management strategies.

Cost, while significant, must be evaluated relative to value. For many ultra-affluent individuals, the time saved, health outcomes improved, and crises averted more than justify the investment. Furthermore, when considering the economic value of maximizing productive years and reducing preventable illnesses, the ROI becomes clear. Pros: Elevated care quality, time efficiency, reduced health risks. Cons: High upfront costs, limited insurance coverage integration if unmanaged. Action Step: Frame concierge healthcare costs as an investment in human capital—you and your family's well-being—and budget accordingly.

Family-wide healthcare planning is an emerging trend. Rather than individual memberships, many families establish group concierge plans, ensuring that spouses, children, and even extended family members receive consistent, coordinated care. This not only simplifies administration but also fosters a culture of health and well-being across generations. Action Step: Explore family concierge plans that offer tailored care coordination for all members, integrating generational wellness and preventive strategies.

Concierge medicine, properly integrated, becomes more than healthcare—it becomes an essential pillar of wealth preservation and life optimization. For the ultra-affluent, health is not a reactive endeavor; it is a proactive, strategic pursuit that deserves the same level of planning and excellence applied to financial affairs.

The call to action is unambiguous: Elevate healthcare to the level of every other critical wealth pillar. Build a healthcare strategy that is proactive, personalized, and seamlessly integrated into your global life.

The goals—maximized longevity, optimal performance, generational wellness—are achievable. But they demand intentional selection of elite concierge partners, strategic alignment with insurance and wealth planning, and a commitment to proactive, continuous care. For those who have achieved extraordinary success, ensuring extraordinary healthcare is not indulgent—it is essential.

Chapter 50: Legacy Letters and Ethical Wills: Passing on Stories, Not Just Wealth

Wealth, at its core, is about far more than financial capital. For the ultra-affluent, the most enduring legacies are not measured in balance sheets but in the transmission of values, stories, wisdom, and purpose. Legacy letters and ethical wills are powerful, often overlooked, tools that allow individuals to pass on not just wealth, but the essence of who they are—the beliefs, lessons, and narratives that have shaped their journey and that can guide future generations long after financial inheritances are spent.

A legacy letter, sometimes called an ethical will, is a personal document intended to convey the intangibles: family history, moral and spiritual beliefs, life lessons, hopes for the future, and expressions of love and forgiveness. Unlike traditional wills, which distribute financial assets, legacy letters distribute intellectual and emotional assets. They are an opportunity to create continuity between generations, to articulate not just what you are leaving behind but why it matters. Real-Life Scenario: A family patriarch, before his passing, wrote a legacy letter that was read aloud at the family's annual retreat. It chronicled his humble beginnings, his principles for success, and his hopes for unity among his descendants. Decades later, it remains a guiding document for family culture and philanthropy. Action Step: Schedule time to begin drafting a legacy letter, focusing first on key life events and values you wish to impart.

The process of creating a legacy letter can be profoundly clarifying. It forces reflection on core beliefs, pivotal moments, and lessons learned. It is not an exercise in autobiography but a distillation of the essential. What principles guided your decisions? What mistakes taught you the most? What do you hope your descendants will know and remember? Pros: Provides clarity and meaning to wealth transfer, fosters family unity, bridges generations. Cons: Emotionally demanding, requires vulnerability and thoughtful articulation. Action Step: Start by outlining key themes: perseverance, integrity, gratitude, responsibility, philanthropy—and weave personal stories around these pillars.

Unlike legal documents, legacy letters have no formal structure. They can be essays, a series of letters, video recordings, or even audio messages. The format should match the individual's personality and the family's traditions. Some choose a chronological approach, recounting their life story; others opt for thematic letters, each addressing a particular value or lesson. Real-Life Scenario: An entrepreneur created a "values anthology," a series of letters, each dedicated to one of the family's ten core values, accompanied by anecdotes illustrating each principle in action. Action Step: Decide on a format that feels authentic and sustainable—start small if necessary, building incrementally.

The timing of delivery can vary. Some legacy letters are shared during significant life events: weddings, births, graduations, or family gatherings. Others are intended to be read posthumously. Some families integrate legacy readings into annual retreats, ensuring that values are reinforced regularly. Action Step: Consider the right moment for delivery—not just the end of life, but milestones where their impact will be most profound.

Ethical wills also serve as a complement to formal estate planning. While trusts, wills, and family constitutions provide the "what" and "how" of wealth transfer, legacy letters provide the "why." They give context, helping heirs understand the decisions behind charitable bequests, governance structures, and even disinheritance if necessary. Without context, financial inheritances can breed resentment, confusion, or a sense of entitlement. With context, they become part of a purposeful narrative. Action Step: Pair legacy letters with estate planning documents, ensuring that heirs receive not just assets but a framework for understanding them.

Writing a legacy letter is also a powerful personal legacy exercise. It clarifies the writer's own life—what mattered, what didn't, what endures. It shifts the focus from accumulation to contribution, from success to significance. Real-Life Scenario: A venture capitalist wrote a letter to his grandchildren, recounting not his financial victories but the lessons learned from his failures. His honesty became a touchstone for the family's ethos around risk, resilience, and humility. Action Step: Reflect not only on achievements but on challenges and how they shaped your values.

Families that embrace legacy letters often report increased cohesion and reduced conflict. When values and expectations are clear, fewer misunderstandings arise around wealth distribution and family roles. Heirs feel connected to something larger than themselves—a lineage of wisdom and purpose. Pros: Reduces family disputes, enhances meaning and direction for heirs, strengthens family identity. Cons: Requires commitment and thoughtful communication, may surface difficult emotions. Action Step: Encourage multiple generations to participate—legacy letters are most powerful when they become a family tradition, not a one-time exercise.

Professional support can elevate the process. Legacy advisors, family wealth counselors, and even ghostwriters can assist in articulating complex life stories and values. Structured interviews, guided writing prompts, and family storytelling sessions can facilitate a richer, more comprehensive document. Action Step: Consider engaging professional support to ensure that your legacy letter is clear, impactful, and preserved appropriately.

Technology now plays a role as well. Secure digital vaults allow families to store legacy letters, videos, and audio messages for future access. Some even integrate legacy communications into broader family governance systems, ensuring that they remain living documents updated over time. Action Step: Explore digital solutions for storing and sharing legacy letters, ensuring that they are accessible to future generations without risk of loss or degradation.

Legacy letters and ethical wills are gifts of the rarest kind. They offer descendants a map—not of how to spend wealth, but of how to live well.

They transform an inheritance from a transfer of resources to a transfer of meaning.

The call to action is heartfelt: Begin writing. Begin reflecting. Begin crafting a narrative that will outlast fortunes and institutions. Pass on not just what you built, but who you became.

The goals—preserving values, strengthening family identity, guiding future generations—are within reach. But they require intentionality, reflection, and thoughtful articulation. For the ultra-affluent, the true legacy lies not only in wealth amassed but in wisdom shared—a gift that will compound across generations.

Part VIII: Strategic Philanthropy and Social Impact

Part VIII: Strategic Philanthropy and Social Impact focuses on elevating giving from reactive donations to purposeful, impactful strategy. For the ultra-affluent, philanthropy is not just an obligation or an afterthought—it is a central pillar of legacy building, reputation management, and societal contribution. This section explores how to approach philanthropy with the same rigor, discipline, and vision applied to wealth creation.

Readers will learn how to craft philanthropic mission statements, structure private foundations and donor-advised funds, and measure impact with precision. It addresses how to engage the next generation in charitable work, ensuring that values and vision are preserved across decades. Global giving strategies, social entrepreneurship, and blending investment returns with social outcomes are also covered, reflecting the evolving landscape of modern philanthropy.

Ultimately, this part empowers readers to align personal passions with strategic outcomes, creating legacies that are not only generous but transformative. It is about moving beyond check-writing to designing initiatives that leave an indelible mark on the world.

Chapter 51: Mission-Aligned Philanthropy for the Ultra Affluent

Philanthropy, at its highest form, is not just about giving; it is about aligning wealth with values, passion with purpose. For the ultra-affluent, mission-aligned philanthropy offers the opportunity to transform charitable giving from a series of transactions into a legacy of meaningful, measurable impact. It is about creating intentional, disciplined, and strategic pathways that not only address today's challenges but also shape the world you envision for generations to come.

Mission-aligned philanthropy begins with clarity—understanding the "why" behind your giving. Defining a philanthropic mission statement is the essential first step. It focuses your resources, aligns your family's interests, and provides a guiding light through the complexities of charitable work. Without a mission, philanthropy risks becoming reactive, scattered, or driven by external solicitations rather than internal convictions. Action Step: Develop a concise, powerful philanthropic mission statement that articulates the values and causes you are most committed to.

The structure through which you give is equally important. Private foundations, donor-advised funds (DAFs), charitable trusts, and direct giving each offer distinct advantages and limitations. Foundations offer control and legacy potential but require significant administrative oversight and public reporting. DAFs provide simplicity and privacy but less flexibility in governance. Real-Life Scenario: A family with $100 million in charitable capital established a private foundation for long-term legacy building, complemented by a DAF for responsive, near-term giving. Action Step: Conduct a structural analysis to determine the optimal philanthropic vehicles for your mission, risk tolerance, and administrative appetite.

Mission-aligned philanthropy requires discipline in grantmaking. Grants should be evaluated not only for alignment with mission but also for organizational strength, scalability, and impact metrics. Engaging in due diligence—assessing leadership, financial health, operational capacity—ensures that grants amplify impact rather than simply fund activity. Pros: Focused giving enhances impact, minimizes waste, and builds credibility. Cons: Requires time, expertise, and willingness to say "no" to worthy but misaligned causes. Action Step: Develop a structured grant evaluation process, including clear criteria and review protocols.

Impact measurement is non-negotiable. Ultra-affluent philanthropists should demand the same accountability from their charitable initiatives that they expect from their investments. This includes setting clear goals, defining key performance indicators (KPIs), and conducting regular impact assessments. Metrics will vary—lives improved, policies changed, ecosystems restored—but measurement must be embedded into the giving strategy. Real-Life Scenario: A philanthropist focused on education reform established a metrics dashboard to track student outcomes, teacher retention, and graduation rates across funded programs, enabling real-time adjustments to strategy. Action Step: Incorporate impact metrics into all major grants and regularly review outcomes against objectives.

Next-generation engagement is a cornerstone of sustainable mission-aligned philanthropy. Involving heirs early, providing philanthropic education, and encouraging them to participate in grantmaking decisions fosters a sense of ownership and continuity. It also ensures that the family's philanthropic vision evolves with new generations without losing its foundational values. Action Step: Establish family philanthropic councils or advisory boards where next-generation members can contribute meaningfully to strategy and decision-making.

Mission alignment can and should extend beyond traditional giving into impact investing—allocating a portion of philanthropic capital or personal assets into investments that generate both financial return and social or environmental benefit. Whether through social impact bonds, ESG-focused funds, or direct investment in social enterprises, impact investing ensures that your capital is working full-time toward your mission. Pros: Leverages full balance sheet for change, enhances legacy impact. Cons: Complexity, often lower returns or higher risk relative to traditional investments. Action Step: Explore impact investing strategies that align with your philanthropic mission and integrate them into your overall wealth strategy.

Global giving introduces additional layers of complexity—legal, tax, and cultural—but also magnifies impact potential. Issues like poverty, education, health, and climate know no borders. Ultra-affluent philanthropists are increasingly looking beyond their home countries to effect change on a global scale. However, international giving demands deep local knowledge, trusted intermediaries, and rigorous compliance with anti-terrorism and anti-money laundering regulations. Real-Life Scenario: A philanthropist focused on clean water initiatives partnered with international NGOs and established field offices in target regions, ensuring cultural competency and operational effectiveness. Action Step: Partner with global NGOs, advisors, and legal counsel to navigate international giving safely and effectively.

Philanthropy should also be integrated into broader estate and wealth planning strategies. Charitable lead trusts, charitable remainder trusts, and testamentary gifts can achieve philanthropic goals while optimizing tax outcomes and preserving family wealth. Action Step: Work with estate planning experts to embed philanthropy into your legacy planning, ensuring alignment with both personal values and financial goals.

Communication matters. Sharing your philanthropic mission publicly—through websites, annual reports, media engagement—can inspire others, attract collaborators, and enhance your family's legacy of impact. However, balance is key. Transparency must be weighed against privacy and security considerations. Action Step: Develop a communications strategy that authentically conveys your mission and impact without compromising privacy.

Mission-aligned philanthropy is a discipline, not a destination. It requires continual reassessment, adaptation, and learning. Societal needs evolve, best practices emerge, and family dynamics shift. A philanthropic strategy that is mission-driven today must remain agile to stay relevant tomorrow. Real-Life Scenario: A long-standing family foundation originally focused on healthcare expanded into climate initiatives after a family values retreat and comprehensive impact review, ensuring alignment with evolving family priorities. Action Step: Schedule regular strategic reviews of your philanthropic mission and practices, inviting external perspectives where appropriate.

The call to action is clear: Elevate philanthropy to the level of strategy, discipline, and rigor that built your wealth in the first place. Define your mission, structure your giving thoughtfully, measure impact meticulously, and engage future generations deliberately.

The goals—meaningful impact, enduring legacy, family unity, and personal fulfillment—are within reach. But they demand intentionality, structure, and expert guidance. For the ultra-affluent, mission-aligned philanthropy is not just about giving; it is about transforming wealth into a lasting force for good.

Chapter 52: Setting Up and Managing Private Family Foundations

Establishing a private family foundation is one of the most profound expressions of purpose and legacy an ultra-affluent individual can create. It transforms wealth into a structured, enduring force for good, channeling resources toward causes that align with deeply held values. Done thoughtfully, a family foundation is not only a vehicle for philanthropy but also a mechanism for educating heirs, fostering family unity, and building a reputation for leadership and stewardship.

The first step in setting up a private family foundation is clarifying its mission and vision. These elements should reflect the family's values, passions, and long-term goals. A clear mission statement provides direction and coherence, ensuring that the foundation's activities remain aligned with its core purpose over generations. Real-Life Scenario: A multigenerational family created a foundation with a mission to improve global access to education, a cause rooted in the founder's personal journey. This clarity allowed the family to focus its grants and leverage its influence effectively. Action Step: Host a family retreat to collectively define the foundation's mission and guiding principles.

Choosing the right legal structure is critical. Most private foundations are established as nonprofit corporations or charitable trusts. Each structure has specific governance, tax, and operational implications. A nonprofit corporation typically offers more flexibility and easier governance updates, while a trust provides greater asset protection and control over amendments. Action Step: Consult with legal counsel specializing in tax-exempt organizations to select the appropriate structure based on long-term vision and regulatory considerations.

Initial funding requires careful planning. While the IRS requires private foundations to distribute at least 5% of their net investment assets annually, the initial endowment must be sufficient to sustain meaningful impact over time. Funding can be accomplished through cash contributions, appreciated securities, real estate, or even closely held business interests. Each asset class has unique tax implications and liquidity considerations. Pros: Immediate charitable deduction, potential capital gains tax avoidance. Cons: Ongoing administrative burden, excise taxes on investment income. Action Step: Work with tax advisors and investment professionals to structure initial and ongoing funding optimally.

Governance is the backbone of a successful foundation. Selecting the board of directors or trustees is a pivotal decision. Board members should possess a blend of passion for the mission, expertise in relevant fields, and a commitment to fiduciary responsibility. Including family members fosters legacy and unity, but many families balance this with independent directors to enhance objectivity and credibility. Real-Life Scenario: A family foundation combined family board members with external experts in education and global development to enrich decision-making. Action Step: Establish clear governance policies outlining board composition, terms, and duties.

Administrative infrastructure must be built deliberately. Foundations must adhere to stringent IRS regulations, file annual Form 990-PF returns, manage grants compliantly, and maintain detailed records. Depending on size and complexity, foundations may hire in-house staff, engage outsourced management firms, or a hybrid approach. Action Step: Develop an operational plan including staffing, compliance, accounting, and reporting protocols to ensure sustainable administration.

Investment management is another crucial pillar. Foundation assets must be invested prudently to balance growth, income, and liquidity needs to meet the annual 5% distribution requirement. Some families establish investment committees or engage outsourced chief investment officers (OCIOs) to oversee portfolios. Aligning investments with the foundation's mission through ESG (Environmental, Social, and Governance) or impact investing strategies is an emerging best practice. Action Step: Create an Investment Policy Statement (IPS) tailored to the foundation's mission, time horizon, and risk appetite.

Grantmaking strategy should be intentional and disciplined. Effective foundations move beyond reactive giving to proactive, strategic philanthropy. This involves identifying high-impact opportunities, conducting due diligence on potential grantees, setting measurable objectives, and evaluating outcomes. Real-Life Scenario: A foundation focused on healthcare innovation established a strategic partnership with a leading research hospital, funding a multi-year study on pediatric disease prevention. Action Step: Develop a formal grantmaking framework that includes application processes, evaluation criteria, and impact measurement protocols.

Family engagement across generations strengthens the foundation's continuity and purpose. Engaging younger family members in board meetings, site visits, and grant evaluations instills philanthropic values and leadership skills. Some families establish junior boards or family councils to cultivate next-generation involvement. Action Step: Design a generational engagement plan that includes educational initiatives and leadership pathways within the foundation.

Transparency and communication enhance credibility. Publishing annual reports, maintaining a website, and engaging in thoughtful public relations amplify the foundation's impact and inspire confidence among stakeholders. However, discretion is equally important to balance privacy and security concerns. Action Step: Craft a communication strategy that authentically conveys the foundation's mission and achievements while safeguarding the family's privacy.

Private family foundations must also be resilient and adaptable. Over decades, family dynamics, societal needs, and regulatory environments evolve. Building flexibility into the foundation's charter and periodically reviewing mission and strategy ensure that it remains relevant and effective.

Real-Life Scenario: A family foundation originally focused on literacy expanded its mission to include digital access as technology transformed education, ensuring continued relevance and impact. Action Step: Schedule regular strategic reviews to assess and adapt the foundation's mission, structure, and practices.

Establishing and managing a private family foundation is a profound endeavor—a testament to vision, discipline, and commitment. It demands the same rigor, foresight, and governance that built the family's wealth, but it yields dividends measured not in profits but in purpose, impact, and legacy.

The call to action is clear: If philanthropy is to be a cornerstone of your legacy, consider the transformative potential of a private family foundation. Approach it with the same precision and passion that defined your professional success.

The goals—enduring impact, family unity, societal contribution, and personal fulfillment—are within reach. But they require expert structuring, disciplined management, and multigenerational engagement. For the ultra-affluent, a private family foundation is not just a philanthropic tool—it is a living legacy.

Chapter 53: Engaging Multiple Generations in Philanthropy

Engaging multiple generations in philanthropy is not merely an exercise in charitable giving; it is a profound investment in legacy, values transmission, and family unity. For the ultra-affluent, strategic philanthropy must move beyond individual acts to become a living, breathing tradition that binds generations together in purpose and impact. When structured correctly, family philanthropy becomes a dynamic platform for leadership development, values education, and legacy preservation.

The starting point is recognizing that each generation approaches philanthropy differently. Founders often see giving through the lens of gratitude and community responsibility, shaped by personal experiences of building wealth. Second and third generations, however, may view philanthropy through lenses of social justice, innovation, or environmental sustainability. Bridging these perspectives requires open dialogue and mutual respect. Real-Life Scenario: A three-generation family foundation brought together elders committed to local community support and younger members passionate about global climate change. Through facilitated retreats, they crafted a mission that honored both local impact and global initiatives. Action Step: Organize intergenerational family meetings focused specifically on sharing philanthropic values and visions.

Creating structured opportunities for engagement is essential. This means more than inviting younger members to attend board meetings;

it requires giving them meaningful roles. Junior boards, youth grantmaking committees, or advisory panels allow emerging family leaders to gain hands-on experience. These roles cultivate skills in due diligence, grant evaluation, and strategic decision-making—skills transferable to broader leadership roles within the family enterprise. Pros: Fosters leadership skills, ensures continuity, deepens family bonds. Cons: Requires time, mentorship, and a willingness to share authority. Action Step: Develop a formal structure for junior participation and mentorship within your family's philanthropic activities.

Education must be woven into the process. While passion is vital, strategic philanthropy requires knowledge—understanding nonprofit management, financial stewardship, impact measurement, and legal compliance. Offering educational workshops, inviting guest speakers, and encouraging attendance at philanthropy-focused conferences enriches the family's intellectual capital around giving. Action Step: Create a "philanthropy curriculum" tailored to different generational needs and experience levels.

Establishing a shared mission statement that reflects intergenerational input ensures alignment and ownership. A family mission that evolves with each generation but remains anchored in core values provides coherence and direction. Real-Life Scenario: A family foundation initially focused on literacy redefined its mission to "expand educational opportunities in all forms" to embrace younger generations' interests in digital education and technology access. Action Step: Facilitate a collaborative mission-building exercise involving all generations.

Grantmaking strategies should reflect generational diversity while staying true to the foundation's mission. One approach is allocating a portion of the annual grants budget to discretionary grants—giving different generations the freedom to support causes they are passionate about. Another is collaborative grantmaking, where teams comprising members from different generations work together to select and vet grant recipients. Pros: Balances tradition with innovation, empowers all voices. Cons: Requires clear guidelines to maintain cohesion and prevent mission drift. Action Step: Incorporate discretionary and collaborative grantmaking mechanisms into your family's philanthropy model.

Storytelling is a powerful tool for transmitting legacy. Founders and senior family members should share their philanthropic journey—the successes, failures, motivations, and lessons learned. Capturing these stories through videos, written narratives, or live storytelling sessions embeds them into the family's collective memory. Real-Life Scenario: A family documented its philanthropic milestones in a "legacy book" featuring essays, interviews, and historical photographs, presented to each new family member at age 18. Action Step: Launch a family storytelling project to document and share your philanthropic journey.

Conflict, while inevitable, can be constructive if managed well. Different viewpoints on causes, giving strategies, and operational practices can be channeled into creative tension that strengthens outcomes. Establishing clear governance structures, decision-making processes, and conflict-resolution protocols ensures that disagreements are productive rather than divisive. Action Step: Develop governance policies that define roles, responsibilities, and procedures for resolving disagreements.

Technology can be a powerful enabler. Digital grant management platforms, virtual meetings, and online learning modules make it easier for geographically dispersed families to collaborate and stay engaged. Younger generations, in particular, are comfortable with these tools and can lead their integration. Action Step: Invest in technology infrastructure that facilitates virtual participation, data management, and knowledge sharing.

Celebrating milestones together strengthens family bonds and reinforces commitment to philanthropy. Hosting annual retreats, site visits to grantee organizations, and family award ceremonies honoring exceptional contributions build a sense of shared purpose and pride. Real-Life Scenario: A family foundation hosts an annual "Impact Week" where family members visit funded projects, meet grantees, and participate in community service activities together. Action Step: Plan annual family philanthropic events that combine celebration, learning, and service.

Succession planning ensures that family philanthropy remains vibrant across generations. Formalizing leadership transition processes, mentoring emerging leaders, and setting term limits for board service create pathways for new voices and perspectives while honoring the contributions of founding members. Action Step: Create a succession plan that identifies, mentors, and transitions leadership roles to the next generation in an intentional, transparent manner.

Engaging multiple generations in philanthropy is not an incidental benefit of family wealth; it is a deliberate, strategic undertaking. It transforms giving from an individual act into a family legacy—a shared enterprise that nurtures leadership, transmits values, and magnifies impact.

The call to action is clear: Build an intergenerational philanthropic strategy that empowers, educates, and unites your family. Approach it with the same intentionality and sophistication that defined your success in business.

The goals—family unity, leadership development, legacy preservation, and societal impact—are within reach. But they require structured engagement, ongoing education, and thoughtful governance. For the ultra-affluent, engaging multiple generations in philanthropy is not just a pathway to lasting impact—it is a pathway to enduring family purpose.

Chapter 54: Creating a Sustainable and Enduring Charitable Legacy

Creating a sustainable and enduring charitable legacy is perhaps one of the most profound achievements an ultra-affluent individual can aspire to. Beyond the balance sheets and financial returns, it is the chance to leave an imprint that echoes across generations and geographies. A true charitable legacy is not defined merely by the magnitude of the gifts given but by the lasting impact they generate—impact that endures, adapts, and inspires long after the founder is gone.

The first step in building a sustainable legacy is defining clear philanthropic intent. It must move beyond broad generosity to specific, mission-driven objectives. Whether focused on education, healthcare, climate change, social justice, or the arts, clarity of purpose gives a legacy the anchor it needs to withstand the shifts of time and circumstance. Real-Life Scenario: A technology entrepreneur passionate about digital literacy outlined a philanthropic mission to ensure technology education access for underprivileged youth worldwide. Over time, this clear mission guided multiple programs, partnerships, and grant cycles with unwavering focus. Action Step: Craft a formal philanthropic mission statement that precisely articulates the intended impact and legacy you aim to leave.

The structure chosen to house your philanthropy plays a critical role in its endurance. Private foundations, donor-advised funds, and charitable trusts each offer different advantages. Private foundations allow for direct control and long-term legacy building but demand significant administrative commitment and regulatory compliance. Donor-advised funds offer flexibility and simplicity but lack permanence unless converted into an enduring fund. Pros: Foundations ensure longevity; DAFs ensure efficiency. Cons: Foundations can become bureaucratic; DAFs risk becoming dormant without active stewardship. Action Step: Evaluate all structural options with legal and philanthropic advisors to determine which aligns best with your legacy vision.

Endowment funding ensures sustainability. Relying on one-time or sporadic gifts leaves philanthropic efforts vulnerable to market fluctuations and changing family fortunes. An endowment—a pool of invested capital that generates income to fund grants or programs—provides the stability needed for a legacy to endure. However, endowments must be carefully managed to balance risk, return, and mission alignment. Real-Life Scenario: A family foundation established an endowment invested with a mission-aligned ESG strategy, ensuring both financial returns and alignment with its philanthropic values. Action Step: Work with investment experts to create an endowment strategy that reflects both financial prudence and mission adherence.

Governance structures underpin longevity. A sustainable legacy demands more than financial assets; it requires clear governance policies, succession plans, and a framework for decision-making. A foundation or charitable entity should have a diverse and committed board, ideally blending family members with independent directors who bring expertise and objectivity. Terms, roles, and leadership development pathways must be established to prevent stagnation and promote renewal. Action Step: Draft and implement governance documents that establish leadership terms, succession planning, and board responsibilities.

Engaging multiple generations ensures continuity. Legacy is as much about people as it is about capital. Future generations must not only inherit the resources but also the values and vision that fueled the original mission. Structured involvement—junior boards, philanthropic retreats, educational initiatives—can cultivate commitment and capability among heirs. Real-Life Scenario: A fourth-generation family foundation conducts annual philanthropic retreats where next-gen family members present new initiatives and participate in grant-making, keeping the legacy alive and evolving. Action Step: Develop a next-generation engagement plan that includes mentorship, leadership training, and gradual assumption of responsibility.

Programmatic flexibility must be embedded. While the core mission should endure, the methods and focus areas may need to adapt to shifting societal needs, technological advancements, and evolving best practices. Locking future generations into narrow mandates can hinder relevance. Instead, legacy structures should allow for innovation and adaptation within the framework of core values. Action Step: Include adaptability clauses in governance documents and mission statements to allow for evolution while preserving intent.

Measurement and accountability ensure impact. Sustainable philanthropy is measured not by dollars given but by lives changed, ecosystems preserved, opportunities created. Establishing rigorous monitoring and evaluation frameworks ensures that resources are deployed effectively and lessons are captured for continuous improvement. Real-Life Scenario: A global health foundation developed a robust metrics dashboard tracking key outcomes like maternal health improvements, informing ongoing strategy and program refinement. Action Step: Implement an impact measurement framework that aligns with your mission and guides strategic adjustments.

Collaborations and partnerships amplify reach. Enduring legacies are rarely built in isolation. Partnering with like-minded organizations, public institutions, and private entities can leverage resources, enhance expertise, and expand impact. Strategic partnerships allow philanthropic efforts to achieve scale and sustainability beyond the founder's direct involvement. Action Step: Identify and cultivate strategic partnerships that align with your mission and extend your legacy's reach.

Communication and storytelling cement legacy. A compelling narrative about the mission, the journey, and the impact not only inspires beneficiaries but also galvanizes future family members and external stakeholders. Transparent, authentic communication—through annual reports, documentaries, books, or digital platforms—ensures the legacy's values and vision are clearly understood and carried forward. Action Step: Develop a legacy communication plan that captures and shares the essence of your philanthropic journey.

Lastly, periodic strategic reviews preserve relevance. A truly sustainable legacy evolves without losing its soul. Regular reviews of mission alignment, operational effectiveness, governance structures, and impact outcomes ensure that the philanthropic endeavor remains dynamic and effective. Real-Life Scenario: A century-old foundation convenes a strategic review every five years, bringing together board members, advisors, grantees, and beneficiaries to assess progress and recalibrate strategies. Action Step: Institutionalize strategic reviews into your legacy framework, ensuring periodic realignment and revitalization.

The call to action is direct: Build a charitable legacy that is not only impactful today but resilient and relevant tomorrow. Approach it with the strategic foresight, governance discipline, and human investment that have characterized your life's greatest achievements.

The goals—enduring impact, multigenerational engagement, societal contribution, and personal fulfillment—are attainable. But they demand careful design, thoughtful stewardship, and a long-term vision. For the ultra-affluent, creating a sustainable charitable legacy is not merely an act of generosity; it is a final, defining masterpiece of leadership.

Part IX: Specialized Wealth Planning

Part IX: Specialized Wealth Planning focuses on the sophisticated, nuanced strategies required to manage, preserve, and transition significant wealth in an increasingly complex financial and regulatory environment. This section is tailored for the ultra-affluent who require more than conventional planning—it demands solutions that anticipate cross-border challenges, protect against unseen risks, and build a multigenerational legacy.

Topics include advanced estate planning techniques, bespoke trust structures, cross-border tax strategies, asset protection mechanisms, succession planning for family businesses, and the integration of philanthropy into overall wealth strategies. It explores the design of private trust companies, the management of complex illiquid assets, and strategic liquidity planning around major life events, such as business exits or generational wealth transfers.

This part empowers readers to go beyond wealth preservation and actively engineer sustainable, resilient financial ecosystems that endure. It invites the ultra-affluent to think strategically, globally, and holistically—transforming wealth from a static asset into a dynamic, enduring legacy.

Chapter 55: Crypto and Digital Asset Transfer Planning

For the ultra-affluent, wealth today increasingly extends beyond traditional assets. Crypto and digital assets have matured from a fringe experiment into a substantial, sometimes dominant, component of sophisticated portfolios. Yet, despite their meteoric rise, these assets introduce complexities few traditional wealth structures are equipped to handle. Effective crypto and digital asset transfer planning is no longer optional; it is essential to preserving and transitioning wealth securely and efficiently.

Crypto assets—Bitcoin, Ethereum, stablecoins, NFTs, and other blockchain-based holdings—operate on fundamentally different principles than traditional assets. They are decentralized, pseudonymous, and often lack the custodial frameworks that banks and brokerages offer. Without a private key, control over a crypto asset is impossible; without proper planning, those assets can become inaccessible, lost forever. Real-Life Scenario: A tech founder with significant crypto holdings failed to leave clear access instructions. After his unexpected passing, tens of millions in digital assets were permanently inaccessible. Action Step: Start by creating a comprehensive inventory of all digital assets—currencies, tokens, wallets, exchanges—and ensure secure, documented storage.

Custody is foundational. Self-custody via hardware wallets offers maximal control but increases personal responsibility and risk of loss. Third-party custodians—regulated digital asset trust companies—offer security and insurance but introduce counterparty risk. Some ultra-affluent investors opt for multi-signature solutions, requiring multiple private keys to authorize transactions, thereby enhancing security and control. Pros: Self-custody maximizes privacy; custodians simplify estate transition. Cons: Self-custody risks loss through mishandling; custodians require trust and due diligence. Action Step: Choose a custody strategy that balances security, accessibility, and ease of transfer in the event of incapacity or death.

Access planning is the cornerstone of digital asset inheritance. Traditional estate plans assume financial institutions can be contacted to transfer ownership. With crypto, knowledge of private keys and recovery phrases is critical. Without them, even an executor cannot access the assets. Solutions include secure, encrypted storage of keys and recovery instructions—ideally in a vault, safe deposit box, or encrypted digital vault—with clear instructions in estate documents on how to retrieve them. Action Step: Work with estate planning attorneys specializing in digital assets to draft clear, legally sound access protocols.

Beneficiary designations require special attention. Unlike brokerage accounts or insurance policies, crypto holdings do not natively allow for "pay on death" instructions. Digital assets must be explicitly included in wills or trusts, and care must be taken to avoid triggering taxable events or jurisdictional complications. Some strategies involve transferring crypto into revocable trusts or creating bespoke digital asset trusts. Real-Life Scenario: A family office created a digital asset trust, structured to manage, trade, and distribute crypto holdings tax-efficiently across multiple generations. Action Step: Evaluate whether a specialized trust structure is appropriate for your crypto holdings.

Taxation is a minefield. Crypto assets are treated as property by the IRS, meaning transfers, sales, and even some gifts can trigger capital gains events. Estate transfers of appreciated crypto assets benefit from a step-up in basis, but only if properly documented and executed. Additionally, the valuation of crypto for estate tax purposes can be volatile; IRS scrutiny is increasing. Pros: Step-up in basis eliminates capital gains for heirs; charitable donations of crypto can yield large deductions. Cons: Improper reporting can trigger audits and penalties. Action Step: Engage tax advisors with expertise in crypto to ensure compliant reporting and optimal tax strategies.

International considerations are magnified with digital assets. Crypto is inherently borderless, but tax jurisdictions are not. Different countries treat crypto assets in wildly divergent ways—from taxation policies to inheritance rules to outright bans. For globally mobile families, careful coordination is required to ensure that digital assets do not inadvertently trigger unfavorable tax treatment or regulatory exposure. Action Step: Conduct a jurisdictional audit if you hold or plan to transfer crypto assets across borders.

Charitable giving strategies with crypto are evolving. Donating appreciated crypto directly to charities or donor-advised funds can eliminate capital gains and provide a fair market value deduction. However, many charities are still not equipped to accept crypto, requiring intermediaries or crypto-savvy DAFs. Real-Life Scenario: A philanthropist donated $5 million in Bitcoin to a university endowment, structured through a donor-advised fund specializing in digital assets, thereby maximizing tax efficiency and donor control. Action Step: Pre-plan charitable crypto gifts by identifying capable recipient organizations and structuring donations appropriately.

Privacy and security must remain paramount throughout the planning process. Unlike traditional assets, crypto transactions are publicly traceable—yet the holders' identities often are not. Maintaining anonymity requires careful design, but total anonymity can complicate probate or trustee duties. Balancing transparency with privacy is critical. Some families use LLCs or trusts to hold crypto, providing a legal entity to streamline transfer and administration while shielding individual identities. Action Step: Implement privacy-enhancing structures that still allow for clear, efficient asset transfer.

Succession planning must extend beyond ownership transfer to operational readiness. Crypto is not static—wallets require maintenance, security protocols evolve, and technological literacy is paramount. Future heirs must be educated on basic crypto principles and operations. Without this knowledge, even inherited access can be useless or dangerous. Real-Life Scenario: A family foundation established a "crypto literacy" curriculum for next-generation members, ensuring they could responsibly manage and grow inherited digital assets. Action Step: Include digital asset education in your family's broader wealth education programs.

Finally, regulatory evolution must be monitored continuously. Crypto regulation is in flux globally, with new laws emerging around taxation, anti-money laundering, and securities treatment. A static plan risks obsolescence. Ongoing review and updates to crypto estate plans are mandatory to stay compliant and optimize outcomes. Action Step: Establish an annual or biannual review process for your digital asset transfer plan, incorporating input from legal, tax, and technical advisors.

The call to action is urgent and clear: Treat crypto and digital assets with the same strategic rigor as traditional wealth components. Plan proactively. Secure access. Educate heirs. Integrate crypto into your estate and legacy frameworks thoughtfully and comprehensively.

The goals—wealth preservation, smooth succession, family education, and regulatory compliance—are fully achievable. But they demand specialized expertise, dynamic strategies, and a willingness to address the unique challenges and opportunities that digital assets present. For the ultra-affluent, digital asset transfer planning is not just a technical necessity—it is a vital element of a future-proof legacy.

Chapter 56: Managing Concentrated Stock Positions Like a Pro

Managing a concentrated stock position is one of the most complex and delicate aspects of ultra-high-net-worth wealth management. Many fortunes are made by building concentrated positions—whether through founding a company, executive compensation, or early investment in a growth story. However, the same concentration that fuels wealth creation often becomes the greatest threat to wealth preservation. The art and science of managing concentrated stock positions lie not in abrupt liquidation but in strategic, deliberate unwinding that preserves value, mitigates risk, and optimizes tax outcomes.

The first and most pressing risk of a concentrated position is simple: lack of diversification. While a concentrated holding can deliver outsized returns, it also exposes wealth to single-stock volatility, corporate governance risks, sectoral shifts, and regulatory surprises. For example, a technology founder holding 80% of their net worth in one company is acutely vulnerable to market sentiment swings, competitive threats, or leadership transitions. Action Step: Begin with a formal risk assessment quantifying the impact of various downside scenarios on your overall net worth.

Tax considerations loom large. Large blocks of appreciated stock carry significant embedded capital gains. Immediate liquidation could trigger enormous tax liabilities, eroding net proceeds by 20%-30% or more, depending on jurisdiction. Strategic deferral or minimization of taxes must be front and center in any unwinding plan. Real-Life Scenario: A healthcare executive used a combination of charitable remainder trusts (CRTs) and donor-advised funds (DAFs) to gift appreciated shares, securing substantial tax deductions and spreading out recognition of gains over time. Action Step: Engage tax counsel and wealth advisors to map out tax-efficient liquidation or transfer strategies before selling a single share.

Several tools are available to manage concentrated positions. The most straightforward—gradual liquidation—involves selling shares over time, taking advantage of market windows and managing tax brackets. Rule 10b5-1 plans provide a compliant, systematic mechanism for executives subject to insider trading restrictions to sell shares in a prearranged, SEC-sanctioned manner, reducing both legal risk and market impact. Action Step: Work with legal advisors to design and implement a Rule 10b5-1 plan customized to your liquidity needs and market dynamics.

Hedging strategies can provide downside protection without immediate sale. Equity collars, for instance, involve buying a protective put option while simultaneously selling a covered call option, capping upside but limiting downside. Variable prepaid forward contracts allow an individual to monetize a portion of their position today in exchange for a future delivery of shares, deferring recognition of capital gains. Pros: Liquidity and downside protection without triggering taxes. Cons: Complexity, counterparty risk, and regulatory scrutiny. Action Step: Evaluate hedging instruments in collaboration with a sophisticated investment banker or derivatives specialist.

Exchange funds are another powerful but often underutilized tool. They allow individuals with concentrated stock positions to pool their shares with other investors' holdings, gaining diversified exposure without triggering a taxable event. Participation typically requires lock-up periods and carries liquidity restrictions, but for patient capital, it is an elegant solution. Real-Life Scenario: A tech entrepreneur placed $50 million worth of stock into an exchange fund, diversifying into a broad market basket and mitigating single-company risk without paying immediate taxes. Action Step: Assess whether your holdings qualify for exchange fund participation and weigh the liquidity constraints.

Gifting strategies are doubly effective. Transferring highly appreciated stock to family members in lower tax brackets, directly or via irrevocable grantor trusts, can reduce overall family tax burdens. Similarly, using appreciated stock to fund private foundations or donor-advised funds can unlock both charitable impact and tax savings. Action Step: Develop a comprehensive gifting strategy that aligns with both philanthropic goals and family wealth transfer objectives.

Psychological attachment is an often overlooked but potent barrier. Many ultra-affluent individuals have deep emotional ties to the companies that created their wealth. Disentangling pride, loyalty, and identity from financial prudence is challenging. A structured, phased approach—gradually reducing exposure while maintaining a meaningful stake—can ease this transition. Action Step: Incorporate behavioral coaching into your advisory relationships to navigate the emotional aspects of diversification.

Family governance and communication are critical. Future generations may inherit concentrated positions without the founder's insights or emotional ties, potentially exposing them to unmanaged risk. Proactively involving heirs in discussions around risk, diversification, and strategic liquidation fosters continuity and wisdom. Real-Life Scenario: A family transitioned $200 million in single-stock holdings into a diversified investment portfolio over a decade, involving next-generation family members in quarterly reviews and strategic decisions. Action Step: Develop an intergenerational wealth governance structure that includes concentrated stock management as a core component.

Monitoring and adjusting the strategy over time is essential. Markets evolve, tax laws change, family dynamics shift. What works today may not be optimal tomorrow. Concentrated position management must be a living strategy, reviewed and recalibrated periodically in response to internal and external developments. Action Step: Schedule annual or semi-annual reviews with your advisory team to reassess concentrated holdings and update strategies accordingly.

Managing concentrated stock positions is not about reacting to volatility or chasing market timing; it is about engineering a disciplined, strategic unwinding process that preserves wealth, honors legacy, and maintains financial flexibility. It demands sophistication, patience, and a willingness to deploy advanced tools and structures.

The call to action is clear: Do not let the success that built your wealth become the Achilles' heel that threatens it. Approach your concentrated positions with the same strategic discipline that built your fortune.

The goals—risk mitigation, tax optimization, family continuity, and financial flexibility—are attainable. But they require customized strategies, expert counsel, and unwavering commitment to prudent wealth stewardship. For the ultra-affluent, mastering the management of concentrated stock positions is not merely a defensive maneuver—it is a cornerstone of enduring legacy and success.

Chapter 57: Planning for Non-Traditional Assets: IP, Royalties, Private Brands

When it comes to building and preserving wealth at the ultra-affluent level, traditional assets like stocks, bonds, and real estate are just one part of the equation. Increasingly, the modern portfolio of the ultra-wealthy includes non-traditional assets—intellectual property (IP), royalties, private brands—that defy conventional valuation and require a specialized approach to planning. These assets are dynamic, often highly personal, and can be some of the most powerful legacy-building tools available when managed correctly.

Intellectual property—patents, copyrights, trademarks, trade secrets—represents the monetization of creativity and innovation. IP assets can generate ongoing income streams, appreciate in value, and serve as collateral for financing. Yet their valuation can be subjective, and their protection requires constant vigilance. Unlike stocks that can be liquidated in seconds, IP requires strategic licensing, enforcement, and renewal. Real-Life Scenario: A tech entrepreneur with a robust patent portfolio licensed her innovations across multiple industries, generating a diversified, recurring revenue stream. Action Step: Conduct an IP audit to identify, value, and protect all intellectual property assets within your portfolio.

Royalties from creative works—music catalogs, literary rights, film franchises—offer another layer of non-traditional wealth. These income streams can be highly lucrative and long-lasting but also volatile based on market trends, technological disruption, and consumer preferences. Proper structuring is critical to ensure royalties are collected efficiently, taxed optimally, and transferred seamlessly across generations. Pros: Predictable cash flow, potential for appreciation. Cons: Exposure to market tastes, complex rights management. Action Step: Engage specialists to establish royalty management systems and review existing contracts for optimization opportunities.

Private brands—luxury goods, fashion labels, lifestyle companies—represent a unique class of assets that blend business, culture, and personal identity. Building and managing a brand requires more than operational expertise; it demands rigorous intellectual property protection, reputation management, and succession planning. Without careful stewardship, private brands can lose value rapidly. Real-Life Scenario: A family-owned luxury brand maintained its cachet and value through three generations by codifying brand values, operational practices, and intellectual property protections in a formal brand constitution. Action Step: Develop a comprehensive brand governance framework to institutionalize values and operational excellence.

Valuation is an enduring challenge for non-traditional assets. Unlike public equities, where price discovery is instantaneous, valuing IP, royalties, and brands often involves complex, subjective methodologies. Income-based, market-based, and cost-based approaches each have a role, depending on the asset and context. Underestimating or overestimating value can have significant tax, legal, and strategic implications, particularly in estate planning or transactions. Action Step: Retain valuation experts with experience in non-traditional asset classes to conduct periodic, defensible appraisals.

Taxation introduces another layer of complexity. IP and royalty income can be taxed as ordinary income, capital gains, or even subject to self-employment taxes, depending on how they are structured and exploited. Additionally, international IP and royalties may trigger complex cross-border tax obligations. Action Step: Develop an integrated tax strategy that optimizes the structure of non-traditional asset holdings, potentially using

IP holding companies or royalty trusts.

Succession planning for non-traditional assets is critical but often overlooked. Future generations must not only inherit ownership but also understand management and strategic decision-making. Without a robust plan, these assets can quickly erode in value. Trust structures, family governance policies, and professional management teams ensure continuity. Real-Life Scenario: A musician established a trust to manage his song catalog, appointing an independent trustee with industry expertise to protect royalties for future generations. Action Step: Integrate non-traditional assets into broader estate plans, ensuring management continuity through specialized governance structures.

Liquidity is another consideration. IP, royalties, and brands can be difficult to monetize quickly without significant discounts or strategic partnerships. Securitization—the process of packaging future royalties or brand revenues into tradable securities—offers one pathway to liquidity, but it requires sophisticated structuring and market timing. Action Step: Explore strategic liquidity options well in advance of potential needs, balancing cash flow requirements with asset preservation.

Risk management must be proactive. IP theft, brand dilution, piracy, and royalty disputes are ongoing threats. Insurance products such as IP infringement coverage, cyber liability, and business interruption policies can mitigate some of these risks. Ongoing legal vigilance—trademark renewals, patent maintenance, licensing audits—is equally critical. Action Step: Conduct a risk audit to identify vulnerabilities and implement robust protective measures for non-traditional assets.

Philanthropic planning can also leverage non-traditional assets. Donating IP rights, royalties, or shares in private brands to charitable foundations can unlock significant tax advantages while supporting personal causes. However, careful structuring is required to avoid unintended tax consequences or operational challenges. Real-Life Scenario: An author donated the future royalties of her literary works to a charitable trust, funding scholarships in perpetuity while receiving an immediate tax deduction. Action Step: Consult with philanthropic advisors to structure charitable giving strategies involving non-traditional assets.

Finally, ongoing education and governance are essential. Future family stewards must be equipped to understand and manage these complex assets. Educational programs, advisory boards with industry experts, and mentorship pathways ensure that non-traditional assets remain vibrant contributors to the family's wealth and legacy. Action Step: Incorporate non-traditional asset management into your family's wealth education curriculum.

The call to action is simple but bold: Treat non-traditional assets with the same strategic rigor as traditional portfolios. Plan proactively. Educate diligently. Govern thoughtfully.

The goals—wealth preservation, legacy enhancement, multigenerational continuity, and purposeful impact—are within reach. But they demand bespoke strategies, expert counsel, and unwavering attention to the unique complexities of intellectual property, royalties, and private brands. For the ultra-affluent, non-traditional asset planning is not an add-on; it is a critical pillar of enduring wealth stewardship.

Chapter 58: Divorce Planning for Ultra High Net Worth Individuals

Divorce, at any level of wealth, is an emotionally and financially disruptive event. For the ultra-high-net-worth individual, however, the stakes are magnified. Not only are the sums involved exponentially larger, but the complexity of assets, the interwoven business interests, the exposure to public scrutiny, and the generational legacy considerations make divorce planning a high-stakes exercise in precision and foresight. When approached with discipline and strategic foresight, divorce need not destroy wealth or fracture family stability. Instead, it can be managed in a way that preserves dignity, privacy, and financial integrity.

The first principle in UHNW divorce planning is preparation. Prenuptial agreements, postnuptial agreements, and marital agreements are the first line of defense. These legal instruments, when thoughtfully crafted, set clear expectations and protect complex asset structures—private companies, trusts, family offices, and cross-border holdings. Real-Life Scenario: A tech founder with $300 million in pre-marital assets established a comprehensive prenup that preserved ownership of his business while providing fair, structured support for his spouse in the event of divorce. Action Step: Before marriage or as circumstances evolve, invest in a professionally drafted marital agreement that anticipates future wealth and life changes.

Asset characterization is fundamental. Divorce proceedings hinge on distinguishing between separate property and marital property. Separate property—assets owned before marriage, inheritances, gifts—typically remains with the original owner, while marital property—acquired during the marriage—is subject to division. However, asset commingling, transmutation agreements, and contributions to asset growth can blur these lines. Pros: Proper documentation preserves separate property claims. Cons: Poor record-keeping or casual commingling can expose separate assets. Action Step: Maintain meticulous records and consult legal counsel regularly to preserve clear asset characterization.

Valuation of complex assets presents another layer of challenge. Private equity stakes, hedge fund interests, intellectual property, and unique real estate holdings require specialized appraisals. Valuation dates, discount rates, and assumptions can materially impact settlement outcomes. Real-Life Scenario: An investor used strategic valuation experts to accurately assess carried interests in private equity funds, avoiding gross overestimations of marital assets. Action Step: Retain independent, credentialed valuation experts experienced in complex, illiquid assets.

Privacy is paramount. Divorce proceedings, unless sealed by the court, are public record. For ultra-affluent individuals, this can lead to unwanted publicity, reputational harm, and even business disruption. Private mediation, arbitration, and collaborative divorce processes offer pathways to confidential resolution. Action Step: Explore alternative dispute resolution mechanisms to minimize public exposure and preserve discretion.

Trusts are often the bedrock of UHNW wealth management, but they can become contentious in divorce. Irrevocable trusts established before marriage generally protect assets, but courts may scrutinize trust structures, especially if they appear to be alter egos or vehicles to defraud a spouse. Additionally, beneficiary designations and discretionary powers must be carefully managed. Action Step: Periodically review trust structures and administration practices to reinforce their legitimacy and resilience against divorce claims.

Liquidity planning is critical. Divorce settlements often require significant liquidity to fund property divisions and support obligations. Illiquid portfolios—private businesses, venture capital, collectibles—can create cash flow challenges. Structured settlements, property transfers in lieu of cash, and installment payments are often employed to balance liquidity needs. Real-Life Scenario: A family office structured a phased buyout of marital interests in a private real estate portfolio, preserving asset integrity while meeting settlement obligations. Action Step: Develop a liquidity strategy early in the divorce process to avoid fire sales and suboptimal asset dispositions.

Tax implications must not be overlooked. The transfer of assets incident to divorce is generally non-taxable, but post-divorce income streams, capital gains from forced asset sales, and the elimination of alimony deductibility under U.S. tax law can create hidden costs. Thoughtful structuring can minimize tax burdens and optimize financial outcomes. Action Step: Integrate tax counsel into the divorce planning team to ensure settlements are structured tax-efficiently.

Family dynamics and legacy planning are intricately tied to UHNW divorces. When children are involved, especially adult children poised to inherit family wealth, divorce can ripple through generational plans. Coordination between divorce attorneys and estate planners ensures that trusts, inheritance plans, and family business succession strategies are updated accordingly. Action Step: Conduct a post-divorce estate plan review to realign family governance and legacy structures.

International assets and multi-jurisdictional issues add further complexity. Different countries have widely varying divorce laws, community property standards, and trust recognition statutes. Domicile, residency, and the location of assets can influence division outcomes. Real-Life Scenario: A family with dual U.S. and European citizenship navigated divergent property division laws by carefully structuring settlement agreements under U.S. jurisdiction. Action Step: Map all cross-border holdings and engage international legal experts to craft jurisdictionally appropriate strategies.

Emotional resilience and decision-making capacity are indispensable. Divorce, even at the UHNW level, can cloud judgment and provoke reactionary choices. Maintaining a disciplined, strategic approach—

anchored by expert advisors—is crucial to achieving favorable outcomes. Consider employing divorce coaches, family counselors, and wealth psychologists to navigate the personal dimensions. Action Step: Build a holistic advisory team that includes emotional support professionals alongside legal, tax, and financial advisors.

Managing divorce at the ultra-high-net-worth level is not about winning or losing; it is about protecting what you've built, ensuring fairness, and preserving your legacy. It demands the same strategic thinking, discipline, and expert guidance that created the wealth in the first place.

The call to action is clear: Approach divorce planning with the same rigor and foresight as every other critical financial decision. Prepare proactively. Structure carefully. Act thoughtfully.

The goals—asset protection, privacy, tax efficiency, family continuity, and emotional stability—are within reach. But they demand bespoke strategies, interdisciplinary expertise, and an unwavering commitment to long-term vision. For the ultra-affluent, mastering divorce planning is not a defeat—it is a definitive expression of disciplined wealth stewardship.

Chapter 59: Custom Lending Solutions: Securities-Backed and Art-Backed Loans

Liquidity is the quiet power behind many of the most strategic financial moves made by the ultra-affluent. Whether acquiring prime real estate, investing opportunistically in a private deal, or smoothing the cash flow of a complex estate plan, access to capital—on your terms—is indispensable. Custom lending solutions, particularly securities-backed and art-backed loans, have become the refined tools of choice for those seeking to leverage wealth without compromising long-term investment strategy or disrupting prized holdings.

A securities-backed line of credit (SBLOC) offers immediate access to liquidity by using a portfolio of marketable securities—stocks, bonds, mutual funds—as collateral. The advantages are profound: interest rates are typically low, approvals are fast, and there is no need to liquidate investments, thereby avoiding capital gains taxes and market timing risks. Real-Life Scenario: A private equity partner needed $10 million quickly to participate in a once-in-a-lifetime co-investment. Rather than liquidating equity positions and triggering massive tax events, he secured an SBLOC against his diversified portfolio and closed the deal within days. Action Step: Review your liquid investment portfolio and assess the borrowing power available through an SBLOC.

The elegance of an SBLOC lies in its flexibility. Funds can be drawn as needed and repaid on your schedule. There are typically no fixed repayment terms, and you retain all dividends, interest, and appreciation within your portfolio. However, SBLOCs are not without risk. Market volatility can erode collateral values, potentially triggering margin calls. Pros: Speed, flexibility, tax efficiency. Cons: Exposure to market downturns, lender-imposed collateral maintenance requirements. Action Step: Work with your private bank to structure an SBLOC with conservative advance rates and robust contingency plans.

Art-backed loans represent another sophisticated avenue for liquidity. Fine art—masterpieces, contemporary icons, sculpture collections—is increasingly recognized not only for aesthetic and cultural value but also for financial leverage. Art lending allows owners to unlock liquidity without selling their pieces, which may carry both financial and emotional costs. Lenders typically advance 40-60% of the appraised value, and interest rates are higher than traditional mortgages but lower than unsecured loans. Real-Life Scenario: A collector secured a $20 million loan against a portfolio of post-war paintings to finance a significant philanthropic initiative while keeping his prized collection intact. Action Step: Conduct professional appraisals on your art holdings to determine lending potential.

Unlike securities, art is illiquid, subjective in valuation, and costly to store and insure. Lenders require rigorous due diligence—provenance verification, condition reports, and insurance coverage—before approving loans. Pros: Liquidity without sale, no market exposure risk. Cons: Higher costs, limited advance rates, complex documentation. Action Step: Engage specialized art advisors and lenders experienced in structuring art-backed loans.

Structuring these custom lending solutions requires sophistication. Cross-collateralization—pledging multiple asset classes, such as securities and art, to back a single loan—can enhance borrowing power and reduce overall interest costs. Real-Life Scenario: A family office structured a blended loan, combining securities and art, to finance a strategic acquisition at terms far superior to a traditional loan. Action Step: Explore integrated collateral strategies to optimize leverage and risk.

Tax considerations must also be factored in. While the proceeds from SBLOCs and art-backed loans are not considered taxable income, interest expenses may or may not be deductible depending on how proceeds are used. Additionally, using loan proceeds to finance personal consumption, like yachts or vacation homes, may preclude deductions. Action Step: Coordinate with tax advisors to structure loans in ways that maximize tax efficiency.

Liquidity risk management is essential. Both securities-backed and art-backed loans carry the risk of forced liquidation if collateral values fall or loan covenants are breached. Maintaining conservative loan-to-value (LTV) ratios, diversifying collateral, and implementing stop-loss strategies can mitigate these risks. Action Step: Establish clear risk management protocols and monitor collateral values regularly.

Custom lending can also be a tool for estate planning. Using loans to fund life insurance premiums, facilitate intra-family transfers, or bridge liquidity gaps for estate tax payments without liquidating legacy assets is increasingly common among sophisticated wealth planners. Real-Life Scenario: An entrepreneur utilized a securities-backed loan to fund premium payments on a large life insurance policy inside an irrevocable trust, preserving liquidity for estate tax purposes without disrupting his core holdings. Action Step: Integrate custom lending solutions into your estate and legacy planning discussions.

Relationship management with lenders is another critical factor. Unlike conventional consumer loans, custom lending relationships are nuanced and dynamic. Terms can often be negotiated based on total client relationships, and maintaining strong communication and trust with lenders ensures flexibility during volatile markets. Action Step: Cultivate and maintain high-level relationships with private bankers and specialty lenders.

Finally, customization is key. No two ultra-affluent portfolios are alike, and lending solutions must be tailored to fit asset composition, risk tolerance, liquidity needs, and long-term goals. Off-the-shelf lending products rarely suffice. Comprehensive, bespoke structuring—often involving multiple advisors, asset managers, and legal counsel—ensures optimal outcomes. Action Step: Build a cross-disciplinary advisory team capable of designing truly customized lending strategies.

The call to action is clear: Leverage your wealth intelligently. Access liquidity strategically. Preserve your core assets while maximizing financial flexibility.

The goals—enhanced liquidity, tax efficiency, asset preservation, strategic agility—are within reach. But they demand thoughtful structuring, proactive risk management, and expert guidance. For the ultra-affluent, custom lending is not just about borrowing—it is about elevating capital strategy to an art form.

Part X: Navigating Risks and Future Trends

Part X: Navigating Risks and Future Trends prepares the ultra-affluent for the dynamic, often unpredictable forces shaping the future of wealth. It recognizes that sophisticated wealth management is not solely about protecting assets today but about anticipating tomorrow's challenges and opportunities.

This section addresses critical areas of risk—economic volatility, regulatory changes, geopolitical shifts, technological disruption, and evolving social expectations. It explores how risks such as cyber threats, ESG pressures, and global taxation reforms can impact wealth preservation. Simultaneously, it highlights emerging trends including digital assets, private markets evolution, sustainable investing, and advancements in artificial intelligence that the ultra-wealthy must understand and harness to maintain and grow their capital.

The goal is to equip readers with the strategic foresight, risk management frameworks, and adaptive mindsets necessary to sustain wealth and influence across generations. It moves from defensive posture to proactive positioning, turning potential risks into strategic advantages.

Chapter 60: Emerging Risks: Regulation, Climate, Cybersecurity, and Geopolitics

In the world of the ultra-affluent, wealth is not a static possession—it is a dynamic system constantly influenced by global forces. Emerging risks—regulation, climate change, cybersecurity threats, and geopolitical volatility—pose significant challenges to the preservation and growth of capital. Ignoring them is not an option. Mastery over these risks requires not just awareness but a proactive, strategic approach to resilience and adaptation.

Regulatory risk is rapidly evolving. Global governments are becoming more assertive in their approach to taxation, wealth transparency, and corporate governance. Initiatives like the OECD's Common Reporting Standard (CRS), the U.S. Corporate Transparency Act, and wealth taxes being floated in various jurisdictions signal a new era of scrutiny. Real-Life Scenario: A family office operating in multiple countries faced increased reporting burdens due to CRS, prompting a complete overhaul of their entity structures to ensure compliance and minimize risk. Action Step: Conduct a comprehensive audit of your wealth structures to ensure alignment with emerging transparency and compliance standards.

The regulatory environment extends beyond taxation. ESG (Environmental, Social, and Governance) regulations are reshaping investment mandates, while anti-money laundering (AML) and Know Your Customer (KYC) requirements are tightening. Pros: Proactive compliance protects reputation and operational continuity. Cons: Increased administrative burden and potential operational disruptions. Action Step: Build a regulatory monitoring team or outsource to specialists who track legislative changes across all relevant jurisdictions.

Climate risk is no longer theoretical. Rising sea levels, extreme weather events, and shifting climate patterns impact not only direct real estate holdings but also the broader portfolio—agriculture, insurance, infrastructure, and energy sectors are all exposed. Moreover, the push toward decarbonization is creating transitional risks as economies shift away from fossil fuels. Real-Life Scenario: An investor's beachfront properties faced plummeting valuations due to revised flood zone maps, prompting a strategic real estate divestiture and relocation of holdings inland. Action Step: Integrate climate risk assessments into all real estate and infrastructure investment decisions.

Beyond physical risk, climate policy risk—carbon pricing, regulation on emissions, disclosure mandates—affects virtually all investment classes. Stranded assets, regulatory penalties, and shifting consumer preferences create both hazards and opportunities. Action Step: Review all portfolio companies and assets for climate transition risk and reallocate capital toward resilient, future-proof sectors.

Cybersecurity has emerged as a top-tier risk for ultra-high-net-worth individuals and family offices. Sophisticated attacks—ransomware, phishing, data breaches—target not just corporations but also wealthy individuals. Cyber breaches can lead to financial loss, reputational damage, and even physical security threats. Real-Life Scenario: A prominent family fell victim to a ransomware attack on their family office, resulting in millions in costs and significant reputational harm. Action Step: Implement enterprise-grade cybersecurity systems, including multifactor authentication, end-to-end encryption, regular audits, and incident response planning.

Personal cybersecurity is equally critical. Digital footprints from social media, online banking, and even smart home devices can create vulnerabilities. Ultra-affluent individuals are high-value targets, necessitating a shift toward digital minimalism and security hygiene. Pros: Enhanced privacy and security. Cons: Potential inconvenience and lifestyle adjustment. Action Step: Conduct a personal cybersecurity audit and implement best practices—secure devices, use privacy-focused services, and limit unnecessary online exposure.

Geopolitical risk is intensifying. Rising nationalism, supply chain disruptions, trade wars, and regional conflicts can impact asset valuations, mobility, and operational continuity. Family offices and UHNW individuals must view geopolitical developments not as background noise but as material risk factors requiring mitigation strategies. Real-Life Scenario: An investor's significant holdings in emerging markets were adversely impacted by abrupt policy shifts, leading to reallocation toward more geopolitically stable jurisdictions. Action Step: Develop a geopolitical risk framework that maps exposure and outlines contingency plans for volatile regions.

Mobility risk—the ability to move people and capital across borders—is becoming more constrained. Visa regimes, capital controls, and shifting immigration policies can trap wealth or limit personal freedom. Residency and citizenship planning through investment programs can provide crucial optionality. Action Step: Diversify residency and citizenship options to ensure freedom of movement and capital access amid geopolitical upheaval.

Insurance plays an underrated role in risk management. Political risk insurance, cyber insurance, climate disaster insurance—each offers a tool to transfer risk from the balance sheet to insurers. However, the complexity of underwriting for UHNW individuals necessitates bespoke policies rather than off-the-shelf products. Action Step: Conduct a comprehensive risk audit and build a tailored insurance portfolio aligned with your risk exposures.

Future-proofing wealth demands agility. Emerging risks are interconnected and rapidly evolving. Static strategies, however well-crafted, can become obsolete quickly. Scenario planning, regular strategy reviews, and access to real-time intelligence are essential components of modern wealth stewardship. Real-Life Scenario: A family office institutionalized quarterly risk review sessions with geopolitical analysts, climate scientists, and cybersecurity experts, transforming risk management into a competitive advantage. Action Step: Institutionalize proactive risk management practices, embedding them into the fabric of your family office or personal advisory team.

The call to action is stark: Shift from passive awareness to active anticipation. Build resilience deliberately. Adapt proactively.

The goals—capital preservation, operational continuity, reputational integrity, and generational security—are attainable. But they require a new mindset—one that treats emerging risks not as rare black swans but as constant, evolving companions. For the ultra-affluent, mastering risk is not merely defensive; it is a critical pillar of enduring success and leadership.

Important Disclaimer

Ultra Affluent is written to educate, empower, and encourage individuals and families with significant wealth to take control of their financial lives, legacy planning, and strategic decision-making. The insights in this book are based on the author's personal experience, professional training, and over two decades of work in financial services, private wealth management, and advising high-net-worth and ultra-high-net-worth clients.

That said, it's important to be clear about what this book is — and what it is not.

Educational Purpose Only

All content in this book is provided for general educational and informational purposes only. It is intended to introduce affluent individuals and families to essential wealth management concepts, strategic frameworks, and deeper awareness of the opportunities and challenges unique to significant wealth.

While this book offers strategies, frameworks, case studies, and real-world examples, it is not personalized financial advice. Every reader's situation is unique. Your goals, business holdings, real estate portfolio, private investments, family dynamics, risk appetite, and tax position must all be considered individually.

Before making significant financial, legal, tax, or business decisions, you should work with licensed professionals who understand your specific circumstances.

No Legal Advice

Although ultra-affluent individuals and families routinely deal with estate plans, trusts, business succession strategies, asset protection structures, and philanthropic entities, this book does not provide legal advice. It is not a replacement for working with a qualified attorney.

If you are:

- Drafting or updating trusts, wills, or succession plans
- Establishing or restructuring family entities or holding companies
- Managing international wealth or cross-border assets
- Structuring charitable foundations or donor-advised funds
- Protecting assets through trusts, prenups, or corporate structures

...you should seek the counsel of an experienced attorney who specializes in estate planning, business law, asset protection, or philanthropy. Legal frameworks vary by jurisdiction and individual circumstances. You are responsible for ensuring compliance with all applicable laws and regulations.

No Financial or Investment Advice

This book covers important topics like asset allocation, private investments, wealth transfer, risk management, liquidity event planning, and long-term wealth preservation — but from an educational standpoint, not an advisory one.

This book is not written by a Certified Financial Planner™, Registered Investment Advisor, or broker-dealer. The strategies and examples are general in nature and may not directly apply to your unique situation.

Before implementing any investment strategies, reallocating capital, executing estate plans, or engaging in liquidity event planning, consult a licensed financial professional who is experienced in managing the complexities of significant wealth.

No Accounting or Tax Advice

Tax efficiency is central to wealth preservation and transfer, but this book is not written by a CPA, Enrolled Agent, or licensed tax advisor. Any discussions around tax optimization, gifting strategies, or estate tax planning are for general educational purposes only.

If you:

- Structure trusts, family partnerships, or holding companies
- Manage multi-generational wealth transfer
- Navigate international tax considerations
- Handle liquidity events, business sales, or investment exits
- Design charitable giving strategies with tax benefits

...you should engage a qualified tax professional. Only a licensed tax advisor can analyze your situation and ensure compliance with current laws while optimizing your outcomes.

No Guarantees or Promises

Reading this book does not guarantee financial success, risk elimination, tax savings, or legacy preservation. Financial literacy, strategic planning, and wealth management are disciplines that require ongoing learning, expert collaboration, and thoughtful action.

The case studies and examples in this book are illustrative. They are not forecasts or assurances of future performance. Your financial outcomes will depend on many factors, including your decisions, economic conditions, tax laws, markets, family dynamics, and unforeseen events.

Limitation of Liability

By reading this book, you agree that the author, Pat Brown, MBA, and affiliated brands — such as FinancialLiteracyForNIL.com and other associated platforms — are not responsible for your financial outcomes, legal challenges, tax liabilities, or business consequences.

Neither the author nor any associated entity shall be liable for financial losses, legal actions, tax penalties, or other negative outcomes associated with your use of the information presented here. You are fully responsible for your financial, legal, and business decisions.

Encouragement to Build Your Professional Team

It is the strong belief of the author that every ultra-affluent individual and family needs a well-structured team of professionals:

- A financial advisor or wealth manager
- A tax advisor (CPA or international tax specialist)
- An estate planning attorney
- A business attorney
- An insurance consultant
- A philanthropic strategist

This book is designed to complement your professional team — not replace it.

If you have not yet assembled a comprehensive advisory team, now is the time. Stewarding significant wealth demands expertise, precision, and coordination. Your financial life deserves the same level of intentionality and strategic design that you bring to your business, investments, and legacy.

You've worked hard to build wealth, create opportunities, and make an impact. Now it's time to ensure you are protecting, preserving, and extending that success for generations to come.

Wealth Manager's Coordination

At the ultra-affluent level, managing wealth is not a singular endeavor—it is a complex, interconnected system requiring constant orchestration across a spectrum of disciplines. A world-class wealth manager must operate not merely as an advisor but as the chief architect and conductor of a sophisticated ecosystem, coordinating estate planning, accounting and tax, insurance, investments, trading, liquidity planning, and philanthropy. Done right, this coordination transforms complexity into clarity, risk into resilience, and assets into an enduring legacy.

Estate planning is foundational. Coordinating trusts, wills, and dynasty structures ensures that wealth transitions seamlessly across generations while minimizing estate taxes and protecting assets from creditors. Irrevocable trusts, grantor retained annuity trusts (GRATs), family limited partnerships (FLPs), and perpetual dynasty trusts are no longer niche concepts—they are standard tools in the ultra-affluent playbook. Real-Life Scenario: A tech founder structured his holdings into a multi-generational trust framework that preserved voting control, mitigated estate taxes, and shielded assets from future divorces within the family. Action Step: Schedule a comprehensive estate planning review to ensure your structures are current, tax-optimized, and aligned with your legacy vision.

Accounting and tax coordination, especially for multi-entity, multi-jurisdictional families, demands precision and foresight. Family offices, partnerships, international holding companies—each layer adds tax complexity. Efficient coordination between wealth managers, CPAs, and tax attorneys is critical to minimize exposure and optimize after-tax returns. Pros: Tax efficiency, risk mitigation. Cons: Requires constant vigilance and cross-disciplinary expertise. Action Step: Assemble a dedicated tax team familiar with multi-jurisdictional structures and insist on quarterly tax strategy reviews.

Insurance planning is the often-underappreciated pillar of wealth protection. Home, auto, yacht, aviation, fine art, disability, life, and umbrella policies must be carefully structured and integrated. For the ultra-affluent, "off-the-shelf" insurance is inadequate—bespoke coverage is required to address the unique risks of complex lifestyles and collections. Real-Life Scenario: A collector's $50 million art collection was underinsured due to outdated appraisals, a situation remedied by engaging a specialist insurer and updating the policy to cover full market value. Action Step: Conduct a full insurance audit across all asset classes and update policies annually to reflect current valuations and risk exposures.

Investment management must be dynamic and bespoke. Direct indexing strategies allow for personalized portfolios that optimize for taxes and factor exposures. Alternative investments—private equity, venture capital, hedge funds, real assets—offer diversification and alpha generation. Increasingly, ultra-affluent portfolios are built not around public markets but private opportunities. Action Step: Develop an investment policy statement that incorporates direct indexing and a disciplined allocation to alternatives, tailored to your long-term goals and risk tolerance.

Trading and execution demand sophistication. Block trading—the sale or purchase of large security positions—requires precision to avoid market impact and slippage. Tax-loss harvesting must be methodical and continuous, especially in volatile markets. For the ultra-affluent, trading is not about chasing returns but about executing strategy with precision and efficiency. Real-Life Scenario: A family office partnered with an institutional trading desk to systematically harvest losses during a market downturn, saving millions in taxes while maintaining strategic exposure. Action Step: Engage a trading specialist or institutional desk capable of executing large trades discreetly and optimizing tax outcomes.

Liquidity and exit planning are non-negotiable for wealth durability. Pre-IPO strategies, business sale readiness, and monetization of illiquid assets require years of preparation. Liquidity is not simply a safety net—it's strategic capital for seizing opportunities, weathering crises, and funding legacy projects. Real-Life Scenario: An entrepreneur planning a $200 million exit engaged a wealth team five years in advance, implementing pre-liquidity estate strategies and diversifying holdings to minimize post-sale tax exposure. Action Step: If liquidity events are on your horizon, begin structuring exit plans early, coordinating with estate and tax planning.

Philanthropy is no longer an afterthought—it is integral to identity and legacy. Foundation structuring, donor-advised funds, and high-impact giving strategies must be coordinated with the broader wealth plan. Mission alignment, family engagement, and impact measurement transform giving from check-writing into enduring legacy-building. Action Step: Develop a strategic philanthropy plan that integrates seamlessly with estate, tax, and family governance frameworks.

The complexity across these domains is not static—it evolves with markets, laws, and family dynamics. Coordinating all of them demands a wealth manager who acts as quarterback, constantly aligning moving parts toward a coherent, strategic whole. A skilled wealth manager brings together estate attorneys, CPAs, investment specialists, insurance consultants, and philanthropic advisors, ensuring that every piece of your wealth strategy operates in harmony. Real-Life Scenario: A multigenerational family office integrated estate planning, tax strategy, investment management, and philanthropy under a single coordinated framework, leading to compounded success across decades. Action Step: Demand a fully coordinated approach from your advisory team, or re-architect your team to deliver it.

The call to action is direct: Insist on orchestration, not isolation. Complexity demands coordination. Strategy demands synchronization.

The goals—wealth preservation, strategic growth, risk mitigation, tax optimization, family unity, and lasting impact—are attainable. But they require a sophisticated conductor guiding the orchestra of estate, tax, insurance, investments, trading, liquidity, and philanthropy. For the ultra-affluent, true wealth mastery lies not in isolated excellence but in seamless coordination—a symphony of strategy that endures and elevates across generations.

While this book has been written for informational purposes, if you find yourself needing deeper guidance and personalized support in implementing this level of coordination, Pat Brown would certainly be honored to be of service. With experience and passion for working alongside ultra-affluent families, he brings the expertise, discretion, and comprehensive vision required to navigate this complexity with precision.

Your First 10 Moves After Reading Ultra Affluent

Financial Literacy Is Powerful—But Only If You Act on It

Here's a strategic checklist to help ultra-affluent individuals and families translate knowledge into meaningful action:

1. **Audit Your Personal and Family Finances**

- Conduct a thorough review of your personal cash flow, savings, and liquidity.
- Assess your family office or private entity structures for efficiency.
- Know your personal runway—and your family's—to maintain lifestyle and flexibility.

1. **Evaluate Business and Private Holdings**

- Review ownership stakes in operating businesses, private equity, and venture investments.
- Understand liquidity timelines, key valuations, and potential exit strategies.
- Confirm governance structures and shareholder agreements are up-to-date.

1. **Strengthen Your Liquidity and Emergency Planning**

- Ensure access to cash equivalents covering 12–24 months of personal

and family obligations.
- Secure standby credit facilities for unexpected capital needs.

1. **Maximize Tax-Advantaged Structures and Retirement Planning**

- Review defined benefit plans, deferred compensation arrangements, and private placement life insurance (PPLI) options.
- Utilize 529 plans, donor-advised funds (DAFs), and other tax-advantaged vehicles.

1. **Protect Yourself, Your Family, and Your Legacy**

- Audit personal insurance policies—life, disability, umbrella, liability, cyber risk.
- Review business insurance—key person, directors and officers (D&O), and corporate liability.
- Update intellectual property protections and asset ownership structures.

1. **Plan for Taxes Early and Strategically**

- Engage tax advisors experienced with complex portfolios and multi-jurisdictional holdings.
- Strategically prepare for liquidity events, including pre-transaction tax mitigation strategies.
- Evaluate opportunities under QSBS, 1031 exchanges, and grantor trust structures.

1. **Establish or Update Your Estate Plan**

- Create or revise wills, revocable and irrevocable trusts, and durable powers of attorney.
- Implement dynasty trusts, GRATs, SLATs, or charitable trusts as

appropriate.
- Address family governance and succession planning proactively.

1. **Diversify Beyond Core Holdings**

- Avoid over-concentration in any single business, asset class, or geography.
- Build a globally diversified portfolio aligned with long-term objectives and risk tolerance.

1. **Build and Maintain Your Professional Advisory Team**

- CPA familiar with multi-entity, multi-jurisdictional structures.
- Financial advisor experienced with ultra-affluent portfolios and family offices.
- Estate attorney skilled in complex trust and legacy planning.
- Insurance consultant attuned to the needs of significant wealth.

1. **Set Quarterly Financial Strategy Reviews**

- Schedule quarterly reviews with your advisory team to assess progress and adjust strategy.
- Monitor wealth transfer plans, investment performance, tax positioning, and family goals.

Final Reminder:

Start where you are. Small, consistent moves compound into significant results over time. Financial literacy at the ultra-affluent level is not about mastering everything overnight—it's about sustained, strategic action aligned with your wealth, values, and legacy.

DIY vs. Professional Management

When it comes to managing significant wealth, the question inevitably arises: Should you manage it yourself, or engage a professional team? For the ultra-affluent, the stakes are far too high for this to be a casual decision. The complexity of assets, the interwoven layers of tax law, risk exposure, opportunity sourcing, and legacy planning turn wealth management from a series of simple choices into a strategic discipline. At this level, DIY may appeal to the independent spirit, but professional management often proves indispensable.

Time is the first and most overlooked factor. Managing an ultra-high-net-worth portfolio is a full-time endeavor. It demands attention not just to investments, but to tax law changes, estate planning opportunities, risk management structures, and family dynamics. Attempting to self-manage these complexities often leads to opportunity costs—time spent managing wealth is time not spent creating more, enjoying it, or nurturing family legacy. Action Step: Conduct an honest audit of the time commitment needed to manage all facets of your wealth—and compare it against the time you want to invest in living your life.

Complexity only compounds the challenge. Multiple legal entities, offshore holdings, private equity partnerships, operating companies, trusts, and charitable foundations all require specialized knowledge and synchronized strategies. Real-Life Scenario: An entrepreneur who sold his business for $500 million initially attempted to manage his affairs solo, only to find that the complexity of tax filings across five jurisdictions made professional help a necessity within two years. Action Step: Map the complexity of your asset base and consult with professionals who can benchmark what institutional-level management would entail.

Emotional distance is a critical, often underestimated advantage of professional management. Ultra-affluent individuals are often deeply tied to the assets they've built—businesses, real estate, legacy investments—which can cloud judgment. A wealth manager provides the necessary emotional neutrality to make decisions based purely on strategy and data. Pros: Objective advice, reduction in cognitive bias. Cons: Potential loss of personal control if not structured properly. Action Step: Evaluate the current emotional bias in your decision-making process and where a neutral third party could enhance outcomes.

Access to opportunities is another differentiator. Many of the best investment opportunities—direct deals, private equity, venture capital, exclusive real estate partnerships—are invitation-only. Professional managers with institutional networks can provide curated access that DIY investors typically can't replicate. Real-Life Scenario: A professionally managed family office secured a seat in an oversubscribed venture fund that produced outsized returns, an opportunity unavailable to individual investors without connections. Action Step: Assess your access to top-tier private investment opportunities and determine whether your network is truly competitive.

Tax mitigation strategies at the UHNW level require deep specialization. From grantor trusts to offshore insurance wrappers, the array of tools available is vast but complex. DIY approaches often result in missed opportunities or costly mistakes. Professionals not only optimize current-year outcomes but also strategically position wealth across generations. Action Step: Engage in a tax strategy review specifically focused on multi-generational optimization rather than just annual minimization.

Risk management requires a holistic, disciplined approach. Insurance, legal structures, investment portfolio hedging, cybersecurity—each risk vector must be managed in concert. DIY investors often focus heavily on market risk but overlook enterprise risk, reputational risk, or personal security. Action Step: Build a comprehensive risk audit into your wealth management process to ensure no blind spots exist.

Family governance and legacy planning are perhaps the most sensitive areas. Managing wealth for one's lifetime is a different discipline than managing it for multiple generations. Effective family governance requires education programs, mission statements, conflict resolution mechanisms, and succession planning. Wealth managers experienced in multigenerational planning can facilitate difficult conversations and put structures in place that families often struggle to implement alone. Real-Life Scenario: A family without governance structures fractured after a patriarch's death, while another, with professional facilitation, transitioned leadership and wealth seamlessly to the next generation. Action Step: Develop a formal family governance structure and engage professional facilitators to support its implementation.

Cost is often raised as an objection to professional management, but it must be weighed against the cost of missed opportunities, suboptimal decisions, and unmanaged risks. Pros: Expert guidance, strategic coherence, risk mitigation. Cons: Management fees, potential misalignment if advisors are not carefully selected. Action Step: Analyze the cost of professional management not just in terms of fees, but in terms of enhanced returns, tax savings, risk reduction, and peace of mind.

Ultimately, the decision between DIY and professional management is not binary. Many ultra-affluent individuals choose a hybrid model—remaining deeply involved in strategy while delegating execution and oversight to trusted professionals. The key is recognizing that wealth at this scale requires a degree of orchestration and expertise that few can master alone.

The call to action is simple but profound: Evaluate not just whether you can manage your wealth alone, but whether you should. Wealth is not merely an asset—it is a responsibility to yourself, your family, and your legacy.

The goals—preservation, growth, risk mitigation, strategic opportunity access, and legacy fulfillment—are achievable. But they demand time, expertise, discipline, and emotional distance. For the ultra-affluent, professional wealth management is not an expense—it is an investment in ensuring that complexity is tamed, opportunities are seized, risks are mitigated, and legacy is secured.

While this book has been designed to inform and empower you, if you recognize the need for more personalized, professional support, Pat Brown would be honored to assist. With deep experience advising ultra-affluent families and individuals, Pat offers the coordination, discretion, and strategic sophistication necessary to navigate these complexities and elevate your wealth to its highest purpose.

Managing Your Wealth Like a Family Enterprise / Important Dates

Managing significant wealth as an ultra-affluent individual or family is not unlike running a highly complex, long-term enterprise. It requires clear milestones, disciplined review cycles, adaptive strategies, and the wisdom to adjust as new information surfaces. Use this month-by-month guide as a blueprint to structure your financial year with precision and intention.

JANUARY

- **January 1**
- New contribution limits for 401(k), 403(b), 457 plans, and IRA/Roth IRA accounts go into effect.
- Health Savings Account (HSA) and Flexible Spending Account (FSA) limits reset.
- Conduct a full review of personal, business, and family office budgets and cash flow.
- Update paycheck withholdings (Form W-4) if there were major life events—marriage, divorce, new family members.
- **January 15**
- Fourth Quarter Estimated Taxes Due (for income earned October 1–December 31 of the prior year) — use IRS Form 1040-ES.
- **Late January**
- Begin receiving W-2s, 1099s, and preliminary tax documents.

FEBRUARY

- **February 1**
- Deadline for employers and payers to issue W-2s and 1099s.
- **Mid to Late February**
- Partnership K-1s may start arriving.
- Begin compiling all tax documents—personal, business, investment accounts, real estate holdings, and alternative assets.

MARCH

- **March 15**
- Tax deadline for Partnerships and S-Corps (Forms 1065, 1120-S).
- File an extension (IRS Form 7004) if needed.
- **March 31**
- Deadline to receive health insurance forms (1095-A, 1095-B, 1095-C) electronically.

APRIL

- **April 1**
- Required Minimum Distributions (RMDs) must begin if you turned 73 last year.
- **April 15**
- Personal Tax Filing Deadline (IRS Form 1040).
- First Quarter Estimated Taxes Due.
- Deadline for prior-year contributions to:
- Traditional IRA/Roth IRA
- SEP IRA (if not filing an extension)
- HSA
- Coverdell ESA
- FAFSA filing deadlines for college-bound dependents.

MAY

- **Early May**
- Review property tax assessments and appeal if necessary.
- **May 29 (5/29 Day)**
- National reminder to review 529 College Savings Plans.

JUNE

- **June 15**
- Second Quarter Estimated Taxes Due.
- U.S. citizens living abroad must file taxes or request an extension.
- **Mid-June**
- Mid-year portfolio review—adjust as needed.
- Reassess charitable giving strategies and donor-advised fund contributions.

JULY

- **July 1–15**
- Conduct a mid-year financial check-in:
- Review spending and savings.
- Update investment allocations.
- Check debt reduction progress.
- Meet with wealth advisors and CPAs.

AUGUST

- **August 1–31**
- Prepare for Open Enrollment periods (healthcare, employer benefits).
- Review HSA/FSA balances.
- Conduct an insurance audit (life, disability, umbrella, property, cyber liability).
- Strategize for year-end charitable giving, appreciated stock donations, and Qualified Charitable Distributions (QCDs).

SEPTEMBER

- **September 15**
- Third Quarter Estimated Taxes Due.
- Final deadline for extended Partnership and S-Corp returns.
- **Late September**
- Review Backdoor Roth IRA strategies.
- Begin tax-loss harvesting evaluations.

OCTOBER

- **October 1**
- Deadline to establish SIMPLE IRAs for current year.
- **October 15**
- Extended Individual Tax Return Deadline (Form 1040).
- Final deadline for SEP IRA contributions (if filing an extension).
- **Late October**
- Review Open Enrollment materials and benefit plan options.

NOVEMBER

- **November 1–30**
- ACA Marketplace Open Enrollment begins.
- Employer benefits enrollment:
- Adjust health, life, disability insurance.
- Max out retirement plan contributions.
- Revisit HSA/FSA elections.
- **Black Friday Weekend**
- Time significant purchases—tech upgrades, luxury goods—aligned with year-end cash flow and deductions.

DECEMBER

- **December 1–15**
- Maximize contributions:
- 401(k), 403(b), 457 plans.
- HSA contributions.
- Complete Backdoor Roth IRA conversions.
- **December 31**
- Final day to:
- Execute charitable donations.
- Complete tax-loss harvesting.
- Take RMDs if age 73+.
- Make annual tax-free gifts (up to $18,000 per recipient).
- Spend down FSA balances (confirm grace period/rollover).
- Complete Roth IRA conversions.
- Issue bonuses or profit-sharing if managing corporate entities.

Rolling & Event-Based Reminders

- **Every Paycheck**
- Check retirement plan and HSA contributions.
- Confirm insurance premium deductions.
- **After Major Life Events**
- Marriage, divorce, birth, adoption.
- Job or role changes.
- Relocation.
- Inheritance or significant liquidity events.
- **Quarterly**
- Review budget and spending.
- Make estimated tax payments.
- Reassess investment portfolios.
- Execute tax strategies like Roth conversions or tax-loss harvesting.

Final Tip: Automate Where Possible

Financial success at the ultra-affluent level thrives on structure and consistency.

- Set automated calendar alerts for major deadlines.
- Automate contributions to savings and investment accounts.
- Schedule quarterly financial reviews.
- Pre-schedule debt payments and strategic giving.

The fewer tasks left to chance, the more disciplined and effective your financial enterprise will be—a steady, deliberate path toward generational wealth stewardship and legacy building.

30 Questions Ultra-Affluent Individuals Should Ask Their Professionals

Questions to Ask a Financial Advisor

1. Are you a fiduciary 100% of the time?
2. Do you have experience working with ultra-affluent families, tech founders, and entrepreneurs with complex equity compensation?
3. How do you get paid—fee-only, fee-based, or commission?
4. Can you help with equity compensation planning, including stock options, RSUs, pre-IPO shares, and liquidity event strategies?
5. Will you coordinate with my CPA, estate attorney, insurance specialist, and other key advisors?
6. What's your investment philosophy, and how do you incorporate private equity, venture capital, and direct deals?
7. How do you help clients prepare for major liquidity events, acquisitions, or IPOs?
8. Can you advise on risk management, including asset protection structures and insurance?
9. Are you familiar with advanced retirement planning for entrepreneurs (e.g., Cash Balance Plans, Defined Benefit Plans)?
10. Do you provide scenario planning and Monte Carlo simulations to stress-test financial strategies?

Questions to Ask a CPA

1. Do you specialize in working with ultra-affluent individuals, en-

trepreneurs, and clients with cross-border or multi-state tax complexities?
2. Do you provide proactive, year-round tax planning instead of only preparing returns?
3. Are you experienced with Qualified Small Business Stock (QSBS) and Section 1202 exclusions?
4. Can you advise on optimizing charitable giving strategies, including Donor-Advised Funds and Private Foundations?
5. How do you handle clients with international holdings, residency considerations, or multi-jurisdictional income?
6. Will you represent me in the event of an IRS audit or tax dispute?
7. Can you consult on real estate investments, 1031 exchanges, and Opportunity Zone strategies?
8. How do you coordinate tax planning with my estate attorney and financial advisor?

Questions to Ask an Estate Planning Attorney

1. Do you have experience working with founders, entrepreneurs, and ultra-high-net-worth families?
2. What core documents should I have in place—wills, revocable living trusts, irrevocable trusts, POAs, healthcare directives?
3. Can you advise on asset protection strategies, including domestic and offshore trusts?
4. How do you handle estate planning for business owners, stock options, and liquidity events?
5. Should I consider advanced structures like GRATs, SLATs, IDGTs, or Dynasty Trusts?
6. Can you help design a family governance framework and succession plan for wealth continuity?
7. How often should I review and update my estate plan given changing tax laws and family dynamics?

Questions to Ask a Business Attorney

1. Do you specialize in startups, venture-backed companies, or scaling tech businesses?
2. Can you advise on entity formation, Delaware incorporation, and ownership structure optimization?
3. Will you review or draft shareholder agreements, IP assignments, employment contracts, and fundraising documents?
4. Can you advise on mergers, acquisitions, and exit strategies, including due diligence preparation?
5. How do you structure your fees—hourly, flat rate, or retainer—and can you provide transparency up front?

Bonus Questions for Other Key Professionals

Insurance Advisor

- Are you independent or affiliated with a carrier (captive agent)?
- Can you tailor a comprehensive insurance portfolio, including personal, business, and estate liquidity needs?
- Should I consider key person insurance or buy-sell agreements for my business?
- How do you balance term life versus permanent life insurance strategies for wealth transfer?

Real Estate Advisor

- Are you experienced with evaluating real estate from an investment and tax optimization perspective?
- Can you guide transactions involving 1031 exchanges or Opportunity Zone investments?

Executive Coach or Career Consultant

- Can you coach on life transitions—founder burnout, post-exit reinvention, or pivoting to venture investing?
- Can you model financial and lifestyle impacts of different career paths or "next chapters" post-liquidity?

Final Thought

Choosing your professional team—financial advisor, CPA, estate attorney, business attorney, insurance consultant, real estate strategist—is one of the highest-leverage decisions you'll ever make. Ask sharp questions. Demand transparent, thoughtful answers. Build a team that matches the scale of your wealth and the ambition of your legacy.

While this guide is for informational purposes, if you require guidance, Pat Brown would be honored to assist—bringing years of experience in advising ultra-affluent individuals through every stage of wealth stewardship and legacy planning.

About The Author

Pat Brown, MBA, is a former Division I football player turned wealth advisor, educator, and nationally respected voice in financial literacy. With more than two decades of experience in financial planning, investment strategy, and insurance, Pat has dedicated his career to helping ultra-affluent individuals, families, and entrepreneurs build wealth with clarity, confidence, and a long-term vision.

After earning his MBA and launching a successful career in wealth management, Pat founded a series of financial literacy platforms designed to serve a wide range of high-achieving, often underserved, communities. His platforms include:

- Financial Literacy For NIL
- Financial Literacy For Student Athletes
- Financial Literacy For The Culture
- Financial Literacy For College Coaches
- Financial Literacy For Parents of Student Athletes
- Financial Literacy For Attorneys
- Financial Literacy For Doctors
- Financial Literacy For Dentists
- Financial Literacy For Pharmacists
- Financial Literacy For Engineers
- Financial Literacy For First Responders
- Financial Literacy For Expats
- Financial Literacy For Architects

Now, through *Ultra Affluent,* Pat brings his mission to the individuals and families managing significant wealth—those who understand that success is not just about accumulation, but stewardship, strategy, and legacy. Ultra-affluent individuals are experts in their professions, industries, and ventures—but even the most accomplished leaders often have not been taught how to apply that same strategic rigor to their personal wealth.

Pat's passion for financial education is deeply personal. Raised in a home where money discussions were scarce, he saw firsthand how the absence of financial literacy could derail even the brightest futures. Today, Pat is committed to bridging the gap between income and enduring wealth—ensuring that success translates into multigenerational security and opportunity.

Over the years, Pat has become a trusted advisor to a diverse and discerning clientele—including entrepreneurs, attorneys, physicians, executives, investors, and high-net-worth families. His approach is practical, culturally aware, and grounded in real-world experience—free from jargon and pretense. Whether you are overseeing a family office, navigating complex business holdings, preparing for a major liquidity event, or planning your family legacy, Pat's guidance is designed to meet you where you are and guide you forward—strategically and thoughtfully.

Beyond his financial work, Pat serves as a Trustee on the Board of Lawrence Memorial Hospital (LMH), contributing to governance and strategic planning initiatives. He is active on multiple nonprofit and civic boards, championing financial literacy, family support services, and improved access to healthcare.

Above all, Pat is a devoted husband and father. When he's not advising clients or speaking at wealth management forums, family office summits, or industry conferences, he translates complex financial concepts into real-world strategies that ultra-affluent individuals and families can immediately apply to secure and elevate their futures.

Pat believes financial literacy at the ultra-affluent level isn't just about wealth—it's about options, freedom, responsibility, and crafting a legacy of purpose and impact. Just as leaders transform bold ideas into world-changing ventures, Pat helps them transform success into significance—and income into enduring wealth.

Final Word

Need Help? Start Here

This book exists because financial education is one of the most powerful tools an ultra-affluent individual or family can possess. When used well, it opens doors, protects legacies, and provides the clarity and confidence to make sophisticated financial decisions with intention.

But just like building a world-class company or managing a complex investment portfolio, enduring financial success isn't achieved through guesswork. You need structure. You need systems. You need the discipline to ask the right questions, weigh the trade-offs, and recognize when it's time to bring in expert guidance. It's not about mastering every detail—it's about navigating decisions with clarity, precision, and long-term vision.

Use this book as a guide—not a rulebook. Let it inspire action. Let it build momentum. But don't mistake it for personalized advice. Stay curious. Stay informed. Keep asking smart questions before making any major financial, legal, or business decision.

Trusted Resources

If you're seeking tailored guidance or want to discuss your next steps in greater detail, reach out to a professional who understands the unique world of the ultra-affluent—complex portfolios, cross-border wealth, business succession, liquidity events, private investments, legacy planning, and family governance.

Pat Brown, MBA

Wealth advisor. Financial literacy advocate. Former Division I athlete.

Advisor to ultra-affluent individuals, entrepreneurs, family offices, executives, and high-performing professionals nationwide.

Website: www.ultraaffluent.com

Email: info@ultraaffluent.com

LinkedIn: linkedin.com/in/patrickbrownmba

Join Our Newsletter

Stay sharp with insights, strategies, and updates designed specifically for the ultra-affluent—delivered directly to your inbox.

Subscribe at www.ultraaffluent.com to receive actionable financial education and strategies tailored to individuals and families managing significant wealth.

Final Word: Use This. Don't Shelf It.

The ideas, frameworks, and tools in this book are not meant to gather dust. Use them. Revisit them. Share them with someone who can benefit. Test what works, refine what doesn't, and keep evolving your process.

This is your playbook—not just for wealth management, but for life management. Personally, professionally, and financially.

Stay sharp. Stay curious. Keep building the future you deserve.

Questions or Need Additional Help?

Pat Brown welcomes inquiries and conversations. For personalized discussions, strategic financial planning, or guidance tailored to your unique wealth journey, visit www.ultraaffluent.com, email info@ultraaffluent.com, or connect with Pat directly on LinkedIn.